# The Right to Legal Personhood of Marginalised Groups

# The Right to Legal Personhood of Marginalised Groups

## *Achieving Equal Recognition Before the Law for All*

ANNA ARSTEIN-KERSLAKE
*Professor of Human Rights, Irish Centre for Human Rights, School of Law, University of Galway, Ireland*
*Associate Professor, Melbourne Law School, University of Melbourne, Australia*

OXFORD
UNIVERSITY PRESS

OXFORD
UNIVERSITY PRESS

Great Clarendon Street, Oxford, OX2 6DP,
United Kingdom

Oxford University Press is a department of the University of Oxford.
It furthers the University's objective of excellence in research, scholarship,
and education by publishing worldwide. Oxford is a registered trade mark of
Oxford University Press in the UK and in certain other countries



Published in the United States of America by Oxford University Press
198 Madison Avenue, New York, NY 10016, United States of America

British Library Cataloguing in Publication Data

Data available

Library of Congress Control Number: 2024934058

ISBN 9780192843944

DOI: 10.1093/9780191926549.001.0001

Printed and bound in the UK by
Clays Ltd, Elcograf S.p.A.

MIX
Paper | Supporting
responsible forestry
FSC® C018072

# Preface

## 1. Human Right to Legal Personhood as a Tool for Social Change

Legal personhood is essential for an individual's participation in society. It is required for voting, marrying, inheriting, contracting, consenting, and other areas that are critical components of social structures and can be predicates to power and privilege.[1] Many groups are experiencing significant marginalisation due to the denial of legal personhood; for example, restrictive guardianship laws limit or deny the legal personhood of disabled people.[2] In addition, several countries continue to restrict the exercise of women's legal personhood by limiting their rights to contracting and inheriting.[3] Stateless people and undocumented migrants around the world are also denied legal personhood when they are denied immigration status or recognition.[4] Although many groups are experiencing injustice due to denials of the right to legal personhood, relatively little scholarship has examined the right and explored its potential as a tool for social change. In this book, I am attempting to fill that gap.

The right to legal personhood has been protected in international human rights law since the 1940s. It is derived from the 'right to equal recognition before the law', which can be found in the 1948 Universal Declaration of Human Rights (UDHR, Article 6) and was made legally binding by the 1966 International Covenant on Civil and Political Rights (ICCPR, Article 16). Its presence in these core human rights instruments illustrates the universal nature of the right and the early recognition of its importance.[5] I provide a detailed description of the right to legal personhood and its history in Chapter 1.

[1] Eilionóir Flynn and Anna Arstein-Kerslake, 'Legislating Personhood: Realising the Right to Support in Exercising Legal Capacity' (2014) 10 International Journal of Law in Context 81.

[2] Robert D Dinerstein, 'Implementing Legal Capacity under Article 12 of the UN Convention on the Rights of Persons with Disabilities: The Difficult Road from Guardianship to Supported Decision-Making Human Rights and the Protection of Persons with Disabilities' (2012) 19(2) Human Rights Brief 8.

[3] Report of the Committee on the Elimination of Discrimination against Women, 40th session (14 January–1 February 2008), 41st session (30 June–18 July 2008).

[4] Human Rights Committee, 'General Comment 15: The Position of Aliens under the Covenant' (11 April 1986) in 'Compilation of General Comments and General Recommendations Adopted by Human Rights Treaty Bodies' (1994) UN Doc HRI/GEN/1/Rev.1; David S Weissbrodt, *The Human Rights of Non-citizens* (OUP 2008).

[5] Anna Arstein-Kerslake, *Restoring Voice to People with Cognitive Disabilities* (CUP 2017); Jack Donnelly, *Universal Human Rights in Theory and Practice* (Cornell UP 2013).

The right was largely ignored by the human rights community until the 1979 Convention on the Elimination of Discrimination Against Women (CEDAW), which includes the first description of the right to legal capacity as a part of the right to equal recognition before the law (Article 15). There is an in-depth discussion of the terms 'legal capacity' and 'legal personhood' at the end of this Preface as well as in Chapter 1, wherein I argue that the right to legal capacity equates to a right to legal personhood.

The use of the term 'legal capacity' in CEDAW is significant because legal capacity encompasses both the recognition of legal personhood and the freedom to exercise that personhood. Elsewhere, the term 'legal personality' has been used instead of 'legal capacity', and 'legal personality' is often defined as only including the static recognition of an individual as a legal person and does not always include the freedom to exercise that personhood.[6] In other words, CEDAW established that the right to legal personhood requires that women are formally recognised as equal to men in the law and that women must have equal powers to act as legal agents under the law—to create, modify, and terminate legal relationships. For example, they must have equal contracting rights and inheritance rights, and their legal decisions must be respected on an equal basis with men's. The drafters of CEDAW recognised that legal personhood is critical for women to have the power and resources necessary to achieve gender equality.

This development of the right to legal personhood in CEDAW was the foundation of the further elaboration of the right in the 2006 Convention on the Rights of Persons with Disabilities (CRPD). In Article 12, the CRPD included similar text and solidified the right to hold *and* exercise personhood as an element of the right to legal capacity.[7] In 2013, I provided expert consultation to the UN monitoring body of the CRPD, the UN Committee on the Rights of Persons with Disabilities, in drafting their General Comment on Article 12, the right to equal recognition before the law.

The General Comment outlines their interpretation of the right to legal capacity—or the right to legal personhood.[8] It provides the first framework for examining denials of the right. It includes: (1) the definitive inclusion of both the right to hold *and* exercise legal personhood; (2) the requirement for laws related to personhood to be non-discriminatory in both purpose and effect; and (3) the

[6] Arstein-Kerslake (n 5); Amita Dhanda, 'Legal Capacity in the Disability Rights Convention: Stranglehold of the Past or Lodestar for the Future Symposium: The United Nations Convention on the Rights of Persons with Disabilities' (2007) 34 Syracuse Journal of International Law and Commerce 429; Flynn and Arstein-Kerslake (n 1); Bernadette McSherry, 'Legal Capacity under the Convention on the Rights of Persons with Disabilities' (2012) 20 Journal of Law and Medicine 22.

[7] Arstein-Kerslake (n 5); Committee on the Rights of Persons with Disabilities, 'General Comment No 1 Article 12: Equal Recognition Before the Law' (19 May 2014) UN Doc CRPD/C/GC/1; McSherry (n 6).

[8] Anna Arstein-Kerslake and Eilionóir Flynn, 'The General Comment on Article 12 of the Convention on the Rights of Persons with Disabilities: A Roadmap for Equality before the Law' (2016) 20 The International Journal of Human Rights 471.

state obligation to provide access to support for the exercise of legal personhood. This General Comment significantly enriches the understanding of how and why marginalised groups are denied full enjoyment of their right to legal personhood because it provides a framework for examining where legal personhood is denied; how such denials are occurring (explicitly or via insidious systemic practices); and whether the state is or is not meeting its obligation to correct this through the provision of support that is appropriate for marginalised populations (eg information in multiple languages for indigenous and immigrant groups; safe and low-cost legal advice for gender minorities facing gender binary barriers; and support for overcoming discrimination faced by women and other minorities). In this book, I provide one of the first analyses of this interpretation of the right to legal personhood as it applies to marginalised groups beyond disabled people.

Article 15 of CEDAW and Article 12 of the CRPD have been controversial globally. Several countries have issued reservations, declarations, or understandings which interpret the articles in a manner that will permit these jurisdictions to continue to deny the recognition or exercise of legal personhood in certain circumstances for women and disabled people—see, for example, reservations made by Australia and Canada on Article 12 CRPD, and reservations made by Algeria and Qatar on Article 15 CEDAW.[9] In addition, many non-state actors have also strongly supported the continued denial of full legal capacity to disabled people and women. For example, many have sought the continuation of restrictive guardianship laws that limit or deny the legal capacity of disabled people.[10] There is also significant resistance to women inheriting property and having equal rights to legal capacity for contracting.[11] Although CEDAW and the CRPD provide the most detail to the right to legal personhood, it is a universal right—as all international human rights are.[12] Many other marginalised groups are also experiencing widespread denials of the right, as I discuss throughout this book. For example, stateless people and undocumented migrants around the world are denied legal personhood when they

[9] Marijke De Pauw, 'Women's Rights: From Bad to Worse—Assessing the Evolution of Incompatible Reservations to the CEDAW Convention' (2013) 29 Merkourios: Utrecht Journal of International and European Law 51; Dinerstein (n 2); Mathieu Dufour, Thomas Hastings, and Richard O'Reilly, 'Canada Should Retain Its Reservation on the United Nation's Convention on the Rights of Persons with Disabilities' (2018) 63 The Canadian Journal of Psychiatry 809; Marsha A Freeman, 'Reservations to CEDAW: An Analysis for UNICEF' (UNICEF 2009); Lauren Bock Mullins, 'CEDAW: The Challenges of Enshrining Women's Equality in International Law' (2018) 20 Public Integrity 257; Joanne Watson and others, 'The Impact of the United Nations Convention on the Rights of Persons with Disabilities (CRPD) on Victorian Guardianship Practice' (2022) 44 Disability and Rehabilitation 2806.

[10] Dinerstein (n 2).

[11] Committee on the Elimination of Discrimination against Women (n 3).

[12] Anna Arstein-Kerslake, *Legal Capacity & Gender: Realising the Human Right to Legal Personhood and Agency of Women, Disabled Women, and Gender Minorities* (Springer 2021); Eva Brems, *Human Rights: Universality and Diversity* (Martinus Nijhoff Publishers 2001); Amita Dhanda, 'Universal Legal Capacity as a Universal Human Right' in Michael Dudley, Derrick Silove, and Fran Gale (eds), *Mental Health and Human Rights: Vision, Praxis, and Courage* (OUP 2012); Jack Donnelly, 'The Relative Universality of Human Rights' (2007) 29 Human Rights Quarterly 281.

are denied immigration status.[13] Such denials are rarely identified as denials of legal personhood—and there would likely be significant resistance to the scale of reform that would be required for the realisation of the right to legal personhood for such groups.

## 2. Applying the Right to Legal Personhood to Marginalised Groups

In this book, I have taken the right to legal personhood, as developed in CEDAW and the CRPD, and applied it to various marginalised groups, including disabled people, migrant groups, indigenous peoples, racial minorities, women, and gender minorities. Previous scholarship has discussed how legal personhood has been denied to these groups and the theoretical underpinnings of the boundaries of legal personhood.[14] However, the concept of legal personhood has conflicting definitions in the literature, and there is, therefore, a lack of clarity regarding the application of related concepts. In this book, I provide clarity in this area of the law by developing definitions of such concepts that will then be applied to the situation of these various minority groups.

Existing scholarship has also given little attention to the human rights implications of denials of legal personhood—particularly in light of the new detail given to the right in Article 12 of the CRPD. This book builds on previous scholarship and incorporates a human rights analysis through the application of the novel definition of the right to legal personhood as it has been illuminated by the UN Committee on the Rights of Persons with Disabilities (CRPD Committee), the UN monitoring body for the CRPD.[15]

The following table provides a non-exhaustive list of some of the legal personhood barriers that marginalised groups face and that are explored in this book.

[13] Human Rights Committee (n 4); Weissbrodt (n 4).

[14] Margaret Jane Davies and Ngaire Naffine, *Are Persons Property? Legal Debates about Property and Personality* (Ashgate 2001); Colin Dayan, *The Law Is a White Dog—How Legal Rituals Make and Unmake Persons* (Princeton UP 2013); Amy Louise Erickson, 'Coverture and Capitalism' (2005) 59 History Workshop Journal 1; Lee Holcombe, *Wives & Property: Reform of the Married Women's Property Law in Nineteenth-Century England* (University of Toronto Press 1983); Ngaire Naffine, 'Who Are Law's Persons—From Cheshire Cats to Responsible Subjects' (2003) 66 Modern Law Review 346; Ngaire Naffine, *Law's Meaning of Life: Philosophy, Religion, Darwin and the Legal Person* (Bloomsbury Publishing 2009); George Pavlich, 'Criminal Justice and Cape Law's Persons' (2014) 23 Social & Legal Studies 55; Mitchell Travis, 'Non-normative Bodies, Rationality, and Legal Personhood' (2014) 22 Medical Law Review 526; Richard Tur, 'The "Person" in Law' in Aurthur Peacocke and Grant Gillett (eds), *Persons and Personality: A Contemporary Inquiry* (Basil Blackwell 1987).

[15] Committee on the Rights of Persons with Disabilities (n 7).

| **Marginalised Group** | **Legal Personhood Barriers (Historic and Modern)** | |
|---|---|---|
| | **Recognition as Rights Holder** | **Recognition of Legal Actions** |
| Disabled people | - Plenary guardianship | - Limited guardianship<br>- Mental health law<br>- Criminalisation of sex<br>- Discrimination<br>- Forced sterilisation |
| Migrant groups | - Undocumented<br>- Slavery (ownership by another party) | - Visa restrictions<br>- Voting restrictions<br>- Contracting restrictions<br>- Discrimination |
| Stateless peoples | - Non-recognition<br>- Undocumented | - Voting restrictions<br>- Contracting restrictions<br>- Discrimination |
| Indigenous peoples | - Non-recognition<br>- Slavery (ownership by another party) | - Systemic incarceration<br>- Discrimination |
| Racial minorities | - 3/5 persons provision (US Constitution)<br>- Slavery (ownership by another party) | - Systemic incarceration<br>- Discrimination |
| Women | - Coverture (personhood held by husband) | - Inheritance<br>- Driver's license<br>- Voting restrictions<br>- Discrimination<br>- Abortion restrictions |
| Gender minorities | - Non-recognition of gender identity | - Same-sex marriage restrictions<br>- Forced sterilisation<br>- Discrimination |

The arguments in this book are based on the presumption that international human rights are universal and there are no rights that only apply to certain groups of people and not to others.[16] As such, I argue that the right to legal personhood is a universal right that applies to all people and that it stems from the right to equal recognition before the law (discussed more in Chapter 1). Evidence of its universal nature includes the inclusion of the right to equal recognition before the law in both the UDHR and the ICCPR, which are instruments that are explicitly meant to apply universally.[17]

16 Donnelly, *Universal Human Rights in Theory and Practice* (n 5).
17 ibid.

## 3. Universal Nature of Right to Legal Personhood

I explore the history of the right to equal recognition before the law in order to illuminate the universal nature of the right to legal personhood. I also explore the history in order to demonstrate the development of the right as part of the right to equal recognition before the law and to trace the development of the right to legal personhood as including both the entitlement to be a holder of rights and to take legal actions.[18] The right to equal recognition before the law can be found in Article 6 of the UDHR, which states, 'Everyone has the right to recognition everywhere as a *person* before the law.' (emphasis added) The UDHR is not legally binding; however, the UN human rights instruments that have followed the UDHR are legally binding documents that secure the rights already set out in the UDHR. This right was made legally binding by Article 16 of the ICCPR, which states, 'Everyone shall have the right to recognition everywhere as a *person* before the law.'(emphasis added) This language suggests that there was an intention to include a right to legal personhood as a core human right from the very initiation of human rights law, in the post-World War II era, with the creation and adoption of the UDHR.[19]

The development of the right to equal recognition before the law in subsequent international human rights treaties suggests that the right to legal personhood includes both a static element and an active element.[20] The static element is the entitlement to be recognised as a holder of rights—as a person with equal legal standing to others.[21] The active element is the entitlement to be recognised as a legal agent and to have your actions (decisions, omissions, physical movements, etc) recognised and enforced by the law.[22] These two elements have been established by the appearance of the right to equal recognition before the law in CEDAW and the CRPD, as discussed above.

While CEDAW and the CRPD discuss human rights in relation to particular groups, I argue that these instruments are not discussing rights that only apply to those groups.[23] Instead, they are discussing rights that are universal, and they are applying those rights to the particular situations of the relevant groups in an effort to create clarity in how those rights can be realised for these unique groups. On this basis, I analyse the right to legal personhood and the right to equal recognition before the law as universal human rights that apply to all people.

18 Arstein-Kerslake (n 5).
19 Pamela Slotte and Miia Halme, *Revisiting the Origins of Human Rights* (CUP 2015).
20 McSherry (n 6).
21 Arstein-Kerslake (n 5).
22 Anna Arstein-Kerslake and Eilionóir Flynn, 'The Right to Legal Agency: Domination, Disability and the Protections of Article 12 of the Convention on the Rights of Persons with Disabilities' (2017) 13 International Journal of Law in Context 22.
23 Rosemary Kayess and Phillip French, 'Out of Darkness into Light: Introducing the Convention on the Rights of Persons with Disabilities' (2008) 8 Human Rights Law Review 1.

The book will also argue for the interpretation of the right to legal personhood as necessitating 'universal legal personhood'. This concept was introduced by legal scholar and disability rights activist Amita Dhanda, who was one of the first to engage in substantial discussions of 'universal legal capacity'.[24] 'Universal legal capacity' is the demand for the recognition of legal capacity on an equal basis for all, regardless of group membership. Dhanda discusses universal legal capacity primarily in relation to disabled people, although she draws on the history of the right to equal recognition before the law (outlined above) to support her argument that all people, including disabled people, are entitled to legal capacity on an equal basis. Dhanda uses the term 'legal capacity' in order to mirror the terminology of the CRPD; however, as discussed further in Chapter 1, I argue that 'legal capacity' can be conceived of as synonymous with 'legal personhood'.

In this book, I explore the concept that universal legal personhood necessitates not only an examination of where disabled people are disproportionately denied legal personhood but also where other marginalised groups are disproportionately denied legal personhood. Dhanda argues that 'universal legal capacity' should be recognised for disabled people because they are humans and are entitled to the protections of the human rights regime on an equal basis with other groups.[25] I agree with that proposition and extend it to other marginalised groups. I argue that there is an international human right to legal personhood and there is, therefore, a human rights imperative to recognise universal legal personhood—and therefore, a need to examine how all groups are disproportionately denied legal personhood and the human rights implications of those denials.

Disabled people, migrant groups, indigenous peoples, racial minorities, women, and gender minorities are not the only marginalised groups that experience denials of legal personhood; for example, convicted prisoners and children also often experience legal personhood denials. More research and scholarship on these and other groups is needed. I, however, have chosen to focus this book on disabled people, migrant groups, indigenous peoples, racial minorities, women, and gender minorities because of the availability of jurisprudence related to disability and gender as well as the opportunity to undertake a novel analysis of the right to legal personhood in the context of discrimination related to race and national origin. There is jurisprudence on the right to legal personhood related to disability and gender because of the inclusion of the right in CEDAW and the CRPD. To explore the right as it relates to race and national origin, I draw on jurisprudence from the ICCPR as well as other human rights bodies in order to develop novel arguments regarding how the right applies to these groups. The aim is that in future scholarship, these novel arguments will be able to be applied to other groups as well, including groups such as convicted prisoners and children.

[24] Dhanda (n 6); Dhanda (n 12).
[25] Dhanda (n 12).

## 4. Defining the Terms 'Legal Personhood', 'Legal Capacity', and 'Mental Capacity'

As discussed above, and will be discussed elsewhere in this book, I have chosen to use the term 'legal personhood' to describe the right to equal recognition before the law, which includes both legal standing (entitlement to be a rights holder) and legal agency (entitlement to recognition as a legal actor).[26] In some of my past scholarship, I have predominantly used the term 'legal capacity' when discussing the right of an individual to be a holder of rights and to be recognised as a legal actor.[27] Here, I am using 'legal personhood' instead of 'legal capacity'; however, I am using it in the same way that I have used the term 'legal capacity' in the past. In this way, I am using the terms interchangeably, although I am primarily using the term 'legal personhood' in this book.

I chose to use the term 'legal capacity' in past scholarship because it is the terminology used in CEDAW and the CRPD. The use of the term allowed for a clear human rights analysis. However, I have found that although the language of CEDAW and the CRPD is unambiguous in establishing that the concept of 'legal capacity' includes the right to be a holder of rights and a legal actor, the term 'legal capacity' itself carries with it significant history and many people make assumptions about the term that can serve to undermine rights arguments related to the right as it is enumerated in CEDAW and the CRPD.

For example, the term 'legal capacity' is often conflated with the term 'mental capacity'. The right to legal capacity is then denied to individuals who are not deemed to have sufficient mental capacity.[28] However, the definition of legal capacity in CEDAW and the CRPD refers only to the recognition of legal standing and agency. It does not refer to an individual's decision-making skills in relation to the exercise of legal capacity. This definition of legal capacity used in CEDAW and the CRPD is commonly utilised across legal disciplines and is particularly evident when legal capacity is discussed in the context of non-human entities, such as corporations, animals, and the environment.[29] These entities may have their legal capacity recognised but may have no ability to independently engage in decision-making to exercise such legal capacity. In this way, mental capacity only relates to legal capacity in that where mental capacity is lacking there may be a need for

[26] Arstein-Kerslake (n 5); McSherry (n 6).

[27] Arstein-Kerslake (n 5); Arstein-Kerslake (n 12); Flynn and Arstein-Kerslake (n 1).

[28] Arstein-Kerslake (n 5); Committee on the Rights of Persons with Disabilities (n 7).

[29] Margaret M Blair, 'Corporate Personhood and the Corporate Persona Symposium: In the Boardroom' [2013] University of Illinois Law Review 785; Richard A Epstein, 'Animals as Objects, or Subjects, of Rights' (2002) John M Olin Program in Law and Economics Working Paper No 171 <https://papers.ssrn.com/abstract=359240> accessed 8 September 2019; Erin O'Donnell and Julia Talbot-Jones, 'Creating Legal Rights for Rivers: Lessons from Australia, New Zealand, and India' (2018) 23(1) Ecology and Society 7 <https://www.ecologyandsociety.org/vol23/iss1/art7/> accessed 8 September 2019.

additional support in the exercise of legal capacity or a third party to exercise legal capacity on behalf of the individual or entity.[30]

In order to avoid this confusion with the concept of 'metal capacity', in this book, I am using the term 'legal personhood' as equivalent to the term 'legal capacity', as mentioned above. I believe that this is particularly important in the context of marginalised groups beyond disabled people because I want to make sure that it is abundantly clear that I am not discussing the mental capacity or legal decision-making skills of these groups (as I am similarly not discussing when I write about the right to legal capacity in the context of disabled people). What I *am* discussing is the right to equal recognition before the law—the right to be recognised as a legal person on an equal basis with others, including both legal standing and legal agency, as I will discuss more throughout the book.

My aim in this book is to explore the marginalisation that is occurring as a result of barriers to the right to legal personhood. I also aim to explore how this can be rectified—how the right to legal personhood can be realised for these marginalised groups. The book presents a legal argument for the protection of the right, as well as a normative analysis of the importance of the right in maintaining equality in socio-legal systems. My aim is for the book to be a novel contribution to the field of legal personhood and legal capacity law, as well as a tool for creating change towards the realisation of the right to equal recognition before the law for all.

## 5. Relationship to Existing Literature

Significant scholarly work on the right to legal personhood has only recently begun in response to Article 12 of the CRPD. In 2017, I was the first scholar to publish a book on the subject—*Restoring Voice to People with Disabilities* (CUP). Since then, I have published another sole-authored book looking at the right to legal personhood from a gender perspective (*Legal Capacity and Gender* (Springer 2021)), as well as an edited collection on the subject (*Global Perspectives on Legal Capacity Reform* (Flynn, Arstein-Kerslake, de Bhailís, and Serra, Routledge 2018)). To date, no other book has been published that focuses on the right to legal personhood as it applies to groups other than disabled people. Only one additional book specifically on the subject of the right to legal personhood has been published, *A New Era for Mental Health Law and Policy* (Gooding; CUP 2017), which focuses on the right to legal personhood for people with mental health disability.

[30] Flynn and Arstein-Kerslake (n 1); Eilionóir Flynn and Anna Arstein-Kerslake, 'The Support Model of Legal Capacity: Fact, Fiction, or Fantasy' (2014) 32 Berkeley Journal of International Law 124.

There are a number of books that look at legal personhood but are not precisely in the field of legal personhood *rights*, because they are not examining legal personhood using a human rights framework. Other works have sections or chapters devoted to the right to legal personhood but are not wholly focused on the examination or analysis of the right.[31] The work in this book has been influenced by these previous works, and my aim is for this book to further explore legal personhood and to firmly establish it as human rights issue.

[31] Jonas-Sébastien Beaudry, *The Disabled Contract: Severe Intellectual Disability, Justice and Morality* (CUP 2021); Gauthier de Beco, *Disability in International Human Rights Law* (OUP 2021); Oddný Mjöll Arnardóttir and Gerard Quinn (eds), *The UN Convention on the Rights of Persons with Disabilities: European and Scandinavian Perspectives* (Martinus Nijhoff Publishers 2009); Davies and Naffine (n 14); Dayan (n 14); Valentina Della Fina, Rachele Cera and Giuseppe Palmisano (eds), *The United Nations Convention on the Rights of Persons with Disabilities: A Commentary* (1st edn, Springer 2017); Mary Donnelly, *Healthcare Decision-Making and the Law: Autonomy, Capacity and the Limits of Liberalism* (CUP 2010); Áine Hynes, *Irish Capacity Law and Assisted Decision-Making* (Bloomsbury Publishing Plc 2018); Arlene S Kanter, *The Development of Disability Rights under International Law: From Charity to Human Rights* (1st edn, Routledge 2014); Catriona Mackenzie and Natalie Stoljar, *Relational Autonomy: Feminist Perspectives on Autonomy, Agency, and the Social Self* (OUP 2000); Bernadette McSherry and Penny Weller, *Rethinking Rights-Based Mental Health Laws* (Bloomsbury Publishing 2010); Naffine, *Law's Meaning of Life* (n 14); Charles O'Mahony and Gerard Quinn (eds), *Disability Law and Policy: An Analysis of the UN Convention* (Clarus Press 2016); Maya Sabatello and Marianne Schulze (eds), *Human Rights and Disability Advocacy* (University of Pennsylvania Press 2013); Dean Spade, *Normal Life: Administrative Violence, Critical Trans Politics, and the Limits of Law* (Duke UP 2015).

# Contents

# Table of Cases

# Table of Legislation

# 1
# Defining Legal Personhood

## 1. Introduction

There is a robust line of scholarship related to personhood.[1] However, there is little agreement on the definition of personhood and related concepts—such as *moral* personhood, *legal* personhood, legal capacity, legal standing, and legal agency. Such concepts are often poorly defined and conflated in the literature and in law.[2] Drawing on the Convention on the Elimination of Discrimination Against Women (CEDAW), the Convention on the Rights of Persons with Disabilities (CRPD), as well as previous scholarship, I will present new working definitions of these concepts in an effort to provide an original contribution that may serve to provide some clarity in the confusing literature that currently exists.

### 1.1 Legal versus Moral Personhood

Much of the existing philosophical and theoretical scholarship focuses on either legal personhood or moral personhood. While there is often inconsistency in how these terms are used, it is useful to ascribe them general definitions in order to categorise existing literature and to begin to understand modern *legal* personhood. Understanding modern legal personhood is, in turn, important for identifying denials of legal personhood that should be protected by human rights law—which is one of my aims in this book.

We will turn first to moral personhood. It is a more flexible concept than legal personhood because it is purely theoretical. It is also commonly referred to as 'moral status'—it is the philosophical recognition of an individual or entity as a 'person' for the purpose of ascribing moral agency, responsibility, and entitlements.[3] In other words, it is an existential—and often intuitive—assignment of

[1] Margaret Jane Davies and Ngaire Naffine, *Are Persons Property? Legal Debates about Property and Personality* (Ashgate 2001); Eva Feder Kittay, 'At the Margins of Moral Personhood' (2005) 116 Ethics 100; Visa AJ Kurki, *A Theory of Legal Personhood* (OUP 2019); Ngaire Naffine, 'Who Are Law's Persons: From Cheshire Cats to Responsible Subjects' (2003) 66 Modern Law Review 346.

[2] Eilionóir Flynn, 'Law, Language and Personhood: Disrupting Definitions of Legal Capacity' (2021) 30 Griffith Law Review 374; Ngaire Naffine, *Law's Meaning of Life: Philosophy, Religion, Darwin and the Legal Person* (Bloomsbury Publishing 2009).

[3] Peter Singer, 'Speciesism and Moral Status' (2009) 40 Metaphilosophy 567; Mary Anne Warren, *Moral Status: Obligations to Persons and Other Living Things* (OUP 2000).

*The Right to Legal Personhood of Marginalised Groups*. Anna Arstein-Kerslake, Oxford University Press.
 DOI: 10.1093/9780191926549.003.0001

ethical obligations and rights. Legal personhood, on the other hand, is more rigid because it is the recognition of that status in the law.[4] It is not theoretical—or we are not defining it as theoretical for our purposes here. It requires an actual legal instrument granting such legal personhood.[5] Legal personhood and moral personhood intersect, or are related to each other, in that legal mechanisms granting or denying legal personhood often do so in a manner that aligns quite closely with theories of moral personhood.[6] For example, definitions of moral personhood often exclude disabled people—especially cognitively disabled people. Similarly, disabled people experience, arguably, the highest rate of denials of legal personhood via guardianship laws, interdiction, conservatorship, and other mechanisms that deny legal personhood on the basis of actual or perceived cognitive disability.[7] In this way, theory related to moral personhood has the power to influence the development and practical application of legal instruments granting or denying legal personhood to various human or non-human entities.

Exploring the practical nature of legal personhood further, we can identify that its function is often to assign personhood to human or non-human entities when it is necessary to recognise them as legal persons with rights and/or responsibilities, whereas discussions and ascriptions of moral personhood are not tied to such necessity. For example, corporations have quite consistently been recognised as legal persons, because it is important to legally recognise both their responsibilities and their rights. When they act negligently, we need a 'legal person' to hold responsible. Conversely, economic demands—and the nature of capitalism—have required that corporations have certain rights, in order to allow them to act relatively freely within the marketplace.[8] Scholars and legal theorists tackling the ascription of moral personhood to corporations are not tethered to such practical concerns—instead they often focus on the exploration of the nature of the corporation and whether an entity without singular cognition or conscience can be theoretically recognised as a moral person.[9] This flexibility in conceptions of moral personhood is useful in that it allows freedom in the development of such theory without the responsibility to be too concerned with the practical implications of such theory.

[4] Naffine, *Law's Meaning of Life* (n 2).

[5] Eilionóir Flynn and Anna Arstein-Kerslake, 'Legislating Personhood: Realising the Right to Support in Exercising Legal Capacity' (2014) 10 International Journal of Law in Context 81.

[6] ibid.

[7] Anna Arstein-Kerslake, *Restoring Voice to People with Cognitive Disabilities* (CUP 2017).

[8] Margaret M Blair, 'Corporate Personhood and the Corporate Persona Symposium: In the Boardroom' (2013) University of Illinois Law Review 785; Frederick Green, 'Corporations as Persons, Citizens, and Possessors of Liberty' (1945) 94 University of Pennsylvania Law Review 202; Michelle Worthington and Peta Spender, 'Constructing Legal Personhood: Corporate Law's Legacy' (2021) 30 Griffith Law Review 348.

[9] Peter A French, 'The Corporation as a Moral Person' (1979) 16 American Philosophical Quarterly 207; Michael J Phillips, 'Corporate Moral Personhood and Three Conceptions of the Corporation' (1992) 2 Business Ethics Quarterly 435; Susanna K Ripken, 'Corporations Are People Too: A Multi-dimensional Approach to the Corporate Personhood Puzzle' (2009) 15 Fordham Journal of Corporate & Financial Law 97.

I engage in this exploration of the distinctions of moral and legal personhood in order to create a foundation on which to move forward with this discussion—in order to firmly establish what *legal* personhood is and when it should be protected by human rights law. Further exploring such distinctions, it is important to note that while this ascription of legal personhood based on practicality and necessity is true in some areas—such as corporate law—there are many cases in which the impetus for the granting or denying of legal personhood seems to be much more related to social bias and the maintenance of power and privilege of certain groups of people—frequently white, able-bodied, cisgender men. Interestingly, this impetus overlaps with the ascription of moral personhood; even from a theoretical perspective, there seems to be a common theme among theorists—they are often keen to recognise moral personhood for those individuals that are similar to themselves and to exclude those that are different. Recognition of moral personhood along these lines, of course, conveniently allows those theorists and their social group to maintain power and privilege via the recognition of their personhood to the exclusion of others.

## 1.2 Exclusions from Legal and Moral Personhood

Since the earliest written codes of law, scholars and others have been discussing who should and who should not be included as legal persons.[10] Historically, marginalised groups have often been excluded from legal personhood. For example, slaves, racial minorities, and colonised peoples have been excluded from personhood via criminalisation, imprisonment, voting restrictions, and other means, including specific laws that limit personhood for individuals in these groups.[11] Women have been excluded from full legal personhood through inheritance restrictions, through coverture laws that extinguish legal personhood upon marriage, and in other ways.[12] Numerous other examples can be found throughout history.

In addition, moral philosophers have long grappled with the concept of moral personhood and have discussed the exclusion of certain groups. For example, in

[10] Davies and Naffine (n 1); David Gindis, 'Legal Personhood and the Firm: Avoiding Anthropomorphism and Equivocation' (2016) 12 Journal of Institutional Economics 499.

[11] Colin Dayan, *The Law Is a White Dog: How Legal Rituals Make and Unmake Persons* (Princeton UP 2013); George Pavlich, 'Criminal Justice and Cape Law's Persons' (2014) 23 Social & Legal Studies 55.

[12] Mary Beth Combs, '"A Measure of Legal Independence": The 1870 Married Women's Property Act and the Portfolio Allocations of British Wives' (2005) 65 The Journal of Economic History 1028; Amy Louise Erickson, 'Coverture and Capitalism' (2005) 59 History Workshop Journal 1; Eleanor Flexner and Ellen Frances Fitzpatrick, *Century of Struggle: The Woman's Rights Movement in the United States* (Harvard UP 1996); Ngaire Naffine, 'Women and the Cast of Legal Persons' in Jackie Jones and others (eds), *Gender, Sexualities and Law* (Routledge 2011); Mary Lyndon Shanley, *Feminism, Marriage, and the Law in Victorian England* (Princeton UP 1993).

the late 1600s, John Locke influentially theorised that personhood was dependent on memory and 'reflective consciousness'.[13] Therefore, one could only possess moral personhood—and be held responsible for their actions—if they could remember and reflect on inappropriate or criminal behaviour.[14] In this way, Locke excludes any person with cognitive impairment that may impact reflection or memory. Furthermore, in his work on the 'social contract', he went on to exclude cognitively disabled people in general from societal participation.[15] His work explicitly excludes people with cognitive disability from political participation.[16] With this work, Locke has been credited as instigating a movement in moral philosophy to exclude cognitively disabled people from consideration as moral persons.[17] Following this trend, the well-known liberal political philosopher John Rawls's conception of personhood requires that the individual have two moral powers: (1) the capacity for a sense of justice; and (2) the capacity for a conception of the good.[18] Many have regarded this as an explicit exclusion of cognitively disabled people from moral personhood.[19] For example, philosopher Martha Nussbaum revisited Rawls's theories and concluded that they exclude cognitively disabled people.[20] Sophia Wong further explored this line of theory and concluded that it is more morally dangerous to exclude disabled people from moral personhood than it is to include them.[21] The efforts of scholars examining both moral and legal personhood have often focused on who to exclude from these categories and when to exclude them.

I do not want to dwell too long here on the long-overprivileged theories of predominantly white, able-bodied, cisgender men—and the many commentaries that have emerged regarding those theories. While they are, of course, not without merit, they have, I believe, been given enough attention. In addition, as mentioned previously, they have served to maintain the power and privilege of those similar to them—other white, able-bodied, cisgender men. There is little consideration in

[13] John Locke, *An Essay Concerning Human Understanding* (Roger Woolhouse ed, Reprint edn, Penguin Classics 1998); Lawrence A Locke, 'Personhood and Moral Responsibility' (1990) 9 Law and Philosophy 39.

[14] Locke, 'Personhood and Moral Responsibility' (n 13).

[15] John Locke, *The Works of John Locke* (T Longman, B Law 1794); John Locke, *Locke: Two Treatises of Government* (CUP 1967).

[16] Barbara Arneil, 'Disability, Self Image, and Modern Political Theory' (2009) 37 Political Theory 218; Stacy Clifford, 'The Capacity Contract: Locke, Disability, and the Political Exclusion of "Idiots"' (2014) 2 Politics, Groups, and Identities 90.

[17] Simon Jarrett, 'The Extinction of Intellectual Disability: An Enlightenment Project from Locke to Freud', in Stan Booth and Chris Mounsey (eds), *Reconsidering Extinction in Terms of the History of Global Bioethics* (Routledge 2021).

[18] John Rawls, *Political Liberalism* (Columbia UP 2005).

[19] Arneil (n 16); Flynn and Arstein-Kerslake (n 5); Christie Hartley, 'Disability and Justice' (2011) 6 Philosophy Compass 120; Sophia Isako Wong, 'Duties of Justice to Citizens with Cognitive Disabilities' in Eva Feder Kittay and Licia Carlson (eds), *Cognitive Disability and Its Challenge to Moral Philosophy* (John Wiley & Sons 2010).

[20] Hartley (n 19); Martha Craven Nussbaum, *Frontiers of Justice: Disability, Nationality, Species Membership* (Harvard UP 2006).

[21] Flynn and Arstein-Kerslake (n 5); Wong (n 19).

their theories of the perspective of those individuals and groups of people experiencing less privilege. The exclusion of disabled people from personhood is just one example; however, other examples abound. They often ignore the interdependencies inherent in our socio-legal world and instead focus their theories of personhood on the illusion of an able-bodied, autonomous, non-pregnant cisgender male deftly moving through the world.[22]

Theories related to legal personhood—especially more recent theories—have enjoyed some more diversity in both their content and the theorists developing them. For example, feminist legal theorist Ngaire Naffine has explored various aspects of legal personhood, including its boundaries as well as who law is constructed for and whether there are individuals or groups that should not be considered legal persons.[23] She has also challenged the ability to achieve equal recognition of personhood for men and women within legal structures that were created to prioritise the personhood of men.[24] Margaret Davies has similarly contended that gender plays a significant role in the ascription of personhood, often causing personhood to be disproportionately granted to males.[25] Richard Tur also discusses the limits of legal personhood and argues for an expansive view of legal personhood.[26] These newer, more diverse, and nuanced theories have ushered in a new opportunity to further explore the concept of legal personhood—its power, influence, construction, and development.

## 1.3 Legal Personhood as Part of the Human Right to Equal Recognition

The concept of equality has long been a focus of legal and socio-legal scholarship. It has many varied constructions, and a multitude of theories have arisen to propose solutions towards the realisation of equality.[27] For these reasons, as a preliminary

[22] Arneil (n 16); Arstein-Kerslake, *Restoring Voice to People with Cognitive Disabilities* (n 7); Anna Arstein-Kerslake, *Legal Capacity & Gender: Realising the Human Right to Legal Personhood and Agency of Women, Disabled Women, and Gender Minorities* (Springer 2021); Catriona Mackenzie and Natalie Stoljar, *Relational Autonomy: Feminist Perspectives on Autonomy, Agency, and the Social Self* (OUP 2000); Naffine, 'Who Are Law's Persons: From Cheshire Cats to Responsible Subjects' (n 1); Naffine, *Law's Meaning of Life* (n 2); Naffine, 'Women and the Cast of Legal Persons' (n 12).

[23] Davies and Naffine (n 1); Ngaire Naffine, 'When Does the Legal Person Die? Jeremy Bentham and the "Auto-Icon"' (2000) 25 Australian Journal of Legal Philosophy 79; Naffine, 'Who Are Law's Persons: From Cheshire Cats to Responsible Subjects' (n 1); Naffine, *Law's Meaning of Life* (n 2).

[24] Ngaire Naffine, *Criminal Law and the Man Problem* (Bloomsbury Publishing 2019).

[25] Margaret Davies, 'Queer Property, Queer Persons: Self-Ownership and Beyond' (1999) 8 Social & Legal Studies 327; Davies and Naffine (n 1).

[26] Richard Tur, 'The "Person" in Law' in Aurthur Peacocke and Grant Gillett (eds), *Persons and Personality: A Contemporary Inquiry* (Basil Blackwell 1987).

[27] Ronald Dworkin, *Sovereign Virtue: The Theory and Practice of Equality* (Harvard UP 2002); Martha Albertson Fineman, 'The Vulnerable Subject: Anchoring Equality in the Human Condition' (2008) 20 Yale Journal of Law and Feminism 1; Thomas Nagel, *Equality and Partiality* (OUP 1995); Nussbaum (n 20); John Rawls, *A Theory of Justice* (Harvard UP 2009); Amartya Kumar Sen, *Inequality Reexamined* (OUP 1992).

matter, it is essential to clarify what I am referring to when I am discussing equality in this book. I am specifically exploring equality in how the law recognises the legal personhood of an individual or group. In other words, I am exploring how the law recognises an individual's legal standing and legal agency—and whether certain individuals or groups of individuals are subjected to unequal or differential recognition of their standing and agency. Where there is evidence that unequal recognition is occurring on the basis of group membership, I will use the human rights framework to challenge whether that is appropriate.

An expansive view of the right to equal recognition before the law may also include how the law recognises non-human entities, such as animals, the environment, corporations, and others. Some scholars have begun to explore this and have developed fruitful arguments—many of them complementary to those that I am developing in this book.[28] In this book, however, my focus is on the law's recognition of *human* individuals and groups. I am examining how the law grants and denies legal personhood and agency to human individuals or groups.[29] I do think, however, that the arguments that I develop here, in relation to human individuals and groups, may be usefully applied to non-human entities—and I have endeavoured to keep this in mind as I have developed these arguments.

My aim is to build on past scholarship on legal personhood and to explore how a human right to legal personhood can contribute to that scholarship. Ultimately, I aim to construct arguments that will facilitate the use of the human right to legal personhood as a tool to rectify some of the power and privilege imbalances that have been identified by previous scholarship due to the manner in which legal personhood has been historically constructed—especially how it has been historically constructed to exclude certain groups, such as women, disabled people, and others.[30] In the first instance, I will provide an examination of existing international law to develop a definition of the human right to legal personhood as part of the human right to equal recognition before the law.

As discussed above, building on the text of CEDAW, the CRPD confirmed that the right to equal recognition before the law includes the right to 'legal capacity'—which I am equating to the right to 'legal personhood' in this book, as discussed in the preface, in order to clearly distinguish the right from the concept of mental capacity. I have made this choice because the concepts of legal capacity and

[28] Anna Arstein-Kerslake and others, 'Relational Personhood: A Conception of Legal Personhood with Insights from Disability Rights and Environmental Law' (2021) 30 Griffith Law Review 530; Erin O'Donnell and Julia Talbot-Jones, 'Creating Legal Rights for Rivers: Lessons from Australia, New Zealand, and India' (2018) 23(1):7 Ecology and Society <https://www.ecologyandsociety.org/vol23/iss1/art7/> accessed 8 September 2019; Martuwarra RiverOfLife and others, 'Yoongoorrookoo' (2021) 30 Griffith Law Review 505; Worthington and Spender (n 8).

[29] Arstein-Kerslake, *Restoring Voice to People with Cognitive Disabilities* (n 7); Committee on the Rights of Persons with Disabilities, 'General Comment No 1 Article 12: Equal Recognition Before the Law' (19 May 2014) UN Doc CRPD/C/GC/1; Flynn and Arstein-Kerslake (n 5).

[30] Arstein-Kerslake, *Restoring Voice to People with Cognitive Disabilities* (n 7); Arstein-Kerslake, *Legal Capacity & Gender* (n 22); Flynn and Arstein-Kerslake (n 5); Naffine, *Law's Meaning of Life* (n 2).

mental capacity are all too often conflated. In this book, 'mental capacity' will only be used to refer to an entity's decision-making skills.[31] 'Legal capacity' or 'legal personhood', on the other hand, will be used to refer to the law's recognition of an individual's legal standing and agency. The term 'mental capacity' is only related to legal capacity because an individual's decision-making skills are relevant to whether they may need support for legal decision-making, which is an exercise of legal agency and a component of legal capacity and legal personhood.[32]

## 1.4 Right to Legal Personhood beyond Gender and Disability

Article 12 of the CRPD provides unprecedented detail to the rights to equal recognition before the law and legal personhood. Many scholars—including me—have begun to explore how this impacts the rights of disabled people.[33] However, these rights apply not only to disabled people but also to all people. This is because, as described above, the rights within the CRPD are merely reiterations of rights that already existed in the 'International Bill of Rights'—which is made up of the Universal Declaration of Human Rights (UDHR), the International Covenant on Civil and Political Rights (ICCPR), and the International Covenant of Economic, Social and Cultural Rights (ICESCR).[34] There are various groups that are experiencing different forms of denials of these rights. However, little attention has been given to how the right to legal personhood, and the broader right to equal recognition before the law, impacts other marginalised groups. This book begins to explore what the rights to equal recognition before the law and legal personhood mean for various marginalised groups and how those groups are experiencing barriers to those rights. It will then explore solutions for breaking down these barriers.

[31] Arstein-Kerslake, *Restoring Voice to People with Cognitive Disabilities* (n 7).

[32] Anna Arstein-Kerslake and Eilionóir Flynn, 'The General Comment on Article 12 of the Convention on the Rights of Persons with Disabilities: A Roadmap for Equality before the Law' (2016) 20 The International Journal of Human Rights 471; Committee on the Rights of Persons with Disabilities, 'General Comment No 1 Article 12: Equal Recognition before the Law' (n 29); Flynn and Arstein-Kerslake (n 5).

[33] Arstein-Kerslake, *Restoring Voice to People with Cognitive Disabilities* (n 7); Peter Bartlett, 'The United Nations Convention on the Rights of Persons with Disabilities and Mental Health Law' (2012) 75 The Modern Law Review 752; Eilionóir Flynn and others, *Global Perspectives on Legal Capacity Reform: Our Voices, Our Stories* (Routledge 2018); Flynn and Arstein-Kerslake (n 5); Piers Gooding, 'Navigating the Flashing Amber Lights of the Right to Legal Capacity in the United Nations Convention on the Rights of Persons with Disabilities: Responding to Major Concerns' (2015) 15 Human Rights Law Review 45; Bernadette McSherry, 'Mental Health Laws: Where to from Here' (2014) 40 Monash University Law Review 175; Gerard Quinn and Anna Arstein-Kerslake, 'Restoring the Human in "Human Rights": Personhood and Doctrinal Innovation in the UN Disability Convention' in Connor Gearty and Costas Douzinas, *The Cambridge Companion to Human Rights Law* (CUP 2012).

[34] Rosemary Kayess and Phillip French, 'Out of Darkness into Light: Introducing the Convention on the Rights of Persons with Disabilities' (2008) 8 Human Rights Law Review 1.

## 2. Multiple Constructions of 'Legal Capacity' and 'Legal Personhood'

Before progressing to my substantive arguments related to the right to equal recognition before the law, I would like to provide additional clarity on terminology. The discussion that I am outlining here pertains to my arguments for the choices that I have made regarding terminology. There is vast variation across scholars, disciplines, and jurisdictions regarding most of these terms. I have made my decisions related to terminology based on widespread acceptance of such terms, as well as the clarity and consistency that particular terms could offer, if used in the manner that I am suggesting here.

The concept of legal capacity has been construed in various ways. *Black's Law Dictionary* defines 'legal capacity' as the '[l]awful capacity for an entity in its own name to enter into binding contracts, to sue and to be sued'.[35] This definition is widely held as correct, which is evidenced in its use across various different legal fields.[36] Although it does not explicitly specify it in this definition, in order for the concept of legal capacity to include the recognition of an entity's ability to enter into binding contracts and to sue and be sued in its own name, it necessarily must include both the recognition of legal standing and legal agency. Legal standing is an entity's recognition as a holder of rights and responsibilities.[37] Legal agency is the recognition of that entity's freedom to act on those rights and responsibilities—for example, to enter into contracts and to sue and be sued.[38] Legal standing is required for such actions to be taken by an entity in its own name. Legal agency is required for the entity's legal actions themselves to be recognised as valid. If an entity has their legal standing recognised, but not their legal agency, it is recognised as a holder of rights and responsibilities, but any action it takes is not legally valid or enforceable by law. For these reasons, it appears self-evident that legal capacity must include both legal standing and legal agency if it is to include the right for an entity to enter into binding contracts and to sue and to be sued in its own

[35] 'Capacity' and 'Legal Entity' in Bryan A Garner (ed), *Black's Law Dictionary* (11th edn, Thomson Reuters 2019).

[36] Richard A Epstein, 'Animals as Objects, or Subjects, of Rights' (2002) John M Olin Program in Law and Economics Working Paper No 171 <https://papers.ssrn.com/abstract=359240> accessed 8 September 2019; WM Geldart, 'Legal Personality' (1911) 27 Law Quarterly Review 90; Abigail Hutchison, 'The Whanganui River as a Legal Person' (2014) 39 Alternative Law Journal 179.

[37] Arstein-Kerslake, *Restoring Voice to People with Cognitive Disabilities* (n 7); Flynn and Arstein-Kerslake (n 5); Gindis (n 10); Naffine, 'Who Are Law's Persons: From Cheshire Cats to Responsible Subjects' (n 1); Naffine, *Law's Meaning of Life* (n 2).

[38] Anna Arstein-Kerslake and Eilionóir Flynn, 'The Right to Legal Agency: Domination, Disability and the Protections of Article 12 of the Convention on the Rights of Persons with Disabilities' (2017) 13 International Journal of Law in Context 22; Bernadette M McSherry, 'Legal Capacity under the Convention on the Rights of Persons with Disabilities' (2012) 20 Journal of Law and Medicine 22.

name. Importantly, this is consistent with the use of the term 'legal capacity' in both CEDAW and the CRPD.

The term 'legal capacity' is widely used in the legal field; however, beyond the legal field, the concept of 'legal personhood' is more frequently used to refer to an entity's recognition by the state. This use of legal personhood is common in philosophy—as discussed above—as well as in more common parlance. In addition, as also mentioned above, the use of the term 'legal personhood' to refer to an entity's legal standing and agency avoids the conflation of the concepts of legal capacity and mental capacity. For these reasons, I have chosen to primarily use the term 'legal personhood' in this book—when I use the term, I am using it in the same manner that the term 'legal capacity' is used in CEDAW and the CRPD—to encompass both an individual's legal standing and agency.

The use of the term 'legal personhood' in this way is consistent with the definition of the term across many different legal and scholarly platforms. For example, *Black's Law Dictionary* defines 'person' as '[a]n entity ... that is recognized by law as having most of the rights and duties of a human being'.[39] Quoting *Jurisprudence* by John Salmond, a legal scholar from New Zealand, it also states, 'So far as legal theory is concerned, a person is any being whom the law regards as capable of rights or duties.'[40] It also includes a quote from *English Private Law*, which states, 'The word "person" is now generally used in English to denote a human being, but the word is also used in a technical legal sense, to denote a subject of legal rights and duties.'[41] All three emanations of the definition of 'person' include both standing—to be a subject of rights—and agency—to have duties. This mirrors the definition of 'legal capacity'—discussed above—which also includes both. There are uses of the term 'legal personhood' that differ from this definition.[42] However, I believe that it is used in this manner consistently enough that it can be equated to the concept of legal capacity for the purposes of examining the right to equal recognition before the law—as I am endeavouring to do in this book.

For the purposes of further clarity, some of the key terms have been succinctly defined in the following table:

[39] 'Person' *Black's Law Dictionary* (n 35).

[40] Nonhuman Rights Project and Spencer Lo, 'What Is a Legal Person? Law Dictionary Corrects Decades-Old Error' (*Nonhuman Rights Project*, 25 June 2019) <https://www.nonhumanrights.org/blog/legal-person-blacks-law-correction/> accessed 13 March 2023; Sir John William Salmond, *Jurisprudence: Or, the Theory of the Law* (Stevens and Haynes 1907).

[41] Peter Birks, *English Private Law* (OUP 2000) 142–143.

[42] Amita Dhanda, 'Legal Capacity in the Disability Rights Convention: Stranglehold of the Past or Lodestar for the Future Symposium: The United Nations Convention on the Rights of Persons with Disabilities' (2007) 34 Syracuse Journal of International Law and Commerce 429.

| Term | Definition |
| --- | --- |
| Legal capacity | Holder of legal rights **and** obligations/duties |
| Legal personhood | Holder of legal rights **and** obligations/duties |
| Moral personhood | Holder of *ethical* rights **and** obligations/duties |
| Legal standing | Holder of legal rights |
| Legal agent | Holder of legal obligations/duties |

Below is a further discussion of legal agency and its role as an element of legal personhood and legal capacity.

## 2.1 Legal Agency

Legal agency has not been given as much scholarly attention as legal personhood; more broadly, however, there is some scholarship related to defining and attributing legal agency. For example, Manfred Rehbinder has discussed the move, from the 19th century onwards, to evaluate legal agency separately from legal status or personhood.[43] Previously, an individual's social status dictated their legal personhood, which also dictated their ability to exercise legal agency. For example, an individual's status as a woman or slave would dictate their status as a legal person. Legal agency for that class of person would then often be predetermined based on that status. However, from the 19th century onwards, there was a move away from social status being tied to legal personhood and also a move to disentangle legal personhood from legal agency. The result was an evolution towards an emphasis on mental capacity for the exercise of legal agency, as opposed to reliance on social status to dictate personhood and agency.[44]

Based on new conceptions of legal agency arising from human rights law, Eilionóir Flynn and I have also explored the concept of legal agency.[45] We sought to provide a modern definition of 'legal agency' in order to determine when legal capacity is being exercised—and, therefore, when the rights to legal capacity and equal recognition before the law are implicated. We established the following definition of 'legal agency':

[43] Manfred Rehbinder, 'Status, Contract, and the Welfare State' (1970) 23 Stanford Law Review 941.
[44] Arstein-Kerslake, *Restoring Voice to People with Cognitive Disabilities* (n 7); Arstein-Kerslake and Flynn (n 38); Rehbinder (n 43).
[45] Arstein-Kerslake and Flynn (n 38).

An action or inaction that the individual intended and which

1. has legal consequences, or
2. creates, modifies, or extinguishes a legal relationship.[46]

We argue that legal agency must include an element of intention. This is in line with moral philosophy on the subject which discusses elements of moral consideration as essential in order to attribute moral agency to an entity.[47] We also argue that legal agency does not require understanding. An entity can be exercising legal agency without understanding the nature and/or consequences of their action or inaction.[48]

In addition, moral philosophy scholarship on personhood, as discussed above, has delineated the granting of personhood as contingent upon the actual or perceived ability to exercise legal agency—especially when considering the personhood of disabled people. For example, Martha Nussbaum has concluded that people with intellectual disability may be excluded from personhood, as defined by John Rawls, because they may not possess the two required moral powers listed above. She postulates that some people with intellectual disability may not have the required reasonableness to regard others as equal citizens and to engage with others on acceptable terms. In addition, she asserts that some people with intellectual disability may not have the required rationality to determine their own goals and take action to realise those goals.[49] In essence, Nussbaum is suggesting that some people with intellectual disability are excluded from Rawls's highly influential definition of 'moral personhood' on the basis that some people with intellectual disability are not able to exercise the two moral powers identified by Rawls. The exercise of these moral powers is essentially equivalent to the exercise of legal agency in that they require engagement with other actors as well as taking action to realise personal goals.

As may be evident from the above examples, it is not always easy to disentangle a denial of legal standing from a denial of legal agency—they are often contingent upon one another. For example, the denial of voting rights to women is both a partial denial of legal standing—because it effectively excludes women from being counted as political participants—and a denial of legal agency—because voting is an action that an individual must take and it is only recognised as valid if that individual is recognised as a legal person with legal agency.

Scholarly attention has also been given to the granting or denying of legal capacity, particularly in relation to disabled people. However, relatively little scholarly

[46] ibid.

[47] James Stacey Taylor, *Personal Autonomy: New Essays on Personal Autonomy and Its Role in Contemporary Moral Philosophy* (CUP 2005).

[48] Arstein-Kerslake and Flynn (n 38).

[49] Nussbaum (n 20); Wong (n 19).

attention had been given to the concept of legal capacity as an individual right. This changed during the 2003 and 2004 drafting of the UN CRPD, which included a contentious debate regarding what legal capacity meant.[50] One of the main tensions arose around whether legal capacity referred simply to legal standing or whether it also included legal agency. Some of these tensions arose due to differences in conceptions of legal capacity and legal personhood in civil law and common law jurisdictions, which will be discussed below. However, some of these tensions also arose out of a desire to maintain laws that deny legal agency to disabled people—such as guardianship, interdiction, conservatorship, unfitness to plead, insanity defences, and others. Some argued that such laws are necessary to protect disabled people. However, such laws are applied to disabled people and, generally, not applied to non-disabled people, which has created a legal regime in which the legal agency of disabled people is pervasively under threat in a way in which it is not for non-disabled people.

Ultimately, during the drafting of the CRPD, it was determined that legal capacity is the law's recognition of an individual, or other entity, as a holder of rights (legal standing) and a legal actor (legal agency).[51] Although this is not explicitly stated in the text of the convention, it is made clear by the specific inclusion of legal personhood (Article 12(1)) and mentions of protections for exercising legal capacity (Article 12(3)) and various types of legal agency, including inheritance and financial interactions (Article 12(5)). These initial tensions during the drafting of the CRPD is one reason why I am endeavouring to be very explicit in this book, and elsewhere in my work, to ensure that it is clear that I am defining 'legal personhood' and 'legal capacity' to include both legal standing and legal agency.

As discussed above and in the preface, the concept of legal capacity has been conflated with the concept of mental capacity.[52] This is particularly true when the concept of legal capacity is applied to disabled people—especially cognitive disability, including mental health disability, intellectual disability, learning disability, autism, dementia, Alzheimer's, and others. Instead of utilising the definition established above, and widely used throughout the legal field, discussions of legal capacity and disabled people has assumed that the term 'legal capacity' refers to an individual's legal decision-making skills—or mental capacity. Accordingly, laws and practices have developed that delineate a bright line between those who are deemed to have sufficient legal decision-making skills and those who do not. Those who do are considered to have legal capacity, and those who do not are not

[50] Dhanda (n 42).

[51] Office of the United Nations High Commissioner of Human Rights, 'Legal Capacity', Background Conference Document for the Sixth Session of the Ad Hoc Committee on a Comprehensive and Integral International Convention on Protection and Promotion of the Rights and Dignity of Persons with Disabilities, 1–12 August 2005.

[52] Flynn and Arstein-Kerslake (n 5).

recognised as having legal capacity. This is a different use of the concept of legal capacity than has traditionally been used across legal fields, as discussed above in the terminology section.[53]

The problem with the conflation of legal capacity and mental capacity is that it risks discriminatorily denying legal capacity to disabled people who have actual or perceived impairments related to decision-making. If the concept of legal capacity, as defined above, is defined to simply be the recognition that an entity—including a human—can enter into binding contracts and sue and be sued, then the actual decision-making skills of that entity or individual becomes an entirely separate issue. When legal capacity is recognised in corporations, animals, and the environment, it is clear that the mental capacity of these entities is a separate issue. Of course, it is an issue that must be addressed in order for the recognition of legal capacity to be meaningful. For example, a river may be recognised as possessing legal capacity; however, it does not have the mental capacity to exercise that legal capacity—the legal agency element of legal capacity. As such, there must be a representative that acts on behalf of the river. It becomes another question as to what principles should guide that representative decision-maker—which will be addressed later in this book. Similarly, when addressing legal capacity in relation to any group of individuals, including individuals with disability, and using the definition of 'legal capacity' above, mental capacity—or legal decision-making skills—is an entirely separate issue.

This book uses the definition of 'legal personhood' and 'legal capacity' that can be found in *Black's Law Dictionary* and is widely used across legal disciplines.[54] As discussed above, this construction of legal personhood and legal capacity refers to an entity's recognition as a holder of rights and legal agent. The concept of mental capacity—or legal decision-making skills—is a wholly separate concept referring to an individual's decision-making skills and will be discussed as such throughout this book. A more in-depth discussion of the meaning of legal personhood and legal capacity can be found in the following sections—including a discussion of how the meaning of the right to legal personhood is evolving in international human rights law.

## 2.2 Civil Law Jurisdictions

Civil law jurisdictions have traditionally provided for definitions of 'legal standing' and 'legal agency' in statutory code—in both public and private law—and they

[53] Committee on the Rights of Persons with Disabilities, 'General Comment No 1 Article 12: Equal Recognition Before the Law' (n 29); Flynn and Arstein-Kerslake (n 5).

[54] Blair (n 8); Epstein (n 36); 'Legal Capacity' <https://thelawdictionary.org/legal-capacity/> accessed 22 July 2019; Office of the United Nations High Commissioner of Human Rights (OHCHR) (n 51).

serve as important aspects of the legal landscape.[55] Many civil law jurisdictions, such as France and Spain, utilise the concepts of legal personality, legal capacity, legal agency, and legal bearer of rights as separate concepts. Legal personality is acquired at the moment of birth and remains for the duration of the life of an individual. It is a precondition for legal capacity—in other words, an entity must have their legal personality recognised in order to then have their legal capacity recognised. Legal capacity includes the recognition as a bearer of rights as well as a legal agent. Recognition as a bearer of rights is inherent to every individual and cannot be limited. However, recognition as a legal agent requires specific elements, such as majority age[56] and an understanding of the nature and consequences of legal actions.[57] Therefore, an individual can have their legal agency limited or denied. In order to be recognised as a legal agent, an entity must first be recognised as a bearer of rights. However, an entity can be recognised as a bearer of rights without also being recognised as a legal agent.[58] The codified and well-developed literature surrounding these concepts in civil law jurisdictions necessitates a thorough understanding of the right to legal capacity at the international level and a careful incorporation of the right into domestic law in civil law jurisdictions. This is particularly important because of the many different languages of civil law jurisdictions and the variability of legal translations. It may also make it easier to create sweeping change because there are centrally located codified definitions of these concepts.[59]

## 2.3 Common Law Jurisdictions

In contrast, common law jurisdictions, such as the United Kingdom, Australia, and most of the United States, have disparate definitions of 'legal standing' and 'agency' that are spread across case law and legislative instruments. They differ across jurisdictions, as well as within various fields of law, such as criminal law, corporate law, and wills, trusts, and estates law. This has caused a lack of consistency in these definitions, and therefore there is no general understanding or definition of legal

[55] Saru M Matambanadzo, 'Embodying Vulnerability: A Feminist Theory of the Person' (2012) Duke Journal of Gender Law and Policy 20, 39.

[56] For example, Article 488(1) of the French Civil Code states, '*La majorité est fixée à dix-huit ans accomplis ; à cet âge, on est capable de tous les actes de la vie civile.*' Article 315 of the Spanish Civil Code states, '*La mayor edad empieza a los dieciocho años cumplidos …*' Article 322 of the Spanish Civil Code states, '*El mayor de edad es capaz para todos los actos de la vida civil, salvo las excepciones establecidas en casos especiales por este Código.*' As cited in Office of the United Nations High Commissioner of Human Rights (OHCHR) (n 51).

[57] For example, Article 489(1) of the French Civil Code states, '*Pour faire un acte valable, il faut être sain d'esprit.*' As cited in ibid.

[58] ibid.

[59] For example, the entire civil code of Peru has been modified to comply with Article 12 of the CRPD: Antonio Martinez-Pujalte, 'Legal Capacity and Supported Decision-Making: Lessons from Some Recent Legal Reforms' (2019) 8 Laws 4.

standing and agency across common law jurisdictions.[60] This may make it more difficult to establish a uniform definition of 'legal personhood' across common law jurisdictions that is consistent with human rights law. However, it may also leave greater flexibility in establishing a definition of legal personhood that is inclusive of all people because there is less structure established around the concept of legal personhood.

## 3. Legal Personhood and Legal Capacity in International Human Rights Instruments

In international human rights law, the right to legal personhood (or legal capacity) has been tied to the right to equal recognition before the law, as discussed above. Article 12 of the CRPD is the most recent iteration of the right to legal capacity as a part of the right to equal recognition before the law. Prior to that, it was enumerated as a part of equality before the law in Article 15 of the CEDAW. Prior to that, the ICCPR (Article 16) and the UDHR (Article 6) both included articles on the right to equal recognition before the law; however, they gave little detail on the meaning of that right and did not include language on the right to legal capacity. This section will examine the evolution of the right to legal capacity, in detail, as part of the right to equal recognition before the law in international human rights instruments. The aim is to lay out the history and meaning of these rights in order to lay the foundation for applying these rights to law, policy, and practice and analyse where there are barriers to these rights for the various marginalised groups identified in this book.

### 3.1 Distinguishing Equal Recognition from Equal Protection

At the outset, it is important to distinguish 'equal recognition before the law' from 'equal protection of the law.' Although the two concepts are closely tied, this book primarily examines equal recognition before the law. This is for several reasons. The first is that while equal protection of the law has been thoroughly explored, equal recognition before the law has received much less attention and the body of literature as well as law, policy, and practice reform relating to equal recognition before the law is much more in its infancy than that of equal protection before the law. This book aims to contribute to building scholarship related to equal recognition before the law in an effort to draw attention to its importance, its power to shape our socio-legal world, and the social justice potential of reform in this area. In addition, this book explores the individual rights and state obligations related to legal standing and

[60] Matambanadzo (n 55).

legal agency—as part of legal personhood and legal capacity. Equal protection of the law can provide a framework for analysis where legal standing and legal agency have been denied on the basis of membership in a protected class of people, but it does not provide a framework for determining how the law goes about granting or denying standing or agency. An analysis of equal recognition before the law, however, can provide the desired framework for analysis relating to legal standing and agency.

Equal protection of the law is the guarantee that the law will not discriminate based on a protected status and it will provide avenues for justice when an individual is discriminated against on the basis of a protected status.[61] Article 7 of the UDHR states, 'All are ... entitled without any discrimination to equal protection of the law. All are entitled to equal protection against any discrimination in violation of this Declaration and against any incitement to such discrimination.' Equal protection of the law entails the guarantee of non-discrimination. Significant attention has been paid to non-discrimination and equal protection of the law in scholarly work as well as in law, policy, and practice reform movements.[62] For example, the 14th Amendment of the US Constitution guarantees equal protection of the law (US Const. amend. XIV § 1); the Equality Act 2010 in the United Kingdom prohibits discrimination (Equality Act 2010, UK Public General Acts 2010 c. 15, part 2); and Articles 14 and 15 of the Constitution of India guarantees equal protection of the law and prohibits discrimination on protected grounds (Constitution of India, 1950, Art. 14 and 15).

Generally, non-discrimination law and the right to equal protection of the law only provide protection where an individual is detrimentally treated differently on the basis of that individual's status as a member of a protected group—such as race, gender, sexual orientation, religion, or disability. What constitutes a protected group differs based on jurisdiction and can be highly controversial and have significant political and social implications.[63] Often, if an individual cannot show that they are a member of a protected group, then they are not considered to have been discriminated against, and their right to equal protection of the law is not considered to have been violated. For example, not all jurisdictions include sexual orientation as a protected group of people under non-discrimination law.[64] In these

[61] Stephanie Farrior (ed), *Equality and Non-discrimination under International Law*, vol 2 (Taylor & Francis 2015); John P Frank and Robert F Munro, 'Original Understanding of Equal Protection of the Laws' (1950) 50 Columbia Law Review 131; Jospeh Tussman and Jacobus tenBroek, 'The Equal Protection of the Laws' (1949) 37 California Law Review 341.

[62] Gordon A Christenson, 'Using Human Rights Law to Inform Due Process and Equal Protection Analyses' (1983) 52 University of Cincinnati Law Review 3; Farrior (n 61); Frank and Munro (n 61); Tussman and tenBroek (n 61); Lisa Waddington, 'Testing the Limits of the EC Treaty Article on Non-discrimination' (1999) 28 Industrial Law Journal 133.

[63] Nancy Levit, 'Changing Workforce Demographics and the Future of the Protected Class Approach' (2012) 16 Lewis & Clark Law Review 463; Marcia L McCormick, 'Decoupling Employment Business Law Forum: The Protected-Class Approach to Antidiscrimination Law: Logic, Effects, Reform' (2012) 16 Lewis & Clark Law Review 499.

[64] Levit (n 63).

jurisdictions, a person likely cannot avail of a right to equal protection of the law or non-discrimination if they are detrimentally treated differently on the basis of sexual orientation. In many jurisdictions, and at the international level, equal protection of law and non-discrimination law is extended to all via a catch-all phrase in the list of protected groups. For example, Article 26 of the ICCPR states, 'All persons are equal before the law and are entitled without any discrimination to the equal protection of the law. In this respect, the law shall prohibit any discrimination and guarantee to all persons equal and effective protection against discrimination on any ground such as race, colour, sex, language, religion, political or other opinion, national or social origin, property, birth or other status.' This more expansive approach can allow more room for the application of equal protection rights and non-discrimination law to people who may not fit squarely into a group in the delineated list of protected groups. However, such catch-all phrases are used less frequently than the specifically listed protection groups, suggesting that the law is generally primarily applied in the context of the categorisations overtly identified.[65]

Under the right to equal protection of the law and non-discrimination law, once an individual shows that they are a member of a protected group and that they have been treated detrimentally differently on the basis of that group membership, in most jurisdictions, and at the international level, it must also be shown that the treatment did not have an objective or reasonable justification and the aim of the treatment was not legitimate—or the treatment was not a reasonable means of achieving that aim.[66] These are often heavy burdens for an individual to prove. As such, they often significantly limit the situations in which the right to equal protection of the law or non-discrimination law can be applied.[67]

The right to equal recognition before the law does not have this same requirement that an individual be from a protected class—at least there has not been a body of work or law that has arisen that would indicate that the right to equal recognition only applies where an individual can show that they are a member of a protected class. Instead, the right to equal recognition, as it is currently developing, appears to apply to all individuals, regardless of membership in protected classes. This may mean that every individual has a right to equal recognition as a legal person regardless of group membership. In other words, by virtue of being a human person, an individual is entitled to recognition before the law on an equal basis with all others. In addition to the potential for this individual focus of the right, there may also be a group element of the right. This is evidenced by

[65] Rory O'Connell, 'Cinderella Comes to the Ball: Art 14 and the Right to Non-Discrimination in the ECHR' (2009) 29 Legal Studies 211.

[66] BG Ramcharan, 'Equality and Nondiscrimination' in *Equality and Non-Discrimination under International Law*,(Taylor & Francis 2017) 76.

[67] Oddný Mjöll Arnardóttir, *Equality and Non-discrimination under the European Convention on Human Rights* (Martinus Nijhoff Publishers 2003); Sandra Fredman, 'European Community Discrimination Law: A Critique' (1992) 21 Industrial Law Journal 119; Laurence Lustgarten, 'Racial Inequality and the Limits of Law' (1986) 49 The Modern Law Review 68.

the inclusion of the right in group-specific treaties, such as the CEDAW and the CRPD. This may mean that an individual must receive equal recognition before the law—and, in addition, the law must provide equal recognition to protected classes of people. Therefore, any individual who is denied legal standing or agency on a differential basis to others can claim a violation of their right to equal recognition before the law. In addition, any individual who is denied legal standing or agency on the basis of their membership in a protected group, such as disability, can also claim a violation of their right to equal recognition before the law.

Under the right to equal recognition before the law, where there has been a denial of legal standing or agency, those denials do not become permissible simply because they were carried out with an objective or reasonable justification or where the aim of the denials was legitimate—or, in other words, where the denials were a reasonable means of achieving the aim. At least, scholarship, law, and jurisprudence surrounding the right to equal recognition before the law has not developed in such a way to require these elements in the same way that they are required under the right to equal protection of the law. The question then emerges whether there is ever a permissible denial of equal recognition before the law. One possibility is that there is not—every human person must always be equally recognised as a legal person. However, this presents a challenge for situations such as where an individual has been convicted of a crime. The criminal justice system limits the legal agency, at a minimum, of individuals convicted of a crime. For example, in some jurisdictions individuals convicted of a crime cannot vote.[68] This is a limitation on legal agency—therefore, it may be considered a limitation on the right to legal personhood and equal recognition before the law. It also presents challenges for situations in which an individual is unable to exercise legal agency—such as when they are in a coma or otherwise in a state in which they are unable to communicate. If another individual is then appointed to act on the individual's behalf and is ascribed the legal personhood—including legal standing and agency—of that individual, then the individual is likely being denied the right to legal personhood and equal recognition before the law. I will explore these issues more in each chapter. I will identify where the rights to legal personhood and equal recognition before the law may be limited or denied to each marginalised group and explore how that can be rectified and whether there is any circumstance in which the state may be justified in infringing on these rights.

[68] Cormac Behan, *Citizen Convicts: Prisoners, Politics and the Vote* (Manchester UP, 2016); Aman McLeod, Ismail K White, and Amelia R Gavin, 'The Locked Ballot Box: The Impact of State Criminal Disenfranchisement Laws on African American Voting Behavior and Implications for Reform' (2003) 11 Virginia Journal of Social Policy & the Law 66.

## 3.2 Universal Declaration of Human Rights, Article 6, and Beyond

As mentioned above, the right to equal recognition before the law first appeared in a UN instrument in Article 6 of the 1948 UDHR. Examination of the drafting history indicates that there was controversy over the meaning of the right and whether there are permissible grounds on which to allow derogation from the right—for example, whether specific groups of people were not entitled to the full protection of the right. Initial drafts of Article 6 included language that listed age, mental impairment, or commission of a crime as legitimate bases for the restriction of the right. It read, 'Everyone has the right to a legal personality. No person shall be restricted in the exercise of his civil rights except under general law based on reasons of age or mental incompetence, or as punishment for a criminal offence, or as otherwise permitted in this bill.'[69] In a subsequent draft, the text was changed to be much more expansive, including the redaction of the language permitting derogation; it read, 'Everyone has the right everywhere in the world to recognition as a person before the law and to the enjoyment of fundamental civil rights.'[70] The final draft of the text appears as follows: 'Everyone has the right to recognition everywhere as a person before the law' (UDHR Art. 6). This final text reflects the most universal version. It delineates a right for 'everyone' that has no specified limitations on the basis of group membership or otherwise.

Following its appearance in the UDHR, the right to equal recognition was included in the 1966 ICCPR. The ICCPR and the ICESCR were created in order to enshrine the rights established in the UDHR in legally binding international instruments that states parties could ratify and could then be held accountable for upholding the individual rights and state obligations within the instruments. This was essential for the development of the United Nations, including the development of human rights monitoring bodies that could have a legal basis for intervening in domestic issues and making public statements regarding the human rights implications of state's actions.[71]

The right to equal recognition before the law (Article 6 of the UDHR) acquired legally binding status in Article 16 of the ICCPR. The text of Article 16 of the ICCPR is almost identical to Article 6 of the UDHR. It states simply, 'Everyone shall have

[69] United Nations Economic and Social Council, 'Commission on Human Rights, Drafting Committee on an International Bill of Human Rights, First Session Report' (1 July 1947) UN Doc E/CN.4/21; United Nations Economic and Social Council, 'Commission on Human Rights, Draft of a Resolution for the General Assembly Submitted by the Representative of India' (31 January 1947) UN Doc E/CN.4/11.

[70] United Nations Economic and Social Council, 'Commission on Human Rights, Report of the Drafting Committee to the Commission on Human Rights' (21 May 1948) UN Doc E/CN.4/95.

[71] Frans Viljoen, 'International Human Rights Law: A Short History' (2012) 12 Journal of Humanitarian Medicine 4.

the right to recognition everywhere as a person before the law.' Neither Article 6 of the UDHR nor Article 16 of the ICCPR provides any additional explanatory text in the articles themselves. The Human Rights Committee, the monitoring body for the ICCPR, has not provided much additional information regarding the interpretation of the right to equal recognition before the law because they have not published a general comment on the article nor has there been any significant use of Article 16 in the Human Rights Committee case law under the first Optional Protocol to the ICCPR.[72]

The negotiations during the drafting of Article 16 of the ICCPR indicate a hesitance to restrict the right in any way. In both drafting processes, there was some controversy regarding whether the right to equal recognition before the law includes both legal personhood and legal agency. Initially, the article was only intended to guarantee the right to legal personhood—or legal standing—but not the right to legal agency or the ability to be an actor before the law.[73] This is evidenced by the preliminary drafting of the article, which explicitly stated that the State *is* permitted to limit the civil rights of minors, people of 'unsound mind', and people convicted of crimes. However, agreement could not be reached on this language, and it was therefore taken out.[74] This dispute also occurred in the drafting of Article 6 of the UDHR, which took place prior to the drafting of the ICCPR. While this does demonstrate a belief by some that the right can be restricted for certain groups, the fact that it was ultimately decided to remove any limitations on the right indicates an overall acceptance that it is a non-derogable right that applies to all people equally.

In 1979, the Convention on the CEDAW provided further description of the rights to equal recognition before the law and legal capacity. It explicitly attached both personhood and agency. It accomplishes this in Article 15, which guarantees equality before the law for women, requiring the granting of legal capacity (or legal personhood) to women on an equal basis with men and the 'same opportunities to exercise that capacity'. It also describes the rights to equality in contracting, administering property, and judicial procedures—this makes it clear that the rights include agency as well as standing. It was not until 28 years later, with the adoption of the CRPD, that further description of the rights was provided in a binding human rights instrument. As described above, Article 12 of the CRPD embraced CEDAW's interpretation by including in the right to legal capacity both the ability to hold rights and the ability to act under the law.

[72] Sarah Joseph and others, *The International Covenant on Civil and Political Rights: Cases, Materials, and Commentary* (OUP 2000); Office of the United Nations High Commissioner of Human Rights (OHCHR) (n 51).

[73] Marc J Bossuyt, *Guide to the 'Travaux Préparatoires' of the International Covenant on Civil and Political Rights* (Martinus Nijhoff Publishers 1987); Office of the United Nations High Commissioner of Human Rights (OHCHR) (n 51).

[74] Office of the United Nations High Commissioner of Human Rights (OHCHR) (n 51).

It also places an obligation on States to provide access to support for the exercise of legal capacity, which had never before been enumerated in an international human rights instrument.

## 3.3 Convention on the Rights of Persons with Disabilities, Article 12

The right to legal capacity (or legal personhood) had not been given significant scholarly or other attention until the 2006 UN CRPD. Article 12 of the CRPD establishes the right to legal capacity as part of the right to equal recognition before the law.[75] The individual rights and state obligations emanating from Article 12 have been illuminated by the UN Committee on the Rights of Person with Disabilities (CRPD Committee), which is the monitoring body for the CRPD. They wrote their first General Comment on the right to equal recognition before the law in Article 12.[76] A General Comment from a UN human rights body is an explanation or interpretation of international law in a particular field or area. They are considered to be authoritative interpretations of international law.[77]

The General Comment on the right to equal recognition before the law outlines key areas of life that the right to legal capacity commonly impacts. For example, legal capacity must be recognised in order to vote, marry, contract, inherit, consent to sex, consent to medical treatment, consent to mental health treatment, and any other area of life that requires a legal decision to be made and respected.[78] Importantly, the General Comment differentiates legal capacity from mental capacity, as discussed above. The General Comment states that, in accordance with Article 12, legal capacity is a right of every individual and should not be denied on the basis of mental capacity.[79] Instead, legal capacity should be respected in every individual and, where an individual experiences difficulty with mental capacity, the state has an obligation to provide access to support for that individual to utilise their mental capacity to exercise their right to legal capacity. In the narrow range of circumstances where this is not possible,

[75] Frank and Munro (n 61).

[76] Arstein-Kerslake and Flynn (n 32); Committee on the Rights of Persons with Disabilities, 'General Comment No 1 Article 12: Equal Recognition Before the Law' (n 29). The author of this article provided support to the CRPD Committee in the drafting and development of General Comment No 1 on the Right to Equal Recognition Before the Law: Arstein-Kerslake and Flynn (n 32).

[77] Kerstin Mechlem, 'Treaty Bodies and the Interpretation of Human Rights' (2009) 42 Vanderbilt Journal of Transnational Law 905.

[78] Arstein-Kerslake, *Restoring Voice to People with Cognitive Disabilities* (n 7); Arstein-Kerslake and Flynn (n 32); Committee on the Rights of Persons with Disabilities, 'General Comment No 1 Article 12: Equal Recognition Before the Law' (n 29); Flynn and Arstein-Kerslake (n 5).

[79] Committee on the Rights of Persons with Disabilities, 'General Comment No 1 Article 12: Equal Recognition Before the Law' (n 29).

a decision can be made in line with the best interpretation of the individual's will and preferences.[80]

The General Comment on Article 12 also states that the right to legal capacity requires that states move away from substituted decision-making systems and replace them with systems of support. It defines substituted decision-making systems as those in which '(a) legal capacity is removed from a person, even if this is in respect of a single decision; (b) a substitute decision maker can be appointed by someone other than the person concerned, and this can be done against his or her will; or (c) any decision made by a substitute decision maker is based on what is believed to be in the objective "best interests" of the person concerned, as opposed to being based on the person's own will and preferences'.[81] This has significant implications for many existing areas of the law, including guardianship, mental health, consent, and others.[82]

In line with the text of Article 12(4), the General Comment explains that systems of support must respect the rights, will, and preferences of the person in a manner that is non-discriminatory.[83] This support can come in various different forms, ranging from the provision of accessible information necessary for making a legal decision to the practice of supported decision-making—where one or more individuals provide assistance to an individual in the process of making a legal decision.[84]

There has been resistance to the CRPD Committee's interpretation of Article 12. For example, prior to the creation of the General Comment, some states, including Canada, Norway, and Australia, had lodged reservations to Article

[80] Arstein-Kerslake and Flynn (n 32); Michael Bach and Lana Kerzner, 'A New Paradigm for Protecting Autonomy and the Right to Legal Capacity' (Law Commission of Ontario 2010); Committee on the Rights of Persons with Disabilities, 'General Comment No 1 Article 12: Equal Recognition Before the Law' (n 29); Flynn and Arstein-Kerslake (n 5).

[81] Arstein-Kerslake and Flynn (n 32); Committee on the Rights of Persons with Disabilities, 'General Comment No 1 Article 12: Equal Recognition Before the Law' (n 29); Committee on the Rights of Persons with Disabilities, General Comment No 1 Article 12: Equal Recognition Before the Law—Corrigendum Paragraph 27' (2014) UN Doc CRPD/C/GC/1/CORR.1; Mary Donnelly, 'Best Interests in the Mental Capacity Act: Time to Say Goodbye?' (2016) 24 Medical Law Review 318.

[82] Anna Arstein-Kerslake, 'Understanding Sex: The Right to Legal Capacity to Consent to Sex' (2015) 30 Disability & Society 1459; Arstein-Kerslake, *Restoring Voice to People with Cognitive Disabilities* (n 7); Mary Donnelly and Claire Murray, *Ethical and Legal Debates in Irish Healthcare: Confronting Complexities* (OUP 2016); Flynn and Arstein-Kerslake (n 5); Brendan D Kelly, 'Dignity, Human Rights and the Limits of Mental Health Legislation' (2014) 31 Irish Journal of Psychological Medicine 75; Penelope Weller, 'Reconsidering Legal Capacity: Radical Critiques, Governmentality and Dividing Practice' (2014) 23 Griffith Law Review 498.

[83] Arstein-Kerslake and Flynn (n 32); Committee on the Rights of Persons with Disabilities, 'General Comment No 1 Article 12: Equal Recognition Before the Law' (n 29); Convention on the Rights of Persons with Disabilities (adopted 13 December 2006, entered into 3 May 2008) 2515 UNTS 3.

[84] Flynn and Arstein-Kerslake (n 5); Joanne Watson, 'Assumptions of Decision-Making Capacity: The Role Supporter Attitudes Play in the Realisation of Article 12 for People with Severe or Profound Intellectual Disability' (2016) 5 Laws 6.

12, articulating their interpretation of Article 12 as permitting legal capacity denial and substituted decision-making in certain circumstances.[85] The CRPD Committee has stated that these interpretations are inconsistent with the committee's interpretation of Article 12 and with the overall object and purpose of the CRPD.[86] Importantly, other jurisdictions have gone forward and achieved significant reform in line with the CRPD Committee's interpretation of Article 12.[87]

The arguments for maintaining substituted decision-making systems often centre on the rights to life, health, and other forms of protection for the individual. However, it is commonly only disabled people whose rights to legal capacity and autonomy are believed to be subservient to these other rights that are more focused on protection.[88] The balance between autonomy and protection will always be a delicate one. However, the right to legal capacity in Article 12 asks that an individual's autonomy—their recognition as a legal person and agent—is respected on an equal basis for people with and without disability.[89] This appears difficult, if not impossible, to achieve in substituted decision-making systems in which disabled people are disproportionately denied legal capacity in the name of protection.[90]

## 4. Conclusion

In this book, I have adopted the definition of 'legal capacity' as utilised in CEDAW and the CRPD. I have also made the decision to use the term 'legal personhood' interchangeably with the term 'legal capacity', in order to avoid confusion with the concept of mental capacity. The terms 'legal personhood' and 'legal capacity', as I use them here, encompass the recognition of an individual's legal standing and legal agency. Legal standing is the law's recognition of the individual as a holder of rights and responsibilities. Legal agency

85 Bartlett (n 33); Richard W Jr Edwards, 'Reservations to Treaties' (1989) 10 Michigan Journal of International Law 362; Steven J Hoffman, Lathika Sritharan, and Ali Tejpar, 'Is the UN Convention on the Rights of Persons with Disabilities Impacting Mental Health Laws and Policies in High-Income Countries? A Case Study of Implementation in Canada' (2016) 16(1):28 BMC International Health and Human Rights 28 <https://www.ncbi.nlm.nih.gov/pmc/articles/PMC5105274/> accessed 1 May 2019; Ronald McCallum, 'The United Nations Convention on the Rights of Persons with Disabilities: Some Reflections' (2010) Sydney Law School Research Paper 10/30 <https://papers.ssrn.com/abstract=1563883> accessed 1 May 2019.

86 Committee on the Rights of Persons with Disabilities, 'Concluding Observations on the Initial Report of Canada' (8 May 2017) UN Doc CRPD/C/CAN/CO/1.

87 Martinez-Pujalte (n 59).

88 Arstein-Kerslake, *Restoring Voice to People with Cognitive Disabilities* (n 7).

89 Arstein-Kerslake and Flynn (n 32); Committee on the Rights of Persons with Disabilities, 'General Comment No 1 Article 12: Equal Recognition Before the Law' (n 29).

90 Arstein-Kerslake, *Restoring Voice to People with Cognitive Disabilities* (n 7).

is the law's recognition of the individual's freedom to act on those rights and responsibilities and for those actions to be recognised as legally valid. This includes all actions that have legal consequences, such as engaging in, modifying, and terminating legal relationships and legal transactions. It is not dependent upon decision-making skills or mental capacity. Instead, mental capacity is only relevant to legal capacity in that it may influence whether the individual needs support for the exercise of their legal capacity.[91] Throughout this book, this definition of legal capacity (termed 'legal personhood' throughout) will be applied to the situation of various marginalised groups who are experiencing denials of legal capacity. It will explore how and why these denials are occurring, as well as solutions for creating law, policy, and practice that respect the right to legal capacity for all people.

[91] Arstein-Kerslake and Flynn (n 32); Committee on the Rights of Persons with Disabilities, 'General Comment No 1 Article 12: Equal Recognition Before the Law' (n 29).

# 2
# Human Rights Law and the Individual

## 1. Introduction

Before engaging in a discussion of how the right to legal personhood applies to specific marginalised groups, it is important to first explore whether human rights law applies directly to the individual or whether it simply regulates how states act. This is important because it impacts how human rights are implemented and whether the right to legal personhood should apply equally to all people—by virtue of their humanity—or whether states have an entitlement to exercise sovereignty and grant certain groups different versions of legal personhood based on certain characteristics, such as citizenship status, race, disability, and gender.

On the face of the core foundational human rights treaties—including the Universal Declaration of Human Rights (UDHR); the International Covenant on Civil and Political Rights (ICCPR); and the International Covenant of Economic, Social and Cultural Rights (ICESCR)—it seems as though all human rights apply to all individuals. For example, Article 2 of the UDHR states, '[e]veryone is entitled to all the rights and freedoms set forth in this Declaration, without distinction of any kind, such as race, colour, sex, language, religion, political or other opinion, national or social origin, property, birth or other status.'[1] However, in practice, human rights law has not applied directly to individuals.[2] Instead, it has been used as a means of regulating how the individual is treated by the state—focusing more on state action than on individual needs. This use of human rights law is bolstered by the fact that the individual rights created by human rights law are rights that states agree (through treaties) to be legally bound to protect—in other words, the origins of human rights law itself are reliant on state acquiescence.

States have historically been given a relatively wide margin to exercise state sovereignty in determining how and when to implement the human rights that they have agreed to be bound by via international treaties. This wide margin for state sovereignty is at least in part due to the long-held rules of international law, as described in more detail below. It has resulted in a significant lack of clarity in terms of how individual human rights actually apply to the individual—because, although on the face of the treaties it appears that every individual human has an equal entitlement to the recognition, protection, and promotion of their human

[1] David S Weissbrodt, *The Human Rights of Non-citizens* (OUP 2008) 35.
[2] Anne Peters, *Beyond Human Rights* (CUP 2016).

*The Right to Legal Personhood of Marginalised Groups*. Anna Arstein-Kerslake, Oxford University Press.
 DOI: 10.1093/9780191926549.003.0002

rights, in practice, the sovereign states that enter into and agree to be bound by human rights treaties are given significant freedom to determine how they implement human rights in their jurisdictions.[3]

In this way, if we accept that human rights law exclusively regulates the activity of the state, it is highly vulnerable to claims of state sovereignty that include an entitlement of non-intervention into the internal affairs of sovereign states. In such a situation, the implementation of human rights law is purely voluntary—based on the consent of sovereign states. However, if we do not accept this, and instead push for human rights law to attach directly to the individual, then it has considerably more power and a state is not free to the same degree to use the entitlement of non-intervention included with the recognition of state sovereignty as a reason for not upholding human rights and carrying out their accompanying state obligations.

The attachment of human rights law to the individual is particularly relevant for the right to legal personhood because, as will be evident throughout this book, there are various points at which the application of the right to legal personhood becomes meaningless if state sovereignty is given priority over the rights of the individual. For example, migrants and stateless people are denied legal personhood due to issues related to political borders—respecting political borders is generally deemed an inherent part of state sovereignty.[4] In addition, women and disabled people are denied legal personhood based on cultural claims and state assertions of protection needs for these populations (who are often prejudicially assumed to be 'vulnerable').[5] Although many states do not explicitly use claims of state sovereignty when making these arguments in human rights venues, these denials can nonetheless be attributed to state sovereignty claims of non-intervention in internal affairs because the monitoring structures within the United Nations that allow for such claims to be made are constructed to elevate the voices of sovereign states and to permit such claims to be heard on the basis that they have an entitlement to non-interference in internal affairs.[6]

For these reasons, and others, the contested nature of legal personhood is such that in order to effectively protect it as a human right for all individuals, it must attach directly to the individual—or, at a minimum, it will be much easier to protect as a human right if it attaches to an individual and claims of state sovereignty are not permitted to supersede the right. This is also particularly important for the

[3] ibid; Weissbrodt (n 1).

[4] Daniel Philpott, *Revolutions in Sovereignty: How Ideas Shaped Modern International Relations* (Princeton UP 2010); W Michael Reisman, 'Sovereignty and Human Rights in Contemporary International Law' (1990) 84 American Journal of International Law 866.

[5] Anna Arstein-Kerslake, 'Gendered Denials: Vulnerability Created by Barriers to Legal Capacity for Women and Disabled Women' (2019) 66 International Journal of Law and Psychiatry 101501.

[6] Although the creation of the United Nations was a step towards a redefinition of state sovereignty, its structures are still premised on the sovereignty of member states. Philpott (n 4); Samuel M Makinda, 'The United Nations and State Sovereignty: Mechanism for Managing International Security' (1998) 33 Australian Journal of Political Science 101.

larger human rights project because the idea of human rights is that they apply to all people—this means that an individual must be recognised as a person in order for human rights law to even be triggered. If there are persons who a state can claim are non-persons, this obviates the entire human rights system—none of the rights apply if an individual is not recognised as a person. This, of course, is how many groups were excluded from early rights entitlements—such as the rights in the US Constitution which African Americans were excluded from on the basis that they were non-persons or partial persons. Legal personhood was denied and with it the entitlement to rights.[7] It is time that we took a harder look at where similar denials of legal personhood are occurring in modern law and where those denials are leading to exclusion from human rights protection. One of the ways that this appears to be occurring is through claims of state sovereignty—as will be explored below. My aim is to thoroughly explore this claim and to develop arguments for how we can overcome this claim and instead strive to recognise legal personhood in all people and thereby ensure that the full gamut of human rights is available to all people.

In the situation of migrants and stateless people, the recognition of legal personhood is particularly pertinent. As a starting point, if human rights are universal, they must apply to the millions of migrants and stateless people around the globe. This must also be true for the right to legal personhood. In fact, the right to legal personhood may be one of the most important rights for these groups, because without this right they are often legally non-existent—with not only lack of legal recognition but also lack of venue for what legal entity or state should provide that recognition. This lack of recognition makes travel, marriage, employment, contracting, and most engagement with socio-legal structures very difficult, if not impossible. As a universal human right, therefore, it is important to explore how the right could be protected for these groups. However, if state sovereignty is prioritised over the individual right to legal personhood for these groups, states can easily claim that they only have human rights responsibilities to their own citizens and do not have an obligation to protect the right to legal personhood for non-citizens within their borders.[8] This is also true for some indigenous groups who have contentious and/or unique citizenship status within a particular state. These statuses may be different from that of a non-indigenous citizen and may leave a window within which the state could explicitly or implicitly claim sovereignty to treat such individuals differently.

[7] Kasey Henricks, '"I'm Principled Against Slavery, but ...": Colorblindness and the Three-Fifths Debate' (2018) 65 Social Problems 285; William Hughes, 'The Origins and Uses of the Three-Fifths Clause Related to Slavery and Taxation' (Master's thesis, Liberty University 2018).

[8] Alison Brysk, *Globalization and Human Rights* (University of California Press 2002); Vincent Chetail, 'The Human Rights of Migrants in General International Law: From Minimum Standards to Fundamental Rights' in Mary Crock (ed), *Migrants and Rights* (Routledge 2015); Carmen Tiburcio, *The Human Rights of Aliens Under International and Comparative Law* (Martinus Nijhoff Publishers 2001); Rogers M Smith, 'National Obligations and Noncitizens: Special Rights, Human Rights, and Immigration' (2014) 42 Politics & Society 381.

It is pertinent to note, as well, that human rights law is a branch of international law, which originated, in part, as a means to solidify state sovereignty and ultimately legitimise colonialism and imperialism.[9] These origins of international law—which led to widespread oppression, subjugation, and even genocide of particular groups around the world, especially in the Global South—are a stark contrast to the aims of human rights now, which are to secure equality and social justice goals around the globe. Noting these tensions, it feels particularly important to address the human rights of the individual beyond state sovereignty—especially the human right of the individual to be recognised as a legal person and therefore be entitled to human rights. Perhaps this may be one avenue of providing some form of reparations for the severe harm that international law has been used to legitimise.

In this chapter, I will begin by exploring the origins of human rights law and its initial intention to regulate the relationship between a sovereign state and its citizen. I will explore the origins and evolution of the concept of state sovereignty, and I will then argue that human rights law has progressed to now being situated as a global framework for social justice that goes beyond state borders and beyond state sovereignty. In other words, that the individual rights established in human rights law are beginning to take on a meaning globally that may supersede claims of state sovereignty and may require states to prioritise the rights of individuals over their own self-preservation or self-interest—a concept that would have been radical and highly controversial at the inception of human rights law in the 1940s and even more so at the inception of international law in the mid-1600s.[10] Finally, I will explore how this prioritisation of the individual in international law may be relevant for the right to legal personhood and may be a critical tool for the realisation of the right to legal personhood for some groups, such as migrants, stateless people, and indigenous groups.

## 2. Origins of Human Rights Law and Initial Intention to Regulate Relationship between a Sovereign State and Its Citizens

The original intention of human rights law was to regulate the relationship between the state and its citizens. This intention arose out of the atrocities of World War II. Human rights law was created, at least in part, in an attempt to mitigate the possibility of another holocaust and other atrocities such as those perpetrated by the Nazi regime in Germany in the 1930s and 1940s.[11] Even though the Nazi regime did not restrict the atrocities they perpetrated to only German citizens,

[9] Antony Anghie, *Imperialism, Sovereignty and the Making of International Law* (CUP 2005).

[10] Steven Patton, 'The Peace of Westphalia and It Affects on International Relations, Diplomacy and Foreign Policy' (2019) 10(1) The Histories <https://digitalcommons.lasalle.edu/the_histories/vol10/iss1/5> accessed 4 December 2023.

[11] Pamela Slotte and Miia Halme, *Revisiting the Origins of Human Rights* (CUP 2015).

human rights law, nonetheless, was limited to the relationship between a state and its citizen because it was developed as part of international law, which strongly prioritises state sovereignty.[12] The idea appears to be that international law was the most appropriate—and the most palatable—venue for the development of a global human rights legal system. The limitations inherent in prioritising state sovereignty as part of a human rights system was apparently a compromise worth making in order to establish a strong worldwide system for the recognition and protection of human rights.

The prioritisation of state sovereignty in international law arose as part of its inception. The creation of modern international law is generally attributed to the Peace of Westphalia in 1648, the treaty that ended the Thirty Years' War in Europe.[13] It was created to end a largely internal European war; however, the international law concepts that it is credited as creating have developed in a manner that would ensure that colonialism and imperialism could flourish and largely European states could continue to explore and exploit primarily non-European jurisdictions, as described below.[14] It established a set of ground rules for how primarily European states could legitimately conquer and colonise across the world.[15]

The aim of creating international law was to protect the sovereignty of states and to ensure that there were some controls on how state sovereignty was exercised, when the sovereignty of one state was in potential conflict with that of another. It was created largely by European states in such a way that made it almost impossible for non-European jurisdictions to be considered states or to have their sovereignty recognised in international law. For example, most non-European jurisdictions were considered 'uncivilised' and not worthy of recognition as sovereign states and, therefore, could not be subjects of international law—and were instead objects that could be owned, controlled, and conquered by European states who enjoyed recognition as sovereign states.[16] This approach was likely taken both out of prejudice against the Global South and what were considered 'underdeveloped' states, and in an effort to maintain the power and privilege of European states. If these largely non-European 'underdeveloped' jurisdictions were recognised as states, with the accompanying sovereignty and rights of sovereign states, then the European states would have been violating international law in engaging in imperialism and establishing colonies in these jurisdictions. For these reasons, state sovereignty and the definition of which jurisdictions qualify as a 'sovereign state' were core reasons for the inception of international law—to have a means to both

[12] ibid; Anghie, *Imperialism, Sovereignty and the Making of International Law* (n 9).

[13] Patton (n 10); Martin Kintzinger, 'From the Late Middle Ages to the Peace of Westphalia' in Bardo Fassbender and Anne Peters (eds), *The Oxford Handbook of the History of International Law* (OUP 2012).

[14] Anghie, *Imperialism, Sovereignty and the Making of International Law* (n 9).

[15] ibid.

[16] ibid.

manage internal European conflicts between states recognised as sovereign and to legalise colonialism and manage conflicts related to imperialism that may arise between the major European imperial powers (England, Spain, France, Portugal, the Netherlands, etc).[17]

On the other hand, the incorporation of human rights law into the international legal order has, arguably, had a positive impact on international law—perhaps pushing it away from its use as a tool for solidifying imperial powers and towards its use as a potential tool for global social justice. Before progressing into an analysis of how human rights law has changed state sovereignty and how the ongoing notion of state sovereignty may limit the human right to legal personhood, it is pertinent to explore the definition of state sovereignty and how it has evolved over time.

## 2.1 Evolution of State Sovereignty

The idea of sovereignty is that the state is the supreme political authority within its territorial boundaries.[18] It includes the social, legal, political, and economic rules and practices that characterise a particular state. There are two types of sovereignty, both of which are relevant to a discussion of the human right to legal personhood. The first type is internal sovereignty—this concept refers to the power of the state to create and enact laws within its territorial boundaries because of its relationship with the individuals in the territory and their consent to be governed (based on various motivations ranging from fear to peaceful agreement, which has long been the focus of legal theorists).[19] The second type is external sovereignty—this concept refers to international recognition of a state by other states and governing bodies. The recognition of external sovereignty includes an agreement with other states that they have an obligation of non-intervention—or the responsibility to not intervene with political and legal processes that are internal domestic processes for that state.[20]

Importantly, this definition of state sovereignty that currently dominates international law was largely developed by white, European, able-bodied, cisgender men who had a particular perspective on socio-political structures and a vested

[17] ibid; Antony Anghie, 'International Law in a Time of Change: Should International Law Lead or Follow the Grotius Lecture: ASIL 2010' (2010) 26 American University International Law Review 1315; Antony Anghie, 'Towards a Postcolonial International Law' in Prabhakar Singh and Benoît Mayer (eds), *Critical International Law: Postrealism, Postcolonialism, and Transnationalism* (OUP 2014).

[18] Philpott (n 4).

[19] Catharine A MacKinnon, *Toward a Feminist Theory of the State* (Harvard UP 1989); HLA Hart and Leslie Green, *The Concept of Law* (OUP 2012); John Locke, *The Works of John Locke* (T Longman, B Law 1794).

[20] Vaishnavi Pallapothu, 'Exploring Sovereignty through a Feminist Lens' (The Gender Security Project, 4 March 2021) <https://www.gendersecurityproject.com/post/exploring-sovereignty-through-a-feminist-lens> accessed 21 March 2023.

interest in maintaining social and gender hierarchies. They also largely had others—primarily women—who met many of their social and survival needs. Such experiences and perspectives profoundly shaped their worldview and likely played a role in de-prioritising social concerns such as equality, welfare, education, health, and other matters that they were largely insulated from. Instead, they had an interest in conceptualising state sovereignty in a manner that reflected their own experiences with power—a focus on a central locus of power and how to create and maintain that power. They were less concerned with the activities of the individuals under the control of such power.

It was not until very recently that these constructions of state sovereignty were critically analysed and understood with more nuance. Critical social theorists, including feminists, queer theorists, and others, have taken up the task of deconstructing the origins of the concept of state sovereignty and asking whether the way the concept has evolved is actually serving our modern, diverse world and its needs.[21] Although I have immense respect for these theories, and I believe that they should be further explored, my argument here is simply that regardless of the precise constriction of state sovereignty, it should never be allowed to supersede a right to legal personhood—because that is the baseline right for entitlement to human rights, and without universally recognising a right to legal personhood, we cannot claim that human rights are universal. To fully understand how state sovereignty has become a barrier to the right to legal personhood, it is necessary to understand the history behind the development of state sovereignty and how it has become an integral component of international law—and, by extension, human rights law. To achieve this examination, it is unfortunately necessary to turn back to the white, European, able-bodied, cisgender men that have dominated the development of the concept of state sovereignty and often continue to be thought of as the ultimate authority on the concept.

The concept of state sovereignty dates back, at least, to Greek political philosopher Aristotle, who, in his pivotal work *The Politics*, in the 4th century BCE, envisioned a positivist conception of sovereignty that emphasises law as the source of sovereign power. He defined 'sovereignty' as the source of ultimate power within a state and identified it as often being the distinguishing feature between states.[22] Several centuries later, in the 1600s, English philosopher Thomas Hobbes is credited with significantly developing the notion of state sovereignty in his book *Leviathan*, in which he strongly criticises Aristotle's understanding of state sovereignty as not sufficiently incorporating the importance of the men who make and enforce such laws—in particular, men who enforce such laws with 'hands and

[21] MacKinnon (n 19); Anghie, *Imperialism, Sovereignty and the Making of International Law* (n 9); Hilary Charlesworth and Christine Chinkin, *The Boundaries of International Law: A Feminist Analysis* (Manchester UP 2000).

[22] Curtis Johnson, 'The Hobbesian Conception of Sovereignty and Aristotle's Politics' (1985) 46 Journal of the History of Ideas 327; Aristotle, *The Politics* (Penguin 1981).

swords'.[23] He emphasised fear as an important—and perhaps inherent—part of state sovereignty. The distinctions between the theories of Aristotle and Hobbes are much debated—what is clear is that they were both pivotal in establishing and furthering the notion of state sovereignty and its internal power over the individual, as well as its external power in relation to other states.[24]

The concept of state sovereignty—as developed by Aristotle, Hobbes, and others—generally referred to the power of a single individual, such as a monarch, with claimed divine rights to complete power, or other form of totalitarian government, in which one individual or a small number of people held virtually complete power within the state; hence, the term 'sovereign' can refer to an individual holding supreme political power.[25] However, over time, the concept of popular sovereignty came to be accepted as the more legitimate form of sovereignty. This change was spurred over a century after the 1651 publication of Hobbes's *Leviathan*. It was strongly moved forward by both the American Revolution (1775–1783) and the French Revolution (1789–1799), which were successful in establishing some of the first sustainable modern democratic governments. However, international law did not expressly incorporate the concept of popular sovereignty as the guiding definition of state sovereignty until later in history.[26]

The American and French revolutions were followed by more than a century of imperialism, colonialism, and fascism before popular sovereignty became recognised as the politically legitimate form of state sovereignty. It was the development of human rights law in the 1940s that played an important role in solidifying this recognition—and securing the move away from recognising the legitimacy of power resting in a single monarch or other similarly dictatorial regime. The UDHR—the founding document of human rights law—established, in Article 21(3), that state sovereignty must be controlled by the people of that state; it states that '[t]he will of the people shall be the basis of the authority of government; this will shall be expressed in periodic and genuine elections which shall be by universal and equal suffrage and shall be held by secret vote or by equivalent free voting procedures'. This change to only recognise popular sovereignty as true sovereignty is evidenced by the fact that across the globe, including Europe, Africa, and Latin America, the principle of non-intervention that is a critical element of sovereignty has not been upheld in instances where democracy—or popular sovereignty—was at risk. When a dictator or other non-democratically elected political actor has usurped power from the people or from a democratic government or where there is a risk that this may take place, there are several examples across the globe where

[23] Johnson (n 22); Thomas Hobbes, *Leviathan* (Clarendon Press 1909) 533.

[24] Johnson (n 22); Sophie Smith, 'Democracy and the Body Politic from Aristotle to Hobbes' (2018) 46 Political Theory 167.

[25] Hobbes's concept of a covenant of the multitude begins to suggest ideas of popular sovereignty but does not fully develop the concept. Reisman (n 4); Hobbes (n 23).

[26] Reisman (n 4).

regional bodies made up of other sovereign states have come together to intervene with the aim of restoring democracy and reinstating popular sovereignty.[27] In this way, while the origins of international law as a tool for legally sanctioning imperialism and colonialism seem ill-suited for the social justice goals of human rights law, the incorporation of human rights law into international law served to, at a minimum, pivot some of the foundational concepts of international law—such as state sovereignty—to a path that is considerably more focused on social justice and the will of the people than was originally intended when international law was established.[28]

## 2.2 State Sovereignty and International Law

The history of international law has frequently been framed as a Eurocentric one with only the viewpoint of the conquerors and victors on display—leaving aside the multitude of others, including victims of imperialism and colonialism. To truly understand the development of international law and the evolution of the concept of state sovereignty, it is critical to look beyond these traditional Eurocentric histories of international law. The first task in moving beyond a Eurocentric account is viewing non-European jurisdictions as more than just passive objects of European domination. Instead, non-European jurisdictions must be understood and acknowledged as legal entities with their own legal histories and often rich understandings of their relationships with other jurisdictions globally. It is not enough to recognise that international law has served to legitimise European imperialism and colonialism and has generated great harms as a result.[29] Limiting our view of the history of international law to that recognition maintains the perception of non-European jurisdictions as objects of European power. It is essential to simultaneously recognise the histories of non-European jurisdictions and how their own understandings of state sovereignty developed—and, perhaps, were impacted by the development of international law. Unfortunately, this is not a particularly easy task because the predominance of international law scholars have focused on the European history of international law or critiques of the European history of international law—again, both of which often highlight non-European jurisdictions as objects of European power and do not illuminate non-European jurisdictions themselves as sources of knowledge and developments in international law and state sovereignty.[30]

27 Anghie, 'International Law in a Time of Change' (n 17).

28 Reisman (n 4); Bardo Fassbender and Anne Peters (eds), *The Oxford Handbook of the History of International Law* (OUP 2012) 33–36.

29 Anghie, *Imperialism, Sovereignty and the Making of International Law* (n 9); Anghie, 'Towards a Postcolonial International Law' (n 17).

30 Fassbender and others (n 28) 4–8.

My aim here is to explore the concept of state sovereignty and its origins. I have done this by both examining existing international law—which is, unfortunately, quite Eurocentric in many respects—and endeavouring to discover historical understandings of state sovereignty from non-European jurisdictions and to uncover their influence on current global understandings of state sovereignty and where those understandings may be moving towards in the near future. I am taking this approach in recognition that European jurisdictions have had significant influence over the development of international law—including human rights law—and are, therefore, relevant to look to for an understanding of what state sovereignty means. In addition, I am exploring understandings of state sovereignty beyond European jurisdictions because I believe it is important to recognise the influence that other jurisdictions have had on history and their potential to continue to have such influence. I believe it is also important to minimise the fostering and maintenance of the prioritisation of European jurisdictions in the further development of international law and human rights law. In order to achieve this, we must explore beyond European jurisdictions in developing our understandings of core concepts in international law, such as state sovereignty.

## 2.3 History of International Law

As mentioned above, human rights law was developed as a part of international law to regulate the relationship between the state and its citizen.[31] However, international law itself was originally developed for a much different purpose—regulating the relationship between states. At its inception, it largely left aside the relationships between various groups of people or even between the state and its citizens. Its concern was the law between states, as political entities. This version of international law arose from the European Greco-Roman tradition—however, it is now the dominant form of international law that is used across the globe.

This type of international law—with a focus on the relationship between states—evolved through a series of treaties, or formal agreements, between states. These were often peace treaties that were created in an effort to end a particular conflict between states. In other words, international law evolved through the development of treaty law. These treaties were treaties that were constituted primarily between European countries—mostly European countries that were engaged in imperialism and colonisation—and were in conflict with each other due to competition over resources or other valuable assets.[32]

[31] David J Bederman, *International Law in Antiquity* (CUP 2001); Randall Lesaffer (ed), *Peace Treaties and International Law in European History: From the Late Middle Ages to World War One* (CUP 2004).

[32] Fassbender and others (n 28) 71–75.

Importantly, many of the European practices related to peace treaties drew heavily on pre-classical civilisations (800–500 BCE) of the Middle East.[33] This is important to note because although the development of international law is often attributed to European states—which is accurate in many ways because they were a powerful driving force behind the rapid creation and enforcement of inter-state treaties that led to the development of many of the existing international law principles—the foundation of how treaties were created and the practices surrounding treaty creation may not have been as Eurocentric as is sometimes assumed. Instead, it was the pre-classical civilisations of the Middle East that created much of the blueprint for how international states negotiate and develop treaty law.[34]

The development of treaty law began many centuries ago in pre-classical times and has been a consistent part of history.[35] However, many historians identify the Peace of Westphalia as a turning point in treaty law which can be marked as instigating the onset of the creation of many of the principles of modern international law, including the concept of state sovereignty.[36] It marked a move away from strong states acting with impunity in their own interests and encroaching on the weak, including intervention, conquest, and colonisation. It did not end such practices—as colonialism, in particular, was alive and well beyond the Peace of Westphalia—however, it marked a move towards respecting state borders and the individual sovereignty of each state.

The Peace of Westphalia was a treaty created in Westphalia, a region in north-western Germany, in 1648. It marked the end of the Thirty Years' War and the Eighty Years' War, which were two of the most destructive wars to ravage Europe.[37] Its major contributions to the field of international law include the concepts of state sovereignty, mediation between nations, and diplomacy—it was one of the first attempts at codifying an international set of laws, and it remains the basis for the development of the European Union and the United Nations. The process of creating the Peace of Westphalia was significant because it was one of the first times that an international conflict was settled via a process of diplomacy, negotiation, and compromise by multiple parties—as opposed to a dominant state simply dictating policy to a weaker state.[38] In terms of the concept of sovereignty, the Peace of Westphalia is significant because it is credited with establishing the

[33] Bederman (n 31); Lesaffer (n 31).

[34] Bederman (n 31); Lesaffer (n 31).

[35] Fassbender and others (n 28) 73–76.

[36] Kintzinger (n 13); Heinz Duchhardt, 'From the Peace of Westphalia to the Congress of Vienna' in Bardo Fassbender and Anne Peters (eds), *The Oxford Handbook of the History of International Law* (OUP 2012); Philpott (n 4); Leo Gross, 'The Peace of Westphalia, 1648–1948' (1948) 42 American Journal of International Law 20; Anghie, 'Towards a Postcolonial International Law' (n 17).

[37] Geoffrey Parker, *The Thirty Years' War* (Routledge 2006); PA Hayman and John Williams, 'Westphalian Sovereignty: Rights, Intervention, Meaning and Context' (2006) 20 Global Society 521; Gross (n 36).

[38] Patton (n 10).

concept of non-intervention in both internal and external sovereignty. In other words, 'Westphalian sovereignty', as it is commonly termed, is the idea that one sovereign state should generally not interfere with another sovereign state's internal domestic decisions and actions—and that each sovereign state has the right to do as it likes within its own territory and in regards to its own people. Similarly, it includes non-interference with a sovereign state's external sovereignty in that it made it impermissible for one state to attack another state on the basis of a sovereign choice made by a state, such as its religion.[39] Importantly, it also includes the concept of sovereign equality—or the idea that all states that are recognised as sovereign have equal power and equal rights to the entitlements of sovereignty.[40]

While the Peace of Westphalia itself was not directly related to broader imperialism and colonialisation beyond Europe, the concept of sovereignty established as part of the Peace of Westphalia—termed 'Westphalian Sovereignty'—has played a significant role in legitimatising imperialism and colonialism, and in complicitly enabling imperialism and colonialism via international law. Its core principles of non-intervention in the internal affairs and external recognition of a state recognised as sovereign have been used to legitimatise interference in jurisdictions that are deemed to not be defined as 'sovereign states'. This premise of permissible intervention into 'non-sovereign' states has occurred frequently across the globe in the 20th and 21st centuries in the context of states where democracy or popular sovereignty is compromised or at risk of being compromised.[41] It has also occurred throughout history towards jurisdictions labelled as outlaws—which usually occurs for those states who do not enjoy high levels of socio-political power and privilege.[42]

In the context of imperialism and colonialism, Westphalian sovereignty was initially not ascribed to those jurisdictions in which European powers desired imperial control and the establishment of colonies or resource exploitation. This denial of sovereignty was largely done on the basis that non-European jurisdictions were 'uncivilised' or engaged in a version of civilisation that was not recognisable or comparable with European standards.[43] This manipulation of international law for the benefit of primarily European states becomes particularly apparent when such sovereignty was denied to jurisdictions with highly sophisticated and long-developed forms of governance and political systems—such as China and Japan.[44] During the dismantling of colonialism and in the postcolonial era, a newfound recognition of sovereignty has developed for such non-European

[39] Hayman and Williams (n 37); Anghie, 'Towards a Postcolonial International Law' (n 17).
[40] Gerry Simpson, *Great Powers and Outlaw States: Unequal Sovereigns in the International Legal Order* (CUP 2004) 10–14.
[41] Anghie, 'International Law in a Time of Change' (n 17).
[42] Simpson (n 40).
[43] Anghie, 'Towards a Postcolonial International Law' (n 17) 128.
[44] ibid 129–31.

jurisdictions (generally, requiting *popular* sovereignty, as described above). This new recognition of sovereignty continues to frequently be attributed to what is assumed to be the civilising nature of colonialism—or the civilising influence of colonial powers.[45] This is problematic because, while it permits the recognition of the sovereignty of non-European states, it does so in a manner that continues to ascribe greater value to European states and their political systems and histories—as opposed to recognising the immense value that the political systems and histories outside of Europe possess and how they have influenced and contributed to the development of our modern systems.

It is important to note that 'states', as we currently conceptualise them globally via international law, have borders that were almost exclusively created by the forces of European colonialism and imperialism. However, they were not created by delineations established between European powers and local powers—instead, they were primarily created via conflicts or agreements between European powers or via administrative acts of colonial powers. This is true for most borders in the Americas, Africa, the Pacific, the Caribbean, and many in Asia.[46] This is significant because it means that state sovereignty, as we currently understand it, is ascribed to states which were mostly constituted by European powers. This creates challenges for many reasons. It creates a challenge in attempting to examine state sovereignty from a non-Eurocentric perspective, because a majority of the states that exist now were created by—or their creation was heavily influenced by—European power. This situation means that even when we are trying to ascertain different non-Eurocentric perspectives on state sovereignty, we are often doing so by looking to the history of states that are heavily influenced and often created by European power.

As discussed above, the evolution of state sovereignty in European jurisdictions has emphasised sovereign equality and the doctrine of non-intervention. These concepts have, in many respects, been adopted by modern non-European states—especially during periods of history when such concepts could be used to the benefit of non-European states; for example, in the early postcolonial period when non-European states could use state sovereignty to argue for the removal of colonial powers and interests from their jurisdictions.[47] However, such concepts were not wholly foreign to non-European states prior to the Peace of Westphalia. There is a common misperception that state sovereignty—including sovereign equality and non-intervention—is a Western invention simply imposed on the non-Western world. As mentioned above, this is likely due to the tendency for even critiques of international law to lean towards objectifying non-European states

[45] ibid 130; Simpson (n 40); Philpott (n 4).
[46] Fassbender and others (n 28) 31.
[47] Michael C Davis, 'Sovereignty and the State in Asia: The Challenges of the Emerging International Order' (2005) 99 American Society of International Law Proceedings 411.

and viewing them as merely pawns of European powers, as opposed to sources of international law wielding power in their own right.[48]

There is no denying that European states held significant power and did, in fact, objectify non-European states at various points throughout history and in modern times. However, many non-European states have long histories of well-developed systems of international collaboration—including evidence of specific understandings of sovereignty, many that are not far removed from that developed in the Peace of Westphalia and which predate the Peace of Westphalia; for example, the foundation of interstate agreement developed in the Middle East, as mentioned above.[49] In addition, there is evidence of understandings and use of the concept of sovereignty in ancient China far before it appeared in Europe. The word 'China' or 'zhongguo' originally referred to 'central states'—these states were sovereign to the extent that they claimed final authority over specifically demarcated geographic spaces.[50] In addition, in China, in the 6th to 5th century BCE, Confucianism developed concepts of sovereignty similar to that in the Peace of Westphalia around two thousand years ahead of Europe. Confucianism contained notions similar to Westphalian sovereignty in both its inter- and intrastate relations. In interstate relations, it taught that war was unnecessary and should only be used to restore moral-political order. It also taught that benevolent rule was the means to state strength because both the internal population of the state would be sympathetic to benevolent rule and external powers would respect and be sympathetic towards such rule.[51] It could be argued that such philosophy demonstrates a more sophisticated understanding of sovereignty than that developed in the Peace of Westphalia. It not only recognises the existence of state power and the need for respect between states but also asserts that benevolence is a critical component of effective rule. This can be compared to the emergence of popular sovereignty in Europe, which moved beyond previous notions of sovereignty that relied on fear and violence of a supreme ruler. However, the emergence of popular sovereignty happened much later in European history, beginning around the late 18th century, as mentioned above.[52] Unfortunately, many of the concepts of state sovereignty developed in Confucianism were overshadowed by successive eras of militarism and legalist authoritarianism.[53] Nonetheless, it is relevant to highlight that

[48] Bardo Fassbender and Anne Peters, 'Introduction: Towards a Global History of International Law' in Bardo Fassbender and Anne Peters (eds), *The Oxford Handbook of the History of International Law* (OUP 2012).

[49] Bederman (n 31); Lesaffer (n 31).

[50] Victoria Tin-bor Hui, 'Toward a Confucian Multicultural Approach to a Liberal World Order: Insights from Historical East Asia' (2005) 99 American Society of International Law Proceedings 413, 414.

[51] ibid 415.

[52] Reisman (n 4).

[53] Hui (n 50) 415–16.

the non-European world had developed an understanding of sovereignty that far predates the Peace of Westphalia.

These origins of international law and human rights law are relevant because this history highlights the tensions with the social justice goals of human rights law. International law was created, at least in part, to legitimise the exploitation of certain peoples—this legitimisation was established via the prioritisation of state sovereignty and the doctrine of non-intervention that gave states relative impunity to treat their citizens as they choose. Human rights law was created as part of international law to temper that power given to sovereign states—to attempt to provide some regulations and boundaries around how a sovereign state can treat its citizens. Herein lies the tension—international law recognises state sovereignty and an entitlement to non-intervention and human rights law, a part of international law, attempts to remove some of that entitlement; however, it does so within the confines of an international legal system that was created to prioritise state sovereignty.

This tension presents problems for the realisation of the right to legal personhood. Ironically—or, perhaps, completely naturally—these problems are particularly exacerbated for some of the groups most profoundly affected by imperialism and colonisation—migrants, stateless people, and indigenous groups, as discussed above. However, the relationship of human rights law to the individual is relevant for all people seeking to secure their right to legal personhood. It is critical to know whether the right to legal personhood is a universal right that supersedes state sovereignty or whether the right to legal personhood is limited by an attachment only to the state. In other words, it is critical to know if the state is only obligated to protect the right to legal personhood insofar as such protection does not infringe on state sovereignty or whether the right to legal personhood must be protected by all states in respect of all people, regardless of decisions or actions a state takes as part of its entitlement to sovereignty in international law.

## 3. Moving Away from State Sovereignty: Towards Rights and Responsibilities of Individuals Separate from the State

Several scholars have begun to explore the evolving nature of the individual within international law.[54] As described above, international law was originally intended as a means to regulate relations between sovereign states. Over the past several decades, this has changed considerably. International law is now relevant not only for states but also for individuals. Human rights law, largely created after World War II as a part of international law, is one of the key forces behind this change—it was

[54] PK Menon, 'The Legal Personality of Individuals' (1994) 6 Sri Lanka Journal of International Law 127; Peters (n 2) 1–10; Antônio Augusto Cançado Trindade, *International Law for Humankind: Towards a New Jus Gentium* (2nd rev edn, Brill Nijhoff 2010).

an explicit attempt to regulate even a sovereign state's treatment of its citizens.[55] As discussed above, this has created a palpable tension between the social justice goals of human rights law and the supremacy of state sovereignty in international law.

There are also many other international law developments that are contributing to the individualisation of international law. For example, individual rights and duties have been created and/or enforced in international law in extradition treaties, double taxation agreements, transport treaties, intellectual property treaties, investment protection treaties, treaties on the legal status of foreigners, the Vienna Convention on Consular Relations, and ad hoc criminal tribunals and the International Criminal Court.[56] Increasingly, international law is addressing the rights and duties of the individual, and human rights bodies and tribunals are enforcing those rights and duties in relation to the individual. This is significant because it signals a move towards a global legal order, which the world has never seen before. While international law is still far from developing legal structures and enforcement mechanisms similar to domestic law, the move towards international law attaching directly to the individual transforms the nature of international law from a diplomatic mechanism to regulate relationships between states to a new rule of law at the international level.[57]

This individualisation of international law is not without its critics. For example, China and Russia have often emphasised the importance of state sovereignty, even at the expense of individual rights and human security.[58] In addition, it has been suggested that the focus and paradigm shift towards individualisation of international law has been largely due to the US and (to a lesser extent) European preoccupation with individual rights—which may not be reflective of global cultural norms or the desires of other jurisdictions in terms of the reach of international law.[59] Furthermore, there is a real concern about whether our global socio-legal structures are ready for a robust international legal order—do we have sufficient protections against abuse of such global power? Do we have sufficient processes to ensure checks and balances of global power? Do we have sufficient enforcement powers at the international level? Do we *want* strong enforcement powers at the international level?[60] Nonetheless, a paradigm shift is gradually occurring that is creating increasing rights and duties for individuals in international law.[61]

[55] Frans Viljoen, 'International Human Rights Law: A Short History' (2012) 12 Journal of Humanitarian Medicine 4; Fassbender and others (n 28).

[56] Peters (n 2) 1.

[57] Rafael Domingo, *The New Global Law* (CUP 2010).

[58] Peters (n 2) 3–6.

[59] William W Burke-White, 'Power Shifts in International Law: Structural Realignment and Substantive Pluralism' (2015) 56 Harvard International Law Journal 1.

[60] Neil Walker, *Intimations of Global Law* (CUP 2015); Andreas Fischer-Lescano and Gunther Teubner, 'Regime-Collisions: The Vain Search for Legal Unity in the Fragmentation of Global Law Diversity or Cacophony: New Sources of Norms in International Law Symposium' (2003) 25 Michigan Journal of International Law 999; Domingo (n 57).

[61] Peters (n 2).

There are a myriad of issues that can be debated and discussed in relation to the individualisation of international law, including critiques of individual rights themselves. However, for my purposes, the argument that I am making here is that in our existing international legal order it is essential to move towards the recognition and enforcement of the individual right to legal personhood on a global scale and to disallow claims of state sovereignty to deny or derogate from that right. It may be that there are other rights that we should similarly recognise as taking precedence over state sovereignty—however, here, I am arguing that it is particularly important for the right to legal personhood to take precedence over state sovereignty claims because the right to legal personhood is the predicate for the application of the whole of the human rights framework. Without the right to legal personhood recognised and enforced for the individual, the human rights framework becomes meaningless. Throughout this book, I have emphasised the many areas of law where this is demonstrated—where the denial of the right to legal personhood by a sovereign state has resulted in the obviation of the human rights framework. If we have a desire to achieve global social justice goals through the use of the human rights framework, the only way to do so is to ensure that the right to legal personhood supersedes state sovereignty, that global legal structures can intervene and require the recognition and enforcement of legal personhood on an equal basis for all people.

## 4. Conclusion

The implications of the arguments raised in this chapter have the potential to require immense change to our socio-legal order. The right to equal recognition before the law has already been delineated as a particularly important right[62] and has even been referred to as one of the 'absolute rights'.[63] Article 4 of the ICCPR designates it as one of the handful of rights that are non-derogable in times of emergency or crisis.[64] Some have argued that this already positions the right to equal recognition at the top of any hierarchy of rights that may exist.[65] It is an indication that there are circumstances, at least, in which state sovereignty will not be respected if it is used to attempt to undermine the right—such as in states of emergency or

[62] Tom Farer, 'The Hierarchy of Human Rights Conference on Human Rights, Public Finance, and the Development Process' (1992) 8 American University Journal of International Law and Policy 115, 115; Teraya Koji, 'Emerging Hierarchy in International Human Rights and Beyond: From the Perspective of Non-derogable Rights' (2001) 12 European Journal of International Law 917.

[63] Attorney-General's Department, 'Absolute Rights' <https://www.ag.gov.au/rights-and-protections/human-rights-and-anti-discrimination/human-rights-scrutiny/public-sector-guidance-sheets/absolute-rights> accessed 30 August 2023.

[64] International Covenant on Civil and Political Rights (adopted 16 December 1966, entered into force 23 March 1976) 999 UNTS 171 (ICCPR) s 4(2); Sarah Joseph and others, *The International Covenant on Civil and Political Rights: Cases, Materials, and Commentary* (OUP 2000).

[65] Farer (n 62) 115; Koji (n 62).

crisis. My argument here extends that proposition. It proposes that the right to equal recognition before the law should be respected without limitation; for example, regardless of state of emergency, cultural relativity, or state borders.

Taken expansively, this could mean a reassessment of our international border and immigration systems—and may demand a complete dismantling of those systems if they are denying the right to equal recognition before the law to non-citizens or non-nationals. It may also mean assertively calling for an end to practices that limit equal recognition before the law to women, disabled people, racial minorities, and other groups. In the following chapters I will begin to explore these possibilities—I will begin to explore how various marginalised groups are denied legal personhood via denials of the right to equal recognition before the law, analyse the human rights implications of such denials, and argue that the only path forward towards the realisation of the universal right to equal recognition before the law is to disallow the exercise of state sovereignty to limit the right and instead to recognise the right as attaching directly to each individual regardless of where the individual is in relation to state borders.

# 3

# Legal Personhood and Marginalised Groups

## 1. Introduction

In the first two chapters I have given the history, background, and definition of the human right to legal personhood. I have also argued for why state sovereignty and the accompanying doctrine of non-interference should not be given precedence over the human right to legal personhood—in other words, states should not be able to use sovereignty as a justification for denying or limiting the right to legal personhood. In this chapter, I am turning to an exploration of how the right to legal personhood applies to marginalised groups.

As described previously in the Preface, I began exploring the right to legal personhood in the context of disabled people. I was initially focused on disabled people because of my personal and professional background which led me to see firsthand the widespread and profound denials of legal personhood that disabled people are experiencing across the globe through guardianship, conservatorship, mental health laws, and in other discrete areas of the law, such as determinations of unfitness to plead in criminal trials. I have written about the denials that disabled people are experiencing in various forums, including in my 2017 book, *Restoring Voice to People*, my 2021 book, *Legal Capacity and Gender*, as well as in a range of articles and conference papers.[1] I also discuss the application of the right to legal personhood in the context of disability further in Chapter 4.

This examination of the right in the context of disability spurred me to begin thinking about what the right to legal personhood means beyond disability. As

[1] Anna Arstein-Kerslake, *Restoring Voice to People with Cognitive Disabilities* (CUP 2017); Anna Arstein-Kerslake, *Legal Capacity & Gender: Realising the Human Right to Legal Personhood and Agency of Women, Disabled Women, and Gender Minorities* (Springer 2021); Anna Arstein-Kerslake, 'Gendered Denials: Law, Policy and Practice' in Anna Arstein-Kerslake (ed), *Legal Capacity & Gender: Realising the Human Right to Legal Personhood and Agency of Women, Disabled Women, and Gender Minorities* (Springer 2021); Anna Arstein-Kerslake, 'Understanding Sex: The Right to Legal Capacity to Consent to Sex' (2015) 30 Disability & Society 1459; Anna Arstein-Kerslake, 'Gendered Denials: Vulnerability Created by Barriers to Legal Capacity for Women and Disabled Women' (2019) 66 International Journal of Law and Psychiatry 101501; Anna Arstein-Kerslake and Eilionóir Flynn, 'Legislating Consent: Creating an Empowering Definition of Consent to Sex That Is Inclusive of People with Cognitive Disabilities' (2016) 25 Social & Legal Studies 225; Eilionóir Flynn and Anna Arstein-Kerslake, 'Legislating Personhood: Realising the Right to Support in Exercising Legal Capacity' (2014) 10 International Journal of Law in Context 81.

*The Right to Legal Personhood of Marginalised Groups*. Anna Arstein-Kerslake, Oxford University Press.
 DOI: 10.1093/9780191926549.003.0003

described in Chapter 1, several scholars and activists have also thought about the right to legal personhood in the context of gender—in fact, the Convention on the Elimination of Discrimination Against Women (CEDAW) was the first international instrument to provide detail to the right to legal personhood and to clarify that the right to legal personhood includes both a right to legal standing and a right to legal agency.[2] However, the right to legal personhood beyond gender and disability is relatively under-explored. There are several likely reasons for this lack of attention. One may be the issues of state sovereignty that were raised in the previous chapter. For example, for migrant groups and stateless peoples there has historically been a great deal of deference to state sovereignty and a resistance to interfering with a state's citizenship and immigration systems, even when those systems are resulting in infringements on the legal personhood of various migrant groups and stateless peoples, including racial and religious minorities, refugees, and indigenous peoples, among others. Because these issues go to the core of state sovereignty—the entitlement of a state to determine who its citizens are and to respect the borders of that state—challenging such decisions of a sovereign state can be controversial and confronting and have the potential to cause tensions in international relationship between jurisdictions. Such issues go to the core of international law and how we conceptualise and construct statehood.

In addition, perhaps legal personhood has long been overlooked as a human rights issue because of its amorphous nature. It is largely an intangible concept that relies heavily on a sophisticated understanding of legal theory and its role in our socio-legal systems. That being said, when framed in an accessible format most people are acutely aware when they are being denied legal personhood and how that impacts their own power and privilege and their role in the socio-legal world. For example, undocumented migrants are aware of their status as non-persons in the eyes of the law and often make decisions accordingly—such as choosing not to involve law enforcement or engage with public bodies, including social welfare and benefit providers. Nonetheless, they likely are not consciously framing their situation as a denial of the human right to legal personhood. The intangibility and amorphous nature of the concept of legal personhood is perhaps what has made it difficult for individuals who are experiencing denials to identify such denials, and perhaps delayed its use as an advocacy tool for activists or as an analytical tool for scholars.

While the right to legal personhood is denied frequently and with dire consequences, we rarely find international civil society organisations or human rights scholars framing their social justice arguments around the right to legal personhood. Instead, they are often drawn to more tangible, often visceral, rights—such as the right to life and to be free from torture. The focus on such rights is often assumed to reach a wider audience and be more impactful. However, the downside

[2] Arstein-Kerslake, *Legal Capacity & Gender* (n 1).

is sometimes the further victimisation of survivors and individuals experiencing human rights violations, including vulnerability labelling of such groups that can lead to the exacerbation of disempowering assumptions and stereotypes, which can lead to power and privilege deficits.[3] In addition, a focus on such rights risks compartmentalising systemic social justice issues and not eliciting a full picture of the root of such problems. For example, the right to be free from torture is often used to argue for the dismantling of institutional settings such as mental health facilities.[4] Such arguments can be effective in the short term; however, they ignore the root of the problem—that disabled people's legal personhood and, particularly, their agency (which is an element of their personhood, as described in Chapter 1) are often ignored or denied altogether. This denial of legal agency is what facilitates the development of complex systems of 'care' that include practices that amount to torture because the will and preferences of disabled people are overlooked or actively denied. If the root of the problem was addressed—the need for full respect for legal personhood and agency of disabled people—it is possible that such systems of 'care' that perpetrate violations of the right to be free from torture would never emerge because they are so clearly in fundamental opposition to respect for the right to legal personhood and agency of disabled people.[5]

A new focus on using the human right to legal personhood in advocacy and scholarship may provide an avenue for addressing social justice and inequality issues, without further victimising or causing vulnerability labelling issues. It may also get closer to the heart of some profound social justice issues—it may allow us to address the core issue that many social injustices are stemming from—that legal personhood, itself, is only fully respected and granted to an elite group of individuals that enjoy power and privilege generated from long histories of preferential treatment to the disadvantage and exclusion of many other groups. Primarily, it is white, European, able-bodied, cisgender men that have enjoyed this power and privilege and the recognition of full legal personhood that comes with such power and privilege. Identifying this, and identifying the groups that have been excluded

[3] Arstein-Kerslake, 'Gendered Denials' (n 1); Elena Pariotti, 'Vulnerability and Human Rights: Which Compatibility?' (2023) 36 International Journal for the Semiotics of Law—Revue Internationale de Sémiotique Juridique 1401; Kate Brown, '"Vulnerability": Handle with Care' (2011) 5 Ethics and Social Welfare 313; Veronika Flegar and Emma Iedema, 'The Use of the "Vulnerability" Label by the Committee on the Elimination of Discrimination against Women: Protecting or Stigmatizing Women and Girls in the Forced Migration Context?' [2019] Brill Open Law 1.

[4] Laurie Ahern and Eric Rosenthal, 'Torture Not Treatment: Electric Shock and Long-Term Restraint in the United States on Children and Adults with Disabilities at the Judge Rotenberg Center' (Mental Disability Rights International 2010) <https://www.driadvocacy.org/wp-content/uploads/USReportandUrgentAppeal.pdf> accessed 17 May 2023; Priscila Rodriguez and others, 'No Justice: Torture, Trafficking and Segregation in Mexico' (Disability Rights International 2015) <https://www.driadvocacy.org/wp-content/uploads/Sin-Justicia-MexRep_21_Abr_english-1.pdf> accessed 17 May 2023.

[5] Arstein-Kerslake, *Restoring Voice to People with Cognitive Disabilities* (n 1); Tina Minkowitz, 'The United Nations Convention on the Rights of Persons with Disabilities and the Right to Be Free from Nonconsensual Psychiatric Interventions Symposium: The United Nations Convention on the Rights of Persons with Disabilities' (2007) 34 Syracuse Journal of International Law and Commerce 405.

from legal personhood, and the ways in which they have been excluded, may allow us to begin a process of correcting such rights violations and may eventually lead us to a correction of many other rights violations that are perpetuated by an initial and/or underlying lack of respect or recognition of certain groups' right to legal personhood—as is explored throughout this book.

The right to legal personhood has the potential to be an empowering social justice tool because it seeks to address the fundamental issue of recognition as a legal person and the consequences of denials of such legal personhood. As opposed to being a visceral or violent violation, which most people in privileged situations could not relate to or could easily designate as a problem of those existentially designated as the 'other', the right to legal personhood is something that we all experience and, perhaps, holds a stronger equalising power, even across already marginalised groups. In this chapter, I define marginalised groups, further explain the universality of rights—including the right to legal personhood—and then explore the application of the right to legal personhood for marginalised groups, as well as exploring jurisdictional limitations. This will lay the foundation for the following chapters, in which I begin to apply the right to specific marginalised groups.

## 2. Defining Marginalised Groups

I have chosen to focus this book on 'marginalised groups' in order to recognise that a denial of legal personhood is both marginalising and occurring disproportionately to already marginalised groups.[6] I have narrowed the analysis in this book down to a few selected marginalised groups, in order to provide concrete examples of how the right to legal personhood is being denied to marginalised groups and how such denials are further marginalising those groups. In addition, I have provided concrete examples for specific groups because my aim is for this book to be a starting point from which solutions can begin to be created. By providing concrete examples, I aim to point to specific areas of law and practice where reform is needed in order to better realise the right to legal personhood of these groups.

### 2.1 Terminology

The term 'marginalised groups' refers to social groups—or groups of people—who experience low levels of power and privilege. This includes groups, such as women, that may be large in numbers but continue to experience deficits in power and privilege, such as disproportionately low wages, high levels of violence perpetrated

[6] Arstein-Kerslake, *Restoring Voice to People with Cognitive Disabilities* (n 1); Arstein-Kerslake, *Legal Capacity & Gender* (n 1).

against them, disproportionate workloads, and so on.[7] In this way, I am using the term as a synonym for 'minority groups'—which is generally taken to have a similar definition, especially in sociology and social theory scholarship.[8]

In this book, I am focusing on the following marginalised groups: disabled people, migrant groups, stateless peoples, indigenous peoples, racial minorities, women, and gender minorities. While this is a diverse and highly varied selection of marginalised groups, I have chosen them because of the commonalities across the groups in terms of the denials of legal personhood that they are experiencing. In this way, while the task is large—to analyse the denials of legal personhood that are being experienced across these groups—it is narrowly focused on those commonalities across their rights denials. Chapters 4–9 will focus on examining each of these groups and the denials of legal personhood that they are facing.

## 2.2 Intersectionality

It is important to highlight that most of these groups have high numbers of individuals that sit across them. For example, indigenous women are both indigenous peoples and women. Consequentially, indigenous women may be experiencing denials of legal personhood that are commonly experienced by indigenous peoples and denials of legal personhood that are commonly experienced by women. Furthermore, they may be experiencing denials of legal personhood that are uniquely experienced by indigenous women. Where possible, throughout this book, I have endeavoured to identify both denials of legal personhood that are being experienced by one marginalised group, such as indigenous peoples, and those that are being experienced uniquely by individuals that are members of multiple marginalised groups and are experiencing intersecting marginalisation due to those group membership.

Throughout the book, I use intersectionality theory to undertake this analysis. Intersectionality theory was largely developed by Kimberlé Crenshaw, an American legal scholar, critical race theorist, and civil rights advocate.[9] She developed the theory in order to identify the profound level of discrimination that black women in the United States are facing. They are experiencing marginalisation

[7] George Hull, *The Equal Society: Essays on Equality in Theory and Practice* (Lexington Books 2015).

[8] Russell Ferguson and others, *Out There: Marginalization and Contemporary Culture* (MIT Press 1992); Viviane Seyranian, Hazel Atuel, and William D Crano, 'Dimensions of Majority and Minority Groups' (2008) 11 Group Processes & Intergroup Relations 21; Philip Vuciri Ramaga, 'Relativity of the Minority Concept' (1992) 14 Human Rights Quarterly 104.

[9] Kimberlé Crenshaw, 'Mapping the Margins: Intersectionality, Identity Politics, and Violence against Women of Color' (1990) 43 Stanford Law Review 1241; Kimberlé W Crenshaw, 'From Private Violence to Mass Incarceration: Thinking Intersectionally about Women, Race, and Social Control' (2011) 59 UCLA Law Review 1418; Kimberlé Crenshaw, *On Intersectionality: Essential Writings* (The New Press, 2017).

and discrimination on the basis of their race, gender, and the interface between the two. In other words, they are at risk of experiencing social injustice that is common across black people, across women—*and* they are also experiencing their own unique form of social injustice as black women, which black men and white women are not experiencing.

Crenshaw developed the theory as a result of her work on *DeGraffenreid v General Motors* (1976).[10] In *DeGraffenreid*, a group of black women sued General Motors for discrimination on the basis of race and gender. The court found that because there were black men and white women who were not experiencing the discrimination that the black women were alleging, no discrimination could be shown—the court declined to recognise black women as a marginalised group unto themselves who could be experiencing a unique form of discrimination that neither black men nor white women were experiencing. The court noted that if they were to recognise such a 'special sub-category', it could open a pandora's box of protected groups.[11]

Unfortunately, intersectional marginalisation and discrimination remains pervasive and extremely difficult to prove and remedy in a courtroom or other adjudicative forums. However, socio-legal scholarship has developed significantly, and intersectionality is now a widely recognised phenomenon.[12] Globally, it has also been incorporated into international and domestic rights frameworks.[13] It is particularly important for the right to legal personhood because there are widespread intersectional denials of the right to legal personhood that are occurring and causing significant disadvantage to individuals as well as to 'special sub-categories' of people. For example, disabled women experience disproportionate levels of denials of legal agency—a core element of their legal personhood, as described in Chapter 1—especially with regard to reproductive choice. They are disproportionately subjected to forced sterilisation and denial of maternal rights, and often assumed to lack sexual agency or sufficient decision-making skills to make sexual and/or reproductive decisions. This is occurring uniquely for disabled women, in a manner that is distinct from non-disabled women and also distinct from disabled people, more generally.[14] Such instances of intersectional denial of the right to legal personhood are explored in the following group-specific chapters.

10 Crenshaw, 'Mapping the Margins' (n 9).

11 ibid; *DeGraffenreid v General Motors*, 413 F Supp 142 (US District Court for the Eastern District of Missouri 1976).

12 Patricia Hill Collins, *Intersectionality as Critical Social Theory* (Duke UP 2019); Crenshaw, 'On Intersectionality' (n 9).

13 Kseniya A Kirichenko and Agnieszka Król, 'Intersectionality and the CRPD: An Analysis of the CRPD Committee's Discourse and Civil Society Advocacy at the Intersections of Disability and LGBTI' (2022) 17 Global Public Health 3224; MariaCaterina La Barbera, Julia Espinosa-Fajardo, and Paloma Caravantes, 'Implementing Intersectionality in Public Policies: Key Factors in the Madrid City Council, Spain' (2023) 19 Politics & Gender 675.

14 Arstein-Kerslake, *Legal Capacity & Gender* (n 1).

## 3. Universality of Rights: Applying Article 12 of the Convention on the Rights of Persons with Disabilities Beyond Disability

As described in the Preface and in Chapter 1, the right to legal personhood is a universal right. While this may seem self-evident to many international lawyers, I have consistently come across scholars from other fields, as well as government actors, practitioners in various fields, and others, who question whether a right that is enumerated in the Convention on the Rights of Persons with Disabilities (CRPD) is also applicable to other groups. It is a relatively common misconception in international law that a group-specific treaty is creating rights that apply only to the specifically delineated group. However, all international human rights are universal, and all rights can, in theory, be traced back to a right within the 'International Bill of Rights', which is made up of the Universal Declaration of Human Rights (UDHR) and its legally binding counterparts, the International Covenant on Civil and Political Rights (ICCPR) and the International Covenant of Economic, Social, and Cultural Rights (ICESCR). In Chapter 1, I discussed the history of the right to legal personhood, which is rooted in the right to equal recognition before the law and can be found in Article 6 of the UDHR and Article 16 of the ICCPR. Therefore, when we see the right to equal recognition before the law described in CEDAW (Article 15) and the CRPD (Article 12), these are just further descriptions of the universal right to equal recognition before the law that are tailored to the specific needs of women and disabled people, respectively.[15] It is perhaps pertinent to note that the descriptions of this right as they are found in CEDAW and the CRPD are significantly more detailed than was previously found in the UDHR or the ICCPR. They also include a more specific right to 'legal capacity' (termed 'legal personhood' throughout this book), which was not seen before in the UDHR or the ICCPR. However, consistent with the concept of universality of human rights law—and the tenet that all rights can be found in the 'International Bill of Human Rights'—the precipitating argument is that the right to personhood (or the right the legal capacity) was always a part of the right to equal recognition before the law; it was simply an implied part of the right as it is described in the UDHR and ICCPR. The drafting histories of Article 6 (UDHR) and Article 16 (ICCPR) are largely consistent with this argument—they both indicate that negotiations regarding the details of the elements of the right to legal personhood were indeterminate, and therefore a decision was made to keep the text broad and to generally refer to a guarantee of the right to equal recognition before the law.[16] At a minimum, this indicates a hesitation to restrict the right, and it left open the

[15] Rosemary Kayess and Phillip French, 'Out of Darkness into Light—Introducing the Convention on the Rights of Persons with Disabilities' (2008) 8 Human Rights Law Review 1.

[16] Arstein-Kerslake, *Restoring Voice to People with Cognitive Disabilities* (n 1) 6–7.

possibility for the definition and interpretation of the right to evolve in subsequent treaties—as it has in CEDAW and the CRPD.

Importantly, regardless of the history of the development of the right to equal recognition before the law (and the subsidiary right to legal personhood), a core tenet of human rights law is that all rights are universal—there are no rights that are only relevant for a certain group or groups of people. The right to legal personhood, therefore, applies equally to disabled and non-disabled people—even though its most detailed definition can be found in the CRPD. The challenge that I take on in this book, and that we must take on holistically as a social justice movement, is to understand how the right to legal personhood (and the right to equal recognition before the law, more broadly) should be applied beyond disability. The parameters dictated by international law are that the substance of the right must be equal across all groups. Therefore, the application of the right may vary depending upon the specific situation of certain individuals or groups; however, the definition and interpretation of the right itself must be consistent across all individuals and group—meaning that the definition and interpretation of the right in CEDAW, and then developed and provided in further detail in the CRPD, must also be the same definition and interpretation that is applied to other individuals and groups. The definition and interpretation of the right that I use in this book—and elsewhere in my work—can be found in Chapter 1 and is based on an analysis of the text of CEDAW and the CRPD, as well as an analysis of subsequent documents coming out of the UN monitoring bodies for those treaties—such as the General Comment on the right from the CRPD Committee (described in more detail in Chapter 1), which I participated in drafting.[17] This interpretation of the right to legal personhood includes both the right to legal standing and the right to legal agency—the entitlement to be recognised by the law as a legal entity and the entitlement to take legal actions—described more in Chapter 1.[18] Throughout Chapters 4 through 9, I will be using that interpretation of the right to legal personhood and applying it to various marginalised groups—in line with the doctrine of universality of all human rights.

## 4. Importance of Legal Personhood for Equality

It may not be obvious why the right to legal personhood is important for equality. I have already begun to talk about its importance in Chapters 1–3, however it is

[17] Anna Arstein-Kerslake and Eilionóir Flynn, 'The General Comment on Article 12 of the Convention on the Rights of Persons with Disabilities: A Roadmap for Equality before the Law' (2016) 20 The International Journal of Human Rights 471.

[18] Anna Arstein-Kerslake and Eilionóir Flynn, 'The Right to Legal Agency: Domination, Disability and the Protections of Article 12 of the Convention on the Rights of Persons with Disabilities' (2017) 13 International Journal of Law in Context 22.

useful to continue to explore its importance for equality in order to highlight the pressing need for greater attention to the right to legal personhood and the social justice opportunities that may arise if such attention is given by scholars, activists, and human rights bodies and adjudicative forums.

## 4.1 Legal Personhood as the Foundation of Socio-legal Structures

As I have argued elsewhere, legal personhood is the basis for the legitimacy of an individual's or entity's interaction with the socio-legal structures in our world. This importance of legal personhood has arisen out of liberal political theory, which dominates much of the world.[19] Liberal political theory holds that the individual is one of the most important, if not *the* most important, element of our social and legal world. It creates a political structure based on the importance of the individual above all else. Hence the priority of individual rights in liberal political systems.[20] In such systems, law is focused on the regulation of interactions between individuals or entities recognised as legal persons—and responsibility, both criminal and civil, almost exclusively lies with an individual or entity recognised as a legal person.

Because of this prioritisation of the individual, individuals or entities that are recognised as legal persons have legitimacy and are regarded as holders of rights and duties within our society. Those individuals or entities that are *not* recognised as legal persons are relegated to the status of objects within our socio-legal structures, and they can be used and manipulated relatively freely by individuals and/or entities that are recognised as legal persons and have the corresponding legitimacy as legal actors with legal standing—in other words, those who hold the rights and responsibilities of a recognised member of society. In much of the world—and a vast majority, if not all, of the 'Western World'—some version of liberal political theory continues to dominate and underpin our social and legal structures. In addition, even in jurisdictions, such as China, where liberal political theory's focus on the individual is often at odds with the communist focus on the community, there remains a requirement of legal personhood to engender interaction and engagement with legal systems.[21] Therefore, legal personhood is essential for an individual's or entity's legitimacy in a significant portion, if not all, of the world's legal systems.

[19] Arstein-Kerslake, *Restoring Voice to People with Cognitive Disabilities* (n 1); Flynn and Arstein-Kerslake (n 1).

[20] Judith N Shklar, 'Rights in the Liberal Tradition' (2023) 71 Political Studies 279.

[21] Wang Liming and Shi Jiayou, *Chinese Law of Personality Rights I: Theory and Practice* (Routledge 2023).

There is a wealth of scholarship debating the positives and negatives of various versions of liberal political theory.[22] Many argue that the liberal focus on the individual detracts from community responsibility and morality towards a common good.[23] Others argue that it has provided an abundantly fruitful platform for the rampant expansion of capitalism and the drive towards economic profit and competition above all else—often at the expense of social justice and environmental protection.[24] Others still, including myself, have argued that it was created by largely white, European, able-bodied, cisgender men who were under the illusion that they are atomistic actors engaging in a series of legal actions and relationships in order to strive towards the good life, or their understanding of the good life—and that this false understanding of human interaction has led to the development of legal systems around the globe that do not take into consideration the vast dependencies and interconnected nature of our socio-legal world.[25] Of course, there are many who continue to discuss the virtues of liberal political theory—and, for the most part, even our social justice systems continue to be based on liberal political theory and its prioritisation of the individual and the individual's rights. Due to the ongoing pre-eminence of liberal political theory, the individual remains a primary focus of our socio-legal systems, and the individual is only recognised within those systems if the legal personhood of that individual is recognised.

## 4.2 Dominance of Legal Personhood in Daily Life

The ever-present prioritisation of the individual as part of our liberal political systems can be seen in the ongoing need for recognition of legal personhood in daily life activities. The lives of disabled people provide a particularly poignant example, which will be explored more in Chapter 4, including the example of institutional and congregated residential settings, such as group homes. Such living situations frequently require that the disabled residents are either partially or fully denied

[22] Shklar (n 20); John Rawls, *Political Liberalism* (Columbia UP 2005); Joel Anderson and Axel Honneth, 'Autonomy, Vulnerability, Recognition, and Justice' in John Christman and Joel Anderson, *Autonomy and the Challenges to Liberalism: New Essays* (CUP 2005); Amy Gutmann, *Liberal Equality* (CUP 1980).

[23] Leighton McDonald, 'Can Collective and Individual Rights Coexist?' in Peter Jones (ed), *Group Rights* (Routledge 2009).

[24] Katrina Forrester, 'Liberalism and Social Theory after John Rawls' (2022) 44 Analyse & Kritik 1; Steven Lukes, 'Capitalism, Justice, and the Boundaries of Liberalism' (2022) 44 Analyse & Kritik 31; Matthew McManus, *The Emergence of Post-Modernity at the Intersection of Liberalism, Capitalism, and Secularism: The Center Cannot Hold* (Palgrave Macmillan 2022); Lars JK Moen, 'Republicanism as Critique of Liberalism' (2023) 61 The Southern Journal of Philosophy 308.

[25] Arstein-Kerslake, *Restoring Voice to People with Cognitive Disabilities* (n 1); Flynn and Arstein-Kerslake (n 1); Arstein-Kerslake, *Legal Capacity & Gender* (n 1); Anna Arstein-Kerslake and others, 'Relational Personhood: A Conception of Legal Personhood with Insights from Disability Rights and Environmental Law' (2021) 30 Griffith Law Review 530; Catriona Mackenzie and Natalie Stoljar, *Relational Autonomy: Feminist Perspectives on Autonomy, Agency, and the Social Self* (OUP 2000).

legal personhood and that their legal personhood rests with the state, a guardian, or the institution or residential setting itself.[26] In these contexts, nearly every detail of the individual's life is dominated by the lack of legal personhood—for example, they cannot decide independently on their medical treatment, including the use of chemical restraints and psychotropic medication, which often has significant short- and long-term implications for the individual.

In addition, often even the daily activities of individuals living in institutional or congregated settings are dictated by the staff, including the possibility of going for a walk—the staff have the power to control the individual at this level because the legal personhood of the individual does not rest with them and their ability to make decisions about their living conditions and care has been removed and, instead, lies with their legal guardian or other entity or person that the individual's legal personhood has been vested in. When the individual is involved in decisions regarding their daily life, living conditions, and care, that is often done as a courtesy to the individual. However, when legal personhood is not recognised in that individual (which it often is not), when they disagree with the staff of the institutional setting or congregated setting, then such staff can simply not enforce the decisions of the individual. This ever-impending removal of decision-making makes any choice into a mere pretence of choice because there is the ongoing risk that it could be disregarded. This demonstrates the power of legal personhood on the daily life of the individual.

Outside of the disability context, there are also a multitude of other ways in which our legal personhood dictates what our daily lives will look like. For example, to have employment that is legally recognised, you must have your legal personhood recognised because it is required for a legally valid employment contract. Most employers require a legally valid contract with all employees—if you cannot show that you are recognised as a legal person and, therefore, your legal agency to sign an employment contract will be recognised in law, most employers will not hire you. Most high-paying jobs require a legally valid employment contract—the employee must be recognised as a legal person and must exercise their recognised legal agency to enter into the contract. We often do not think about our legal personhood in such a way; however, it becomes imminently relevant to do so when the denial of legal personhood creates a significant barrier such as limiting an individual's employment options.

Let me provide a bit more detail to the example of an employment contract in order to facilitate an understanding of how the recognition of legal personhood relates to such a situation. As established in Chapter 1, legal personhood is an individual or entity's recognition as a holder of rights and a legal agent. Conversely, if the individual or entity is not recognised as a legal person, they do not hold rights

[26] Series Lucy, *Deprivation of Liberty in the Shadows of the Institution* (Policy Press 2022).

and they cannot exercise legal agency (in other words, their actions are generally not legally recognised or enforceable). The legal validity of an employment contract—or any contract—requires that all parties are recognised as legal agents; otherwise they are non-existent before the law, and their rights and obligations under the contract are not valid and do not have to be recognised by a court or other legal entities. Therefore, when signing an employment contract—or any contract—all individuals or parties entering into the contract must be recognised as legal persons in order for the contract to be valid and for both parties to be protected by contract law and other forms of law and law enforcement.

The means for demonstrating that you are a legal person for the purposes of an employment contract—and many other exercises of legal agency—is often via government identification documents and/or proof of immigration status, including permission to work.[27] If you do not have government identification documents and/or evidence of permission to work in that jurisdiction, then your legal personhood is not recognised and, therefore, your legal agency to enter into the employment contract is not recognised. Instead, it is restricted. As there is a human right to legal personhood on an equal basis for all, as described in Chapter 1, the questions then become:

- Is your legal personhood being restricted on a differential and impermissible basis, in violation of your human right to legal personhood?
- If it is being restricted on a differential and impermissible basis, how much discretion should states have to curtail legal personhood in such contexts?

Individuals that are often impacted by such denials—or limitations—on their legal personhood in relation to employment contracts include undocumented migrants, other migrants without permission to work, stateless people, and indigenous peoples who encounter barriers to obtaining identity documents or permission to work, among others.[28] Such limitations on the legal agency to enter into employment contracts have a significant impact on the socio-economic status of such groups. They are often either forced to work without an employment contract—meaning they have little to no legal protection and there is little to no regulation of their labour conditions—or to not work at all. This often results in either very poor labour conditions—including violations of other human

[27] Where an individual has government identification and immigration status, but that immigration status does not include permission to work, they would likely be considered to hold partial legal personhood. They hold some recognition as a legal person—they likely hold some rights—but they are not fully recognised as legal agents because the law will generally not recognise employment contracts that they enter into.

[28] Other groups may also be denied their legal agency to enter into employment contracts for other reasons, such as disabled people who are under guardianship and do not have their legal agency recognised as well as individuals convicted of crimes whose legal agency to engage in certain kinds of employment may not be recognised.

rights, such as those related to fair working conditions—and/or extreme poverty, which also precipitates other human rights violations. In these ways, denial of legal agency to enter into employment contracts can have a profound impact on an individual's—and their family's—daily life.

In relation to employment contracts—and the denial of legal agency to enter into such contracts—it is relevant to note that, for the most part, we recognise that curtailing such agency for children, or those under the age of majority, is a good thing. We generally want states to curtail the legal agency of children to enter into employment contracts. We want this curtailing because we have decided that it is better for children to not enter the labour market and to, instead, seek education. There are many reasons for this, including a terrible history of exploitation of child labour that has resulted in long-term health implications for many individuals, as well as an inability to seek the education that is often required for socio-economic advancement, among other negative effects.[29] However, it is relevant to note that there is a movement to change this assumption that children should not be permitted to work—that their legal agency should be curtailed in such a manner that their legal agency to enter into employment contracts is not recognised. Such arguments are being made on the basis that children and their families who are experiencing poverty are unable to escape such poverty, in part, because children's legal agency to enter into employment contracts is not recognised and they are unable to work.[30] In addition, this lack of recognition of legal agency to enter into employment contracts can leave children in a similar situation to the adults mentioned in the example above—they may be forced to enter labour situations that do not require a legally valid employment contract and are, therefore, largely unregulated and leave the child without recourse to contract law, law enforcement, and other legal protections that are available when an individual has their legal personhood recognised and can enter into a legally valid employment contract.

This lack of recognition of their legal agency is a denial of legal personhood on a differential basis—an unequal basis—for children. It is a denial of their right to legal personhood. The questions that arise are as follows:

- Do we want to allow states to exercise sovereignty and decide to make such denials of children's legal agency to enter into employment contract?

[29] Delphine Boutin and Marine Jouvin, 'Child Labour Consequences on Education and Health: A Review of Evidence and Knowledge Gaps' <https://hal.science/hal-03896700> accessed 5 September 2023; Heloise Weber and Aliya Abbasi, 'Poverty Is Not "Another Culture": Against a Right of Children to Work to Live' (2023) 49 Review of International Studies 409.

[30] Michael FC Bourdillon, Ben White, and William E Myers, 'Re-assessing Minimum-Age Standards for Children's Work' (2009) 29 International Journal of Sociology and Social Policy 106; Angelique Gatsinzi and Gavin Hilson, '"Age Is Just a Number": Articulating the Cultural Dimension of Child Labour in Africa's Small-Scale Mining Sector' (2022) 78 Resources Policy 102779.

- More broadly, when is the denial of legal personhood—or the denial of full legal personhood—appropriate, if ever? Is it appropriate for certain groups, such as children?

These are just two examples of how legal personhood—and the fulfilment of the right to legal personhood—can significantly impact our daily lives. It is also meant to provide a bit of a preview of some of the issues that will be raised in the following chapters regarding the disproportionate denials of legal personhood that certain minority and marginalised groups are experiencing and how that may impact the power and privilege of individuals within that group, as well as the power and privilege of the group, collectively. What I also aimed to have shown in this section is the tip of the iceberg in terms of the, as yet, unanswered legal questions with regard to legal personhood and the right to legal personhood. Because the right to legal personhood has been given so little attention, its boundaries and potential have yet to be defined. In contrast, non-discrimination law has been given considerable attention over the past 50 years, and many of the legal questions are well-defined—if not fully satisfactory in terms of creating non-discrimination law that is an effect tool for social justice and equality/equity goals.

I am attempting to shed light on the right to legal personhood and the many ways in which it can be applied. I believe that it has the potential to be a powerful tool for social change. However, I must also caution that I am concerned that attention on the right may result in a narrowing of the right—which, if taken to the extreme, could render it meaningless. Our challenge is to explore the right to legal personhood and the many ways in which it can be applied—to begin to establish the boundaries of the right—but with a vision towards creating a new, targeted, and robust social justice tool. We must avoid turning the right to legal personhood into merely another tokenistic nod to social justice, which is a risk if state sovereignty, capitalism, and liberal political theory continue to take precedence and cannot allow for the meaningful application and enforcement of the right to legal personhood on an equal basis for all (as has, arguably, occurred with non-discrimination law in some areas[31]). This task is not easy. However, I believe that the time has come to turn our minds to the right to legal personhood as a social justice tool, in part, because many of the other social justice tools—such a non-discrimination law—have failed to provide the protections needed or significant amelioration of socio-economic inequalities.

[31] Shreya Atrey and Sandra Fredman, *Exponential Inequalities: Equality Law in Times of Crisis* (OUP 2023); Shreya Atrey, 'Xenophobic Discrimination' (2023) The Modern Law Review <https://onlinelibrary.wiley.com/doi/abs/10.1111/1468-2230.12829> accessed 5 September 2023; Andrew F Johnson and others, 'Neglected under the Law: A Typology of Stigmatization and Effective Employment Protections' (2022) 32 Human Resource Management Review 100873.

## 4.3 Legal Personhood as a Predicate to Power and Privilege

As I have suggested, the recognition of legal personhood has a strong correlation to an individual's—or group's—power and privilege in our socio-legal world. This correlation is due to the pervasiveness of the importance of legal personhood in our daily lives, as well as in our legal systems that are dominated by liberal political theory and, therefore, prioritise the individual. The recognition of an individual's legal personhood dictates how they are able to operate as a socio-legal actor and what standing they have in the socio-legal world. For example, their legal personhood dictates their employment capabilities (discussed above), their financial freedom and ability to control their finances (because this is tied to their recognition as a legal actor), their ability to move between jurisdictions (because this is tied to their ability to gain legal documents to demonstrate the recognition of their legal standing and agency), their ability to enforce their rights in a court or other legal forum (because without the recognition of their legal standing, they have no ability to enforce such rights), among others. All of these aspects of life that are tied to personhood have the potential to strongly impact the power and privilege of the individual because they are directly related to the individual's socio-economic status as well as the individual's legal standing and power to assert their legal rights, particularly in the face of potential harm from others.

Because legal personhood is often strongly correlated with an individual's and/or group's power and privilege, it has immense potential to be a robust social justice tool. If legal arguments can be successfully made regarding a particular group's right to legal personhood, we may be able to avoid intractable arguments regarding non-discrimination, which have often been very slow to produce social justice benefits. It may also allow us to jump straight to the heart of a social justice issue, as opposed to tinkering around the edges examining social justice harms that are actually caused—at their root—by denials of legal personhood.

For example, if advocates and scholars were able to successfully argue for the right to legal personhood of transgender people to be fully recognised and respected, that would necessitate methods for legally changing gender and appropriate choices for legal gender recognition that align with various gender identities. It would also require equal rights and access to all exercises of legal agency for transgender people, such as marriage, divorce, and medical decision-making. Currently, activists and social justice actors and scholars are often tackling these issues in isolation. However, an argument for the right to legal personhood on an equal basis for transgender people would require all of these injustices to be corrected. It is likely that individual battles would still need to be fought to achieve change in each area; however, the overarching argument that all these areas *must* change because they each are a type of violation of the right to legal personhood has the potential to provide a new, strong legal foundation for demanding reform.

This is true for many areas where social justice reforms have long been needed. Another example is women's equality. In more restrictive jurisdictions, many equality issues for women stem from lack of legal agency due to formal legislative restrictions on women's contracting and inheritance rights. For example, in Saudi Arabia, there is a long-standing guardianship law that places women under the legal guardianship of a man, such as their father, husband, brother, or son. The male guardian then assumes the legal personhood of the woman, and the woman's ability to exercise legal agency is severely limited.[32] (Although it is relevant to note that there has been progress in limiting the control that male guardians have over women, especially in the past ten years, when reforms have occurred that permit women to drive, travel, and carry out some other activities without the permission of their guardian.[33]) In other jurisdictions, where there are no such full-scale formal legislative restrictions on women's legal agency, there are often discrete areas of the law that limit women's legal agency, as well as informal practices that result in restrictions on women's legal agency. These restrictions often either directly limit women's agency or indirectly impact on the ability of women to exercise their legal agency. For example, restrictions on reproductive choice significantly impact women's ability to make decisions about their own bodies, including restrictions on abortions, contraceptive, sterilisation, and other areas. These restrictions also significantly impact the legal agency of all persons who can become pregnant, including trans persons and intersex people, among others. Such restrictions on reproductive choice also indirectly impact women and persons who can become pregnant with regard to other exercises of legal agency that become increasingly difficulty if reproductive agency is not respected. For example, if abortion and/or contraceptives are not freely available as a meaningful choice for this cohort, then they may have children at higher rates, which often limits educational choice, as well as employment choices—both of which can be exercises of legal agency in different ways. Education is an exercise of legal agency, if there are legal implications related to decisions made regarding education[34]—for example, if there are legal penalties for either attending or not attending school. Employment is almost always an exercise of legal agency because it creates an inherently legal relationship between the employee and employer—this is true whether there is a valid employment contract or not because even where there is no valid employment contract, there remain legal implications of the labour relationship between the two parties.

[32] Arstein- Kerslake, *Legal Capacity & Gender* (n 1); Rebekah D Bunch, 'Shackled by Shari'a: Saudi Women Still Controlled by Male Guardianship System despite Present (Cosmetic) Reforms' (2022) 8 Journal of Global Justice and Public Policy 73; فيصل بن عبدالواحد الصانع, 'عدم المساواة بين الجنسين في السعودية Gender Inequality in Saudi Arabia' (2022) 9 مجلة مستقبل العلوم الإجتماعية 63; Rachel Aruna Hasan, Anam Muzamill, and Muhammad Saqib Saleem, 'Unveiling Women's Empowerment: Exploring the Liberation Movement in Saudi Arabia' (2023) 8 Global Sociological Review 166.

[33] Bunch (n 32); Hasan, Muzamill, and Saleem (n 32).

[34] Arstein-Kerslake and Flynn, 'The Right to Legal Agency' (n 18).

This is similarly true for people who are self-employed with regard to the parties that are paying for their services and/or goods. In short, I have provided these examples in order to demonstrate the vast array of areas that the right to legal personhood impacts—and the high level of importance of those areas for either the increase or decrease in an individual's power and privilege levels in our society.

## 5. Jurisdictional Limitations

The jurisdictional limitations related to securing the right to legal personhood for marginalised groups are primarily related to issues of state sovereignty—at least, in theory. As discussed in Chapter 2, the doctrine of non-interference that is a core element of respect for state sovereignty in international law, gives states a significant margin of control over the implementation of human rights law,[35] including the human right to legal personhood. As I argued in Chapter 2, there are strong social justice goals that would be furthered if the right to legal personhood was one area of human rights where states were not permitted to exercise full sovereignty. In other words, I am arguing that the right to legal personhood should not be subjected to the doctrine of non-interreference with regard to states that are recognised as sovereign and are legally bound by international human rights law.

If the doctrine of non-interference does apply to the right to legal personhood (which seems to currently be the situation), then the right becomes largely meaningless for many marginalised groups because there are widespread practices within domestic legal systems throughout the world that limit or deny legal personhood to many marginalised groups. For example, migrants, stateless people, women, gender minorities, disabled people, and others have their legal personhood denied in various ways—as is explored throughout this book. This is a jurisdictional limitation on multiple levels. The first level on which it is a jurisdictional issue is the division between international law and domestic law. The majority of states have signed and ratified at least one international human rights instrument that protects the right to legal personhood—and makes that jurisdiction legally bound to respect, protect, and enforce such a right. However, most jurisdictions—if not all—deny or limit the right to legal personhood at the domestic level on the basis of group membership for many marginalised groups.

There is also a jurisdictional issue due to the existence of political borders between states. This primarily affects the right to legal personhood of migrants, stateless peoples, and indigenous groups. Such borders—and the doctrine of non-interference that applies to the states that are recognised as sovereign within

[35] W Michael Reisman, 'Sovereignty and Human Rights in Contemporary International Law' (1990) 84 American Journal of International Law 866.

those borders as part of international law—create differential relationships between the governments of those sovereign states and individuals with various immigration statuses with the states, as well as individuals that the state chooses not to recognise at all (or in a limited fashion), which often occurs in the context of stateless peoples and indigenous groups. This differential relationship allows the state to limit or deny the legal personhood of these groups. The elimination of political borders would likely alleviate these problems; however, such a goal seems quite lofty at this moment in history. What may be more possible is the acceptance of political border, with the caveat that each government—each sovereign state—must ensure recognition of legal personhood to all persons on an equal basis, including migrants, stateless people, and indigenous groups. In other words, an individual's place of birth, immigration status, ethnic identity, and any other social identity or political label cannot be a justification or basis for the limitation or denial of legal personhood. This would significantly change the nature of political borders because it would likely mean that individuals would have equal legal personhood on either side of all borders. This change would obviate the need for most immigration law and immigration statuses. Of course, such a situation is not without precedent; for example, the European Union and its commitment to 'free movement' ensures that all citizens of the European Union can move and work freely within the European Union, which includes jurisdictions with significantly different levels of wealth and economic stability. This fundamental change in the nature of the political borders within the European Union has been largely successful—it has not led to widespread economic failure or resource scarcity.[36] Success in such a large region suggests the fallacy of arguments related to resource protection and economic stability being tied to political borders that deny legal personhood to non-citizens or individuals with certain immigration status. More research is needed in this area—both from an economic and from a socio-legal perspective—and an overnight transformation could potentially be catastrophic. However, I believe that the right to legal personhood gives us the opportunity to crack open the door and begin to imagine a world in which we respect all persons as full legal persons, and we seek to create a system of political borders that upholds that right for all, including marginalised groups (as opposed to allowing the fear of resource scarcity and economic instability excuse the treatment of some groups as subhuman within our legal systems).

[36] Emiliana Baldoni, 'The Free Movement of Persons in the European Union: A Legal-Historical Overview' (July 2003), STATE OF THE ART REPORT PIONEUR Working Paper No 2 <https://www.academia.edu/21816300/The_Free_Movement_of_Persons_in_the_European_Union_A_Legal_historical_Overview> accessed 18 June 2024; Martin Kahanec, Mariola Pytliková, and Klaus F Zimmermann, 'The Free Movement of Workers in an Enlarged European Union: Institutional Underpinnings of Economic Adjustment' in Martin Kahanec and Klaus F Zimmermann (eds), *Labor Migration, EU Enlargement, and the Great Recession* (Springer 2016).

## 6. Conclusion

We have agreed, as an international community, in multiple different international instruments, that the right to legal personhood is core to an individual's fundamental rights—that we want governments to recognise the legal personhood of all persons on an equal basis. I believe that we now have a responsibility to look closer at how we can achieve that. We need to look closer at how we are denying the right to legal personhood to certain groups, how that is affecting the power and privilege of those groups, and how we can fulfil the promise of the right to legal personhood for all peoples on an equal basis. It is not an easy task because it demands that we re-examine the core principles of international law, such as the doctrine of non-interference with regard to state sovereignty and the existence (and power) of political borders. However, if we are taking human rights seriously—and if social justice is a real goal—it is critical to also take the right to legal personhood seriously. It is, surely, the very foundation of social equality—and it is unlikely that either social justice or the normative principles of human rights law can be achieved without first securing the basic right of every individual from every marginalised group to be recognised as a legal person on an equal basis with others (especially in our socio-legal systems that are dominated by liberal political theory, which does not appear to be fading anytime soon.)

# 4

# Legal Personhood and Disability

## 1. Introduction

The right to legal personhood has been most explored in scholarship in the context of disability because of Article 12 of the 2006 UN Convention on the Rights of Persons with Disabilities (CRPD), which included more detail to the right than had ever been seen before in an international human rights instrument.[1] Scholars and activists quite immediately began exploring what a right to legal personhood looks like for disabled people.[2] Although Article 15 of the 1979 Convention on the Elimination of Discrimination Against Women (CEDAW) preceded the CRPD and provided the most detail, at that time, of the right to legal personhood, it did not seem to generate anywhere near as much attention for the right as Article 12 of the CRPD has generated.[3] Perhaps this is because there was a much greater involvement of activists and civil society in the development of Article 12 of the CRPD[4]—it is difficult to identify exactly why this occurred; however, it is significant to note that although CEDAW provided the first detail to the right to legal personhood in an international human rights instrument, it did not usher in a new era of legal theory related to legal personhood, as I believe Article 12 of the CRPD has done.[5]

[1] Anna Arstein-Kerslake, *Restoring Voice to People with Cognitive Disabilities* (CUP 2017); Eilionóir Flynn and Anna Arstein-Kerslake, 'Legislating Personhood: Realising the Right to Support in Exercising Legal Capacity' (2014) 10 International Journal of Law in Context 81.

[2] Tina Minkowitz, 'The United Nations Convention on the Rights of Persons with Disabilities and the Right to Be Free from Nonconsensual Psychiatric Interventions Symposium: The United Nations Convention on the Rights of Persons with Disabilities' (2007) 34 Syracuse Journal of International Law and Commerce 405; Amita Dhanda, 'Legal Capacity in the Disability Rights Convention: Stranglehold of the Past or Lodestar for the Future Symposium: The United Nations Convention on the Rights of Persons with Disabilities' (2007) 34 Syracuse Journal of International Law and Commerce 429; Bernadette McSherry, 'Legal Capacity under the Convention on the Rights of Persons with Disabilities' (2012) 20 Journal of Law and Medicine 22; Piers Gooding, 'Navigating the Flashing Amber Lights of the Right to Legal Capacity in the United Nations Convention on the Rights of Persons with Disabilities: Responding to Major Concerns' (2015) 15 Human Rights Law Review 45; Penelope Weller, 'Reconsidering Legal Capacity: Radical Critiques, Governmentality and Dividing Practice' (2014) 23 Griffith Law Review 498.

[3] Anna Arstein-Kerslake, *Legal Capacity & Gender: Realising the Human Right to Legal Personhood and Agency of Women, Disabled Women, and Gender Minorities* (Springer 2021).

[4] Rosemary Kayess and Phillip French, 'Out of Darkness into Light: Introducing the Convention on the Rights of Persons with Disabilities' (2008) 8 Human Rights Law Review 1.

[5] Anna Arstein-Kerslake and others, 'Relational Personhood: A Conception of Legal Personhood with Insights from Disability Rights and Environmental Law' (2021) 30 Griffith Law Review 530; Erin O'Donnell and Anna Arstein-Kerslake, 'Recognising Personhood: The Evolving Relationship between the Legal Person and the State' (2021) 30 Griffith Law Review 339.

*The Right to Legal Personhood of Marginalised Groups.* Anna Arstein-Kerslake, Oxford University Press.
 DOI: 10.1093/9780191926549.003.0004

This new era of legal theory related to legal personhood is still evolving, but it has implications for legal fields far beyond disability. It demands a re-examination of legal personhood in light of relational understandings of the person—which challenge the existing liberal political idea of the autonomous man deftly manoeuvring through socio-legal systems to secure his idea of the 'good life'.[6] The requirement of state-provided access to support for the exercise of legal personhood demands this re-examination, and it opens up new possibilities for many different legal entities to exercise their legal personhood in ways that do not require the traditional method of guardianship where the individual or entity is forced to vest some or all of their legal personhood in another person or entity—effectively losing control of most of their legal decision-making power. This new era of legal theory spurred by Article 12 of the CRPD also demands a close examination of how denials or limitations of the right to legal personhood are taking place both for disabled people and for others. As described in Chapter 1, the universal nature of human rights dictates that the right to legal personhood cannot be a right that is only enjoyed by women and disabled people (although they are the only cohorts with group-specific human rights treaties that provide significant detail to the right). It must apply to all humans—if not also to non-human entities (although this book is not aimed at exploring that possibility, it seems that environmental lawyers and animal rights activists, for example, are already taking up that possibility[7]). Therefore, this new era of legal theory can take the detail provided to the right to legal personhood in the context of gender and disability and apply it beyond those groups. In this chapter, I will provide a brief overview of the key new understandings of the right to legal personhood that have developed in Article 12 of the CRPD (on the back of the detail provided in Article 15 of CEDAW) in an effort to create a foundation of knowledge of these new understandings that is sufficient for moving forward and applying them to various other marginalised groups—as is done in the chapters that follow.

In addition, the CRPD uses the social model of disability as a foundation for the enumeration of human rights law as it applies to disability.[8] The social model of disability is a theoretical framework born out of the field of disability studies. It is a form of critical disability studies (which is a form of critical social theory), and it holds that disability is a social construct and social barriers are the source of disability. In other words, it holds that if the social barriers that prevent people with impairments from full societal participation are broken down, then the individual

[6] Arstein-Kerslake, *Restoring Voice to People with Cognitive Disabilities* (n 1); Flynn and Arstein-Kerslake (n 1); Arstein-Kerslake and others (n 5).

[7] Erin O'Donnell and Julia Talbot-Jones, 'Creating Legal Rights for Rivers: Lessons from Australia, New Zealand, and India' (2018) 23(1):7 Ecology and Society <https://www.ecologyandsociety.org/vol23/iss1/art7/> accessed 8 September 2019; Richard A Epstein, 'Animals as Objects, or Subjects, of Rights' University of Chicago John M Olin Law and Economics Working Paper No 171 <https://papers.ssrn.com/abstract=359240> accessed 8 September 2019.

[8] Kayess and French (n 4).

would no longer be disabled.[9] Article 12 of the CRPD (as part of the CRPD) was born out of this understanding of disability—it establishes that the barriers to legal personhood for disabled people are socio-legal structures that deny legal personhood, and a lack of access to support for disabled people who are seeking to exercise their legal personhood via their legal agency. If these social barriers were broken down, disabled people would enjoy their legal personhood on an equal basis with others. Conversely, as described in the UN Committee on the Rights of Persons with Disabilities General Comment on the Right to Equal Recognition Before the Law (which I participated in drafting and supporting the Committee to amend and adopt), a person's legal personhood is not tied to their mental capacity or their decision-making skills. In line with the social model of disability, barriers to legal personhood are due to an inhospitable socio-legal environment, as opposed to an impairment of the individual themselves. This critical social theory lens allows us to explore not just immediate experiences of legal personhood denials or limitations but also the deeper socio-legal and historical roots of these denials or limitations. Therefore, using the CRPD, and Article 12 specifically, as an analytical tool for both disabled people and beyond provides a robust analytical tool that can help us address solutions that take into account these socio-legal and historical foundations of the limitations and denials of legal personhood for these groups. I will also discuss critical race theory and its relation to the social model of disability and Article 12 CRPD in Chapter 6, as well as critical feminist theory and its relation to the social model of disability and Article 12 CRPD in Chapter 7.

## 2. Exclusion from Legal Personhood

### 2.1 Introduction

Disabled people are one of the groups that are most profoundly affected by exclusions from legal personhood—both throughout history and in modern legal systems. Where an individual experiences an intersecting form of marginalisation, in addition to marginalisation related to disability, they are often even more profoundly affected by such exclusions.[10] This intersecting impact from exclusion

[9] Bill Hughes and Kevin Paterson, 'The Social Model of Disability and the Disappearing Body: Towards a Sociology of Impairment' (1997) 12 Disability & Society 325; Mike Oliver, 'The Social Model of Disability: Thirty Years On' (2013) 28 Disability & Society 1024; Tom Shakespeare, 'The Social Model of Disability' in Lennard J Davis (eds), *The Disability Studies Reader* (Taylor & Francis 2016); Rannveig Traustadóttir, 'Disability Studies, The Social Model And Legal Developments' in Gerard Quinn and Oddný Mjöll Arnardóttir, *The UN Convention on the Rights of Persons with Disabilities: European and Scandinavian Perspectives* (Brill 2009).

[10] For a discussion of intersectionality, see Kimberlé Crenshaw, 'Mapping the Margins: Intersectionality, Identity Politics, and Violence against Women of Color' (1990) 43 Stanford Law Review 1241; Patricia Hill Collins, *Intersectionality as Critical Social Theory* (Duke UP 2019);

from legal personhood is particularly true for all disabled people within the groups that I have selected to focus on in this book (migrant groups, stateless peoples, indigenous peoples, racial minorities, women, and gender minorities), which is part of the reason that they have been chosen to be included in this analysis. What I am discussing in this chapter are the exclusions from legal personhood that are uniquely experienced by disabled people—or exclusions that are explicitly made on the basis of disability. I am also discussing some exclusions from legal personhood that affect disabled people who are experiencing intersecting forms of marginalisation because many of those exclusions are being uniquely experienced by individuals at that intersection of multiple forms of marginalisation—for example, disabled women. Some of these exclusions may arise in this chapter as well as in the group-specific chapter related to the other, intersecting, forms of marginalisation. The aim of this discussion is to raise some of the ways in which disabled people are being excluded from legal personhood—and, in doing so, to begin to see how the right to legal personhood can be applied, in order to move on to applying it to other groups in future chapters.

It is important to identify exclusions both in the context of disability alone and in the context of intersecting forms of marginalisation because they each raise unique exclusions of the right to legal personhood—leaving either out would result in significant gaps in analysis. However, while wanting to ensure that both disability and intersectional forms of exclusions of legal personhood are discussed here, I also want to make it clear that the exclusions from legal personhood discussed here, and throughout this book, are not an exhaustive list of exclusions from legal personhood. Instead, they are meant to be examples of some of the most significant exclusions from legal personhood as they affect various groups in order to demonstrate the profound impact of exclusions from legal personhood on the power and privilege of such groups.

## 2.2 Guardianship, Conservatorship, and Interdiction, and Intersectional Marginalisation Based on Gender

Perhaps the most obvious forms of denial of legal personhood for disabled people are formal legal determinations that remove legal personhood—either wholly or in part—from the individual and place it with another individual or entity. The terminology used for these removals of legal personhood varies by jurisdiction—some of the commonly used terms are guardianship, conservatorship, and interdiction. These legal mechanisms are generally used when there is an actual or

Gauthier de Beco, 'Intersectionality and Disability in International Human Rights Law' (2020) 24 The International Journal of Human Rights 1.

perceived difficulty with decision-making.[11] They often conflate the concepts of mental capacity and legal capacity (which, I argue, is synonymous with legal personhood) and deny legal capacity on the basis of actual or perceived deficits in mental capacity. This is in violation of the right to legal personhood, as interpreted by the Committee on the Rights of Persons with Disabilities in their first General Comment. Described in more detail in Chapter 1, they establish that the right to legal personhood must be enjoyed equally by all people, regardless of decision-making skills.[12] Therefore, in order to respect the right to legal personhood, a person must not have their legal personhood denied on the basis of decision-making skills; this is important beyond disability, as other groups have frequently had their legal personhood removed on the basis that they lack decision-making skills or 'rationality', for example, women and gender minorities, which is discussed below and in Chapters 8 and 9.[13]

Such laws are often thought of as laws that are beneficial for disabled people; however, the reality is that disabled people are often disenfranchised and disempowered by such laws because they remove the individual's control and decision-making power in their own lives. I have written about this extensively in other forums, as have many other scholars and activists.[14]

The origins of such laws are often quite paternalistic and arise from prejudicial understandings of disability, as well as other characteristics, such as gender. This paternalism and prejudice stem, at least in part, from the historic creation of law by white, able-bodied, cisgender men, who may both lack a nuanced understanding of disability and gender and often benefit from having mechanisms for removing legal personhood on the basis of gender. I do not say this to paint white, able-bodied, cisgender men as villains. On the contrary, I think it is important to explicitly identify the persons who are in positions of power and who are creating

[11] Arstein-Kerslake, *Restoring Voice to People with Cognitive Disabilities* (n 1); Flynn and Arstein-Kerslake (n 1).

[12] Anna Arstein-Kerslake and Eilionóir Flynn, 'The General Comment on Article 12 of the Convention on the Rights of Persons with Disabilities: A Roadmap for Equality before the Law' (2016) 20 The International Journal of Human Rights 471; Committee on the Rights of Persons with Disabilities, 'General Comment No 1 Article 12: Equal Recognition before the Law' (19 May 2014) UN Doc CRPD/C/GC/1.

[13] Arstein-Kerslake, *Legal Capacity & Gender* (n 3).

[14] Arstein-Kerslake, *Restoring Voice to People with Cognitive Disabilities* (n 1); Flynn and Arstein-Kerslake (n 1); Anna Arstein-Kerslake, 'An Empowering Dependency: Exploring Support for the Exercise of Legal Capacity' (2016) 18 Scandinavian Journal of Disability Research 77; Anna Arstein-Kerslake and others, 'Future Directions in Supported Decision-Making' (2017) 37(1) Disability Studies Quarterly <https://dsq-sds.org/article/view/5070> accessed 6 May 2022; Joanne Watson and others, 'The Impact of the United Nations Convention on the Rights of Persons with Disabilities (CRPD) on Victorian Guardianship Practice' (2022) 44 Disability and Rehabilitation 2806; Dhanda (n 2); Kristin Booth Glen, 'Not Just Guardianship: Uncovering the Invisible Taxonomy of Laws, Regulations and Decisions That Limit or Deny the Right of Legal Capacity for Persons with Intellectual and Developmental Disabilities Selected Works Regarding Government Law' (2019) 13 Albany Government Law Review 25; Kristin Booth Glen, 'Changing Paradigms: Mental Capacity, Legal Capacity Guardianship, and Beyond' (2012) 44 Columbia Human Rights Law Review 93.

laws that have a profound impact on the legal personhood of others. It is important in order to draw out the often flawed reasoning behind such laws—as well as to demand greater diversity in lawmakers—to remove the responsibility of such law creation from such a narrow group of people and reposition that power into the hands of those most significantly affected by such laws.

The history that I am referring to is the history of guardianship laws—and similar laws—being used to silence women, to pathologise female characteristics and gender diverse experiences, to remove disabled people from social participation (often for the sake of convenience or normalisation), to pathologise disabled people, and for other reasons that stem more from a desire to homongenise and eugenise than to provide assistance or to recognise that our socio-legal systems were generally structured to meet the needs of white, able-bodied, cisgender men—and others are often excluded and left in actual or perceived need of assistance when navigating systems that are ill-suited to their needs. There is also an apparent aim of such laws to maintain the power and privilege of certain groups—mostly white, able-bodied, cisgender men.[15] This is evidenced in the use of guardianship laws to control and silence women and wives, in particular—this occurred in Europe, North America, and Australia until the mid-1900s when such laws (often termed coverture laws) were largely eliminated.[16] Such laws operated similar to guardianship laws and allowed husbands to subsume the legal personhood of their wives—it allowed husbands to hold the legal standing and legal agency of their wives. Similar laws continue in many parts of the world, including Saudi Arabia and elsewhere.[17] These laws have been used to explicitly exclude disabled people and others—especially women and gender minorities—from legal personhood. They have also been used in a manner intended to provide assistance to such groups for the exercise of legal personhood; however, functionally, they remove power and recognition from the individual and act as a kind of 'civil death' that leaves the individual in the position of an object before the law, rather than a subject.[18]

I am discussing this form of legal personhood denial—guardianship, conservatorship, and interdiction—because its use and reach have impacts far beyond disabled people—even though disabled people are often thought of as the only ones

[15] Arstein-Kerslake, *Legal Capacity & Gender* (n 3).

[16] Amy Louise Erickson, 'Coverture and Capitalism' (2005) 59 History Workshop Journal 1; Claudia Zaher, 'When a Woman's Marital Status Determined Her Legal Status: A Research Guide on the Common Law Doctrine of Coverture' (2002) 94 Law Library Journal 459.

[17] Jawaher Al-Shamari, 'Legalized Patriarchy: An Examination of Qatari Women's Lived Realities in the Private/Public Spheres' (Honor's thesis, Georgetown University in Qatar, GU-Q 2022) <https://repository.library.georgetown.edu/handle/10822/1067512> accessed 5 September 2023; Rebekah D Bunch, 'Shackled by Shari'a: Saudi Women Still Controlled by Male Guardianship System Despite Present (Cosmetic) Reforms' (2022) 8 Journal of Global Justice and Public Policy 73.

[18] Gerard Quinn and Abigail Rekas-Rosalbo, 'Civil Death: Rethinking the Foundations of Legal Personhood for Persons with a Disability' (2016) 56 Irish Jurist 286.

impacted by such laws. Women and gender minorities, as mentioned above, were historically often subjected to such laws—and, in some jurisdictions, are still subjected to such laws. In addition, they provide a quite clear and concrete example of what the formal legal denial of legal personhood can look like. They specifically and intentionally remove legal standing and/or legal agency—in whole or in part—from the individual and vest it in someone else. As discussed in Chapter 1, this is the essence of legal personhood denial. A thorough understanding of legal personhood denials via guardianship, conservatorship, interdiction, and the like gives us a clear picture of what it can look like, and we can then endeavour to identify similar denials of legal standing and legal agency in other, more discrete, areas of law and practice.

## 2.3 Mental Health Law and Intersectional Marginalisation Based on Gender and Indigeneity

Mental health law is profoundly affected by a newly recognised right to legal personhood. Mental health law includes denials of legal personhood to the extent that it removes legal agency from the individual on the basis that they are a person with a mental health disability. Generally, it places that legal agency in a health professional—such as a psychiatrist or other mental health professional. The professional then has legal protection to make treatment decisions on behalf of the individual—including, frequently, the use of chemical or physical restraints. In other words, once the individual is determined to have a mental health disability, they are at risk of removal of their legal agency to make treatment decisions, including their legal agency to consent to staying in a treatment facility. Under most mental health law, individuals with mental health disability can be detained against their will.

Since the 2006 CRPD, there has been a burgeoning cohort of scholars and activists (including myself) that has provided new analysis of mental health law in light of the right to legal personhood in Article 12 of the CRPD.[19] They have recognised that the vast majority of current mental health law is inconsistent with a right to legal personhood. There has been considerable resistance to this from mental health professionals, many of whom argue that the profession is established—and maintains as its aim—to assist and improve the well-being of people with mental health disability, as well as being committed to preserving the rights of people with

[19] Bernadette McSherry, 'Mental Health Laws: Where to from Here' (2014) 40 Monash University Law Review 175; Weller (n 2); Gooding (n 2); Dhanda (n 2); Minkowitz (n 2); Peter Bartlett, 'The United Nations Convention on the Rights of Persons with Disabilities and Mental Health Law' (2012) 75 The Modern Law Review 752; Anna Arstein-Kerslake, 'Challenging the Foundations of Mental Health Law' (2015) (128) Precedent 32.

mental health disability.[20] While this is often true—it is also true that on a pure legal analysis of the right to legal personhood—the denial of legal agency on the basis of a mental health disability is, at the minimum, a partial denial of the right to legal personhood. The task at hand is to engage in a discussion of whether we would like legal agency to be denied in certain circumstances—as is the task at hand across the board in all fields. What is clear from the way in which the right to legal personhood has evolved over the various human rights treaties and the interpretation from the relevant treaty bodies (discussed in Chapter 1) is that it is a violation of human rights if the right to legal personhood is denied on the basis of membership in a protected group. Disabled people are widely accepted as a protected group—therefore, legal personhood (including both legal standing and agency) cannot be denied on the basis of disability. If there are instances in which we, as a society, would like to deny legal agency, it must be applicable to all people, not just those in certain groups.

In order to address this challenge—creating law that may curtail legal agency in certain crisis situations but is disability neutral—we have to ask the question of why we allow mental health law to curtail legal agency. Is there a necessary aspect of such limitations on legal agency, and, if there is, what are those necessary aspects and how can we create law that addresses those necessary aspects but is disability neutral? This challenge then often raises some concerning issues related to why we allow mental health law to limit legal agency at all. Is it because we want to protect people from harming themselves and/or others? If this is the case, then a determination of an individual's 'dangerousness' comes into play—and can have some concerning outcomes. One outcome is that disabled people are prejudiciously labelled as 'dangerous' and subsequently experience the removal of their legal agency. This is problematic because it disadvantages disabled people and leaves them more likely to be subject to denials of legal agency; it is also problematic because there is evidence to suggest that disabled people may actually be less 'dangerous' than non-disabled people, including people with mental health disability.[21] I am raising these issues here to highlight the existing prejudicial nature of existing denials of legal agency, such as exists in mental health law, and also to begin to demonstrate what an analysis of denials of legal personhood looks like and how we can begin to go about moving towards solutions.

[20] Melvyn Colin Freeman and others, 'Reversing Hard Won Victories in the Name of Human Rights: A Critique of the General Comment on Article 12 of the UN Convention on the Rights of Persons with Disabilities' (2015) 2 The Lancet Psychiatry 844.

[21] Eric B Elbogen, Paul A Dennis, and Sally C Johnson, 'Beyond Mental Illness: Targeting Stronger and More Direct Pathways to Violence' (2016) 4 Clinical Psychological Science 747; Martin Sellbom and others, 'Assessment of Psychopathy: Addressing Myths, Misconceptions, and Fallacies' in Luca Malatesti, John McMillan, and Predrag Šustar (eds), *Psychopathy: Its Uses, Validity and Status* (Springer 2022); Seena Fazel and others, 'Schizophrenia and Violence: Systematic Review and Meta-Analysis' (2009) 6 PLOS Medicine e1000120 <https://pubmed.ncbi.nlm.nih.gov/19668362/> accessed 11 January 2024.

I have only scratched the surface here of the implications of the right to legal personhood for mental health law reform. However, it is relevant to acknowledge that although there are significant tensions between respecting the right to legal personhood and existing mental health law, the situation is not intractable. To demonstrate this, it is pertinent to touch briefly on the solutions that have been proposed. They include a paradigm shift in mental health law to focus on protecting the rights of individuals with mental health disability, including the right to legal personhood. In addition, there is a demand to shift mental health law and practice to focus on the protection of the will and preference of the individual—as required by Article 12(4) of the CRPD. This would ask mental health professionals to reorient much of their practice to focusing on discovering and implementing the will and preference of their patients—as opposed to 'curing' or acting in what they believe to be in the 'best interests' of their patients, as is currently the focus on much mental health law and practice. There is also significant evidence to suggest that such a shift towards the will and preference of people with mental health disability would not only be advantageous for meeting international legal obligations related to the right to legal personhood, under international law, but would also create better outcomes for people with mental health disability and for those in their families and communities.[22]

I want to highlight here that disabled people that also experience intersectional marginalisation as a member of another protected group—such as disabled women and disabled indigenous peoples—are often experiencing denials of legal agency as part of mental health law in unique and, sometimes, more profound ways. Disabled women, for example, have long experienced high rates of detention in mental health facilities and high rates of forced treatment, as well as uniquely negative experiences as a result, including gendered violence and disruption to mothering.[23] Disabled indigenous people—including women—have also found themselves subject to high rates of forced treatment and more profoundly negative impacts from such treatment, at least in part, due to the lack of cultural sensitivity

[22] Piers Gooding, *A New Era for Mental Health Law and Policy: Supported Decision-Making and the UN Convention on the Rights of Persons with Disabilities* (1st edn, CUP 2017); Flynn and Arstein-Kerslake (n 1); Eilionóir Flynn and Anna Arstein-Kerslake, 'The Support Model of Legal Capacity: Fact, Fiction, or Fantasy' (2014) 32 Berkeley Journal of International Law 124; Bernadette McSherry and Penny Weller, *Rethinking Rights-Based Mental Health Laws* (Bloomsbury Publishing 2010); Bernadette McSherry and Yvette Maker (eds), *Restrictive Practices in Health Care and Disability Settings: Legal, Policy and Practical Responses* (Routledge 2020).

[23] Arstein-Kerslake, *Legal Capacity & Gender* (n 3); Anna Feeney and others, 'Gender, Diagnosis and Involuntary Psychiatry Admission in Ireland: A Report from the Dublin Involuntary Admission Study (DIAS)' (2019) 66 International Journal of Law and Psychiatry 101472; Ulla-Karin Schön, 'Recovery in Involuntary Psychiatric Care: Is There a Gender Difference?' (2013) 22 Journal of Mental Health 420; Aoife Curley and others, 'Exploring and Explaining Involuntary Care: The Relationship between Psychiatric Admission Status, Gender and Other Demographic and Clinical Variables' (2016) 47 International Journal of Law and Psychiatry 53; James A Holstein, 'Producing Gender Effects on Involuntary Mental Hospitalization' (1987) 34 Social Problems 141; Emma Jane Tseris, Eva Bright Hart, and Scarlett Franks, '"My Voice Was Discounted the Whole Way Through": A Gendered Analysis of Women's Experiences of Involuntary Mental Health Treatment' (2022) 37 Affilia 645.

or accessibility of mental health systems, as well as existing prejudice in such systems that disadvantages disabled indigenous people and often leads to assumptions related to decision-making skills and mental health status.[24]

This brief analysis of mental health law and its denial of the right to legal personhood for disabled people—and other groups—is meant to provide a window into an area of the law that explicitly curtails or denies the right to legal personhood and needs to be urgently addressed. I hope that it also raises questions around why disabled people and other marginalised groups are disproportionately denied legal personhood through mental health law and practices and what methods we could use for rectifying these types of denials of legal personhood.

## 2.4 Forced Sterilisation, Eugenics, and Intersectional Marginalisation Based on Gender

For many similar historical reasons to those discussed above in relation to the denial of legal agency under mental health law, disabled people—and disabled women, in particular—have also experienced denials of legal agency related to reproductive choice, including forced sterilisation. Some of those historical reasons include the assumption that disabled people have diminished decision-making skills, prejudicial disregard for female decision-making and an assumption that those with female traits are 'irrational', as well as the pathologisation of female traits and disability.[25] It appears that many of these historical issues arose around the time that the eugenics movement took hold in North America and Europe. The eugenics movement upheld the idea that there is an ideal human typology that should be striven towards. The ideal typology was generally a white, able-bodied, cisgender individual. The movement included many practices—which are now considered immoral and, in some cases, horrific—that sought to achieve the 'normalisation' of the human race towards that 'ideal' typology. The leaders of the movement were largely white, able-bodied, cisgender men, and they viewed individuals in their own image as the ideal typology.[26]

[24] Tseris, Bright Hart, and Franks (n 23); Joan E Dodgson and Roxanne Struthers, 'Indigenous Women's Voices: Marginalization and Health' (2005) 16 Journal of Transcultural Nursing 339; Tony Butler and others, 'Mental Health Status of Aboriginal and Non-Aboriginal Australian Prisoners' (2007) 41 Australian & New Zealand Journal of Psychiatry 429; Melissa E Lewis, Erica E Hartwell, and Laurelle L Myhra, 'Decolonizing Mental Health Services for Indigenous Clients: A Training Program for Mental Health Professionals' (2018) 62 American Journal of Community Psychology 330.

[25] Arstein-Kerslake, *Legal Capacity & Gender* (n 3); Anna Arstein-Kerslake, 'Gendered Denials: Vulnerability Created by Barriers to Legal Capacity for Women and Disabled Women' (2019) 66 International Journal of Law and Psychiatry 101501.

[26] Tom Shakespeare, 'Choices and Rights: Eugenics, Genetics and Disability Equality' (1998) 13 Disability & Society 665; Dagmar Herzog, *Unlearning Eugenics: Sexuality, Reproduction, and Disability in Post-Nazi Europe* (University of Wisconsin Press 2018); David Pfeiffer, 'Eugenics and Disability Discrimination' (1994) 9 Disability & Society 481.

The eugenics movement heavily influenced Nazi Germany, including the 'scientific' work that took place in many of the internment and concentration camps.[27] Such work was often aimed at manipulating humans and the human population towards this ideal typology. It also seems to have heavily influenced the longer-term project to sterilise—and often forcibly sterilise—people deemed to be unworthy of reproduction, or whose genes were deemed to not be desirable for reproduction.[28] *Buck v Bell*, 274 US 200 (1927), in the US Supreme Court, is an example of such sterilisation. In the case, the plaintiff, *Buck*, had been forcibly sterilised on the basis that she had a cognitive disability, as did many people in her family, and that it was not desirable for her to pass on such traits to further generations. There was a state statute in Virginia allowing for such sterilisations—the Sterilisation Act of 1924. Justice Oliver Wendell Holms, Jr, writing the decision for the court, is often quoted as having written that 'three generations of imbeciles is enough'. The court ruled that the state statute permitting compulsory sterilisation of the unfit, including the cognitively disabled, 'for the protection and health of the state' did not violate the US Constitution. The Supreme Court has never expressly overturned *Buck v Bell*—although there are several subsequent cases and pieces of legislation that make it unlikely that the Supreme Court would arrive at a similar decision today.[29]

Disabled people continue to be subjected to denials of their legal agency to engage in reproductive choice—which amounts to a denial of their right to legal personhood where it disproportionately impacts, either in purpose or effect, disabled people; for example, the case of Ashley X in the United States in which Ashley's parents consented to treatments that resulted in her sterilisation and stunted reproductive system and growth over the course of her life. Ashley was born in 1997 and has significant disability, which is believed to affect both her cognition and physical body. The case spurred many others coming forward, both in support and in protest.[30]

Women are experiencing such denials of legal agency in reproductive matters uniquely. This is likely both due to the historical reasons listed above and the biological reality that it is predominately women who are able to get pregnant. However, it is significant that there tends to be a focus on disabled women's sterilisation as well as a lack of accessible information and services for disabled women in relation to reproductive choices.[31]

[27] Stephen Garton, 'Eugenics in Australia and New Zealand: Laboratories of Racial Science' in Alison Bashford and Philippa Levine (eds), *The Oxford Handbook of the History of Eugenics* (OUP 2010).

[28] Arstein-Kerslake, *Legal Capacity & Gender* (n 3); Susan M Schweik, *The Ugly Laws: Disability in Public* (New York UP 2009); Herzog (n 26).

[29] Kelley D Jacobs, 'Buck v. Bell: Eighty Years of Challenges for Parents with Developmental Disabilities' (2022) 3 LC Journal of Special Education 4; Paul A Lombardo, *Three Generations, No Imbeciles: Eugenics, the Supreme Court, and Buck v. Bell* (Johns Hopkins UP 2022).

[30] Christine Wieseler, 'Disability Bioethics, Ashley X, and Disability Justice for People with Cognitive Impairments' in Joel Michael Reynolds and Christine Wieseler (eds), *The Disability Bioethics Reader* (Taylor & Francis 2022).

[31] Arstein-Kerslake, *Legal Capacity & Gender* (n 3); Hoangmai H Pham and Barron H Lerner, 'In the Patient's Best Interest? Revisiting Sexual Autonomy and Sterilization of the Developmentally

I have raised this example of denial of legal personhood via the denial of legal agency to make reproductive choices, such as sterilisation, in order to provide another example, from disability, of how legal personhood is removed. Of course, reproductive choice—and the removal of reproductive choice—is a form of legal agency denial that reaches far beyond disability. It particularly impacts women and people who can become pregnant. This will be discussed more in Chapter 8 as a quite profound denial of legal personhood based on gender. The hope is that where non-discrimination arguments have fallen short for reproductive justice, arguments around the right to legal personhood may be able to provide a new platform for securing reproductive rights.

## 3. Barriers to Legal Personhood and the Role of State Sovereignty

The examples discussed above are all exclusions from legal personhood on the basis of disability or exclusions from legal personhood that disproportionately affect disabled people. Activists and scholars, including myself, have argued that the right to legal personhood, as developed in CEDAW and the CRPD (and described in Chapter 1), is violated by the exclusions from legal personhood that are described above. Some states have made RUDs stating that they do not believe that some or all of the exclusions from personhood identified above are violations of the right to legal personhood—or that they are interpreting the right to legal personhood to allow for some or all of the exclusions from legal personhood listed above.[32]

RUDs are an opportunity in international law for state parties to international treaties to clarify their interpretation of the treaty text and what they are intending to agree to be bound to by ratification of such treaty. Such statements from state parties are generally respected, unless they are determined to be against the object and purpose of the treaty. It is another state party to the treaty that is required

Disabled' (2001) 175 Western Journal of Medicine 280; Roberta Cepko, 'Involuntary Sterilization of Mentally Disabled Women' (1993) 8 Berkeley Women's Law Journal 122; Emily Ledingham, Graham W Wright, and Monika Mitra, 'Sexual Violence against Women with Disabilities: Experiences with Force and Lifetime Risk' (2022) 62 American Journal of Preventive Medicine 895; David McConnell and Shanon Phelan, 'The Devolution of Eugenic Practices: Sexual and Reproductive Health and Oppression of People with Intellectual Disability' (2022) 298 Social Science & Medicine 114877; Iva Strnadová, Joanne Danker, and Allison Carter, 'Scoping Review on Sex Education for High School-Aged Students with Intellectual Disability and/or on the Autism Spectrum: Parents', Teachers' and Students' Perspectives, Attitudes and Experiences' (2022) 22 Sex Education 361.

32 Ruby Dhand, 'Indigenous Peoples with Disabilities and Canadian Mental Capacity Law' in Camillia Kong and others (eds), *Capacity, Participation and Values in Comparative Legal Perspective* (Bristol UP 2023); Watson and others (n 14); Mary Donnelly, 'Judging Values in a Time of Transition: An Irish Perspective' in Camillia Kong and others (eds), *Capacity, Participation and Values in Comparative Legal Perspective* (Bristol UP 2023); Zahra Hosaneea, 'Reservation on the CRPD from a Mauritian Perspective Section A: Articles: Chapter 6' (2022) 10 African Disability Rights Yearbook 110.

to challenge a reservation, understanding, or declaration as being contrary to the object and purpose of the treaty and to request that it not be upheld as a valid interpretation of the treaty—in essence, the state would then be bound by the plain meaning of the text of the treaty, and the reservation, understanding, and declaration would not have validity and would not be considered in regard to the monitoring of the implementation of the treaty by UN bodies.[33] Such a challenge by another state party is not frequent, which makes reservations, understandings, and declarations from state parties a powerful exercise of state sovereignty because they have relatively high levels of freedom in crafting such statements (they are unilaterally created and there is no negotiation or consultation required). Therefore, where states have made RUDs in relation to the right to legal personhood (the right to equal recognition before the law), it creates a problematic assertion of state sovereignty that undermines the right of the individual to be recognised by the law.

Although these states that have made reservations, understanding, and declarations on the right to legal personhood have negotiated and agreed to be bound by CEDAW and/or the CRPD, they are asserting that they have their own interpretation of the right to legal personhood, which differs from that of the UN monitoring bodies—at least the Committee on the Rights of Persons with Disabilities and their General Comment on the Right to Equal Recognition Before the Law (as discussed in Chapter 1). In addition, many states that have not made formal RUDs are simply maintaining socio-legal structures that likely violate the right to legal personhood for disabled people and others. This is also an exercise of state sovereignty—albeit a more subtle, implicit version.

Our challenge is now twofold—first to determine whether explicit or implicit state action that undermines the right to legal personhood (as it has developed through treaty text and the interpretation by monitoring bodies) is a valid exercise of state sovereignty, or whether such state action undermines the right to legal personhood to such an extent that it is rendered meaningless—and, if that is the case, then do we want states to be allowed to exercise sovereignty in this way—or does it risk rendering all human rights meaningless? (Here, I am arguing that, perhaps, we can develop a new limitation on state sovereignty in international law—that where the assertion of state sovereignty renders a right meaningless, the doctrine of non-interference does not apply and the state is in violation of international law.)

The second challenge is to take this definition and application of the right to legal personhood and apply it to other groups—because the universality of rights dictates that all rights must be equally applicable to all persons. In doing this

[33] Eric Neumayer, 'Qualified Ratification: Explaining Reservations to International Human Rights Treaties' (2007) 36 The Journal of Legal Studies 397; Kelebogile Zvobgo, Wayne Sandholtz, and Suzie Mulesky, 'Reserving Rights: Explaining Human Rights Treaty Reservations' (2020) 64 International Studies Quarterly 785.

application of the right beyond disability, we must then determine the extent to which the right to legal personhood is being denied and begin to challenge states to reform law and practice in order to uphold the right for all groups. There will likely be significant resistant to protecting the right to legal personhood for all people because many of the barriers (some identified below) go to the core of how states define themselves and how they maintain their power—they will likely be hesitant to relinquish such defining features and power.

In order to begin these quite large tasks, it is necessary to turn to the specific barriers that are creating the exclusions from legal personhood. Much of this identification will be done in the group-specific chapters to follow—however, there are some defining features of barriers to legal personhood that can be outlined here. The first is when a group is prevented—in purpose or effect—from the exercise of their legal personhood (otherwise termed legal agency). This barrier exists where state action is either explicitly intended to curtail or deny legal agency of a specific group—or where state action has the effect of disproportionately impacting the legal agency of a specific group. In the context of disability, an example of state action that is an explicit denial of legal personhood is that which occurs under mental health law (discussed above). The second potential defining feature of a barrier to legal personhood is when a group is implicitly or explicitly excluded from being recognised as having legal standing. This defining feature is similar to the barrier to legal agency, described above, but it is in relation to whether the law recognises the individual as a legal entity. In the context of disability, an example of an explicit exclusion from legal standing is guardianship, conservatorship, and interdiction (discussed above). Hopefully, these defining features and the examples provided in the disability context will begin to paint a picture of how the right to legal personhood can be denied and what the main barriers to the right may be.

## 4. Conclusion: Using Disability as Model for Identifying Legal Personhood Barriers for Other Groups

As mentioned above, the aim of this chapter is to provide an explanation of some of the key areas of legal personhood denial that disabled people are experiencing—and to also highlight some intersectional marginalisation that is occurring as a result of these denials. There is more in-depth detail of these denials provided elsewhere—both in my scholarship and in that of others.[34] The purpose of describing such denials in this book is both to provide a snapshot of the denials of legal personhood that are facing disabled people and to use these analyses as a jumping off point for beginning to do similar analyses for other marginalised

[34] Arstein-Kerslake, *Legal Capacity & Gender* (n 3); Arstein-Kerslake, *Restoring Voice to People with Cognitive Disabilities* (n 1); McSherry and Weller (n 22); Gooding (n 22).

groups—as will be done in the following chapters. I have chosen to use this analysis of denials of legal personhood of disabled people as a jumping off point because the most detail provided to the right to legal personhood is found in the CRPD and, as a result, arguably, the richest depth of scholarship is occurring in relation to disabled people.[35] This depth of scholarship provides a good starting point from which to begin to understand how the right to legal personhood should be applied. In the upcoming chapters, I use the knowledge gained in the application of the right to legal personhood in the context of disability and apply it in the context of other marginalised groups. In basic terms, this means identifying where legal agency and legal standing is being denied on the basis of membership in a protected group and then identifying such denials as violations of the right to legal personhood. As in this chapter, I then go on to explore solutions to such denials and to analyse why such denials may be taking place, both from a critical social theory perspective (ie identifying the structures of power and privilege that created and are benefiting from such denials of legal personhood to various groups) and from a practical perspective (ie identifying other structural barriers that may exist).

The aim is to provide a new avenue for social justice analysis—something beyond, or parallel to, non-discrimination arguments—that may get to the heart of many social justice issues and provide answers and solutions to better distribute power and privilege across social groups. I am using the right to legal personhood and redeploying the rich analysis of the right that has occurred in the disability context to explore how other groups are being denied the right, how it may be impacting their power and privilege, and how we can better protect the right for such groups.

[35] Dhanda (n 2); Minkowitz (n 2); Michael Ashley Stein and others, *Mental Health, Legal Capacity, and Human Rights* (CUP 2021); J Fiala-Butora and MA Stein, 'The Law as a Source of Stigma or Empowerment: Legal Capacity and Persons with Intellectual Disabilities' in Katrina Scior and Shirli Werner (eds), *Intellectual Disability and Stigma: Stepping Out from the Margins* (Palgrave Macmillan 2016); Robert D Dinerstein, 'Implementing Legal Capacity under Article 12 of the UN Convention on the Rights of Persons with Disabilities: The Difficult Road from Guardianship to Supported Decision-Making Human Rights and the Protection of Persons with Disabilities' (2011) 19(2) Human Rights Brief 8; Quinn and Rekas-Rosalbo (n 18); McSherry (n 2); Piers Gooding and Charles O'Mahony, 'Laws on Unfitness to Stand Trial and the UN Convention on the Rights of Persons with Disabilities: Comparing Reform in England, Wales, Northern Ireland and Australia' (2016) 44 International Journal of Law, Crime and Justice 122; McSherry and Weller (n 22); Watson and others (n 14); Arstein-Kerslake, 'An Empowering Dependency' (n 14); Arstein-Kerslake and others (n 5).

# 5

# Legal Personhood, Migrant Groups, and Stateless Peoples

## 1. Introduction

As a starting point, it is prudent to define what I mean by 'migrant groups' and 'stateless peoples' and why I have chosen to discuss them here. When I use the term 'migrant group', I am referring to people who have moved from one jurisdiction to another with the purpose of staying, living, and/or working for an extended period of time and, perhaps, indefinitely.[1] Such persons may intend to become citizens of the jurisdiction to which they have migrated, or they may simply intend to be residents there. A defining feature of such a person is that they seek to establish standing as a legal person in the new jurisdiction and to exercise their legal personhood via the exercise of legal agency to some extent, for example, through the ability to sign and execute contracts, vote, and so on. Of course, this may not be an explicit intent of such peoples, because this is seldom an explicit intent of any individual, beyond perhaps legal theorists, such as myself, who have turned their minds to such issues. For most individuals, their intention to establish their legal personhood (standing and agency) is expressed in the form of seeking immigration status or documentation (standing) and in attempting to engage in employment contracts and other forms of creating and extinguishing legal relationships (agency). I have chosen to discuss migrant groups here because they are one of the groups that is most profoundly affected by denials of legal personhood—domestic immigration law in most jurisdictions is specifically created to determine who should and who should not be considered a legal person in that jurisdiction. This determination is made via the granting or denial of immigration status, which is effectively the granting and/or denial of legal personhood to varying degrees. For example, an individual who is granted permission to stay but not permission to work has been granted partial legal personhood in that they have some form of legal standing in the jurisdiction; however, they have been denied the right to exercise their legal personhood in the form of exercising legal agency in engaging in employment via an employment contract that would be

[1] Nasar Meer Modood Tariq, 'Migration and Cultural Diversity Challenges in the Twenty-First Century' in Anna Triandafyllidou (ed), *Routledge Handbook of Immigration and Refugee Studies* (2nd edn, Routledge 2022); James F Hollifield and Neil Foley, *Understanding Global Migration* (Stanford UP 2022).

*The Right to Legal Personhood of Marginalised Groups.* Anna Arstein-Kerslake, Oxford University Press.
 DOI: 10.1093/9780191926549.003.0005

protected by domestic contract and employment law. Hopefully, it is clear that there are large numbers of people that fall under the category 'migrant groups', and these people are being denied legal personhood whenever a state limits their legal personhood via a particular immigration status or simply does not legally acknowledge the existence of such groups, or provide avenues for such groups to gain legal personhood (standing or recognition).

When I use the term 'stateless people', I am referring to the large group of people who are not recognised as citizens by any state and do not have immigration status in any state. Essentially, they are people who are not recognised as legal persons by any state. These groups are often overlooked; however, their numbers are very high.[2] They are, perhaps, the best evidence of the failure of our international legal systems—and the dangers of state sovereignty—because there are huge sections of our population who are left largely unprotected by domestic or international law, including unprotected by human rights law.[3] In our current international legal system, in order to be protected by international human rights law, an individual generally must be a subject of a particular jurisdiction—they must have either citizenship or immigration status in a jurisdiction. States are only responsible for the individuals that are within their jurisdictions—and, generally, if they do not even recognise an individual or group, they are not seeking to protect that individual's or group's human rights. Therefore, stateless people are generally not recognised as legal persons and do not enjoy legal standing or legal agency. This is extremely limiting in terms of the power and privilege of most people within these groups and also undermines the meaning and significance of international human rights law because there is not a clear avenue for its application when there is no jurisdiction that recognises the legal personhood of such individuals or groups as a starting point for the ascription of rights and the assumption of responsibility for the protection of those rights by a particular state. For these reasons, I have chosen to discuss stateless peoples here—they are, perhaps, the epitome of why the right to legal personhood is so important and why we must uncover a method for realising the right to legal personhood for all peoples, including realising it over claims of state sovereignty.

[2] Mary Strode and Melanie Khanna, 'Improving Official Statistics on Stateless People: Challenges, Solutions, and the Road Ahead' (2021) 37 Statistical Journal of the IAOS 1087; Indira Goris, Julia Harrington, and Sebastian Köhn, 'Statelessness: What It Is and Why It Matters' (2009) 32 Forced Migration Review 4.

[3] Dorothy Jean Walker, 'Statelessness: Violation or Conduit for Violation of Human Rights?' (1981) 3 Human Rights Quarterly 106; Laura van Waas, '"Are We There Yet?" The Emergence of Statelessness on the International Human Rights Agenda' (2014) 32 Netherlands Quarterly of Human Rights 342; David Owen, 'On the Right to Have Nationality Rights: Statelessness, Citizenship and Human Rights' (2018) 65 Netherlands International Law Review 299; Lindsey N Kingston, '"A Forgotten Human Rights Crisis": Statelessness and Issue (Non)Emergence' (2013) 14 Human Rights Review 73; David Weissbrodt and Clay Collins, 'The Human Rights of Stateless Persons' (2006) 28 Human Rights Quarterly 245; Michelle Foster and Helene Lambert, *International Refugee Law and the Protection of Stateless Persons* (OUP 2019).

## 2. Limitations of State Sovereignty

As discussed in Chapter 2, one of the most significant barriers for the legal personhood of migrant groups and stateless people is state sovereignty claims regarding territoriality and national borders. Admittedly, this is a very challenging issue to overcome because it goes to the core of statehood and the foundations of international law. The claim is that states negotiate and agree to be bound by international human rights law—to the extent that they are respected as sovereign states within the international legal system and, in particular, that they maintain control over their own borders and the granting or denial of citizenship and immigration status to people within their borders.[4] This is core to the modern understanding of state sovereignty—and the doctrine of non-interference, as discussed in Chapter 2, is very commonly assumed to protect such state sovereignty interests.

There are, of course, some exceptions to state sovereignty claims with regard to citizenship and immigration. Perhaps the most significant exception includes refugee and asylum claims. These claims are generally claims from non-citizen immigrants for status and/or citizenship in a particular jurisdiction on the basis that their home country is unsafe. The particular refugee and asylum system in each jurisdiction is regulated by domestic immigration law. However, such law is subject to binding international human rights instruments that dictate the circumstances under which a state party to such instruments is required to accept asylum and refugee claims and to provide immigration status for such individuals.[5] International treaties related to refugees and asylum seekers are a challenge to state sovereignty to the extent that it regulates how a state should determine who to grant certain types of immigration claims to—the claims of refugees and asylum seekers. However, because this regulation is dictated by international treaties that states have negotiated and agreed to be bound by, it could be argued that states are exercising their sovereignty in agreeing to be bound by such international law.

[4] W Michael Reisman, 'Sovereignty and Human Rights in Contemporary International Law' (1990) 84 American Journal of International Law 866; Andrew Geddes, 'International Migration and State Sovereignty in an Integrating Europe' (2001) 39 International Migration 21; Laura Thompson, 'Protection of Migrants' Rights and State Sovereignty' (2013) 50 UN Chronicle 8; Linda S Bosniak, 'Human Rights, State Sovereignty and the Protection of Undocumented Migrants under the International Migrant Workers Convention Part II: Interpreting the Convention' (1991) 25 International Migration Review 737; Myron Weiner, 'Ethics, National Sovereignty and the Control of Immigration' (1996) 30 International Migration Review 171; Linda S Bosniak and Aristide Zolberg, 'State Sovereignty, Human Rights and the New UN Migrant Workers Convention' (1992) 86 Proceedings of the Annual Meeting (American Society of International Law) 634; Virginie Guiraudon and Gallya Lahav, 'A Reappraisal of the State Sovereignty Debate: The Case of Migration Control' (2000) 33 Comparative Political Studies 163; Brian Opeskin, 'Managing International Migration in Australia: Human Rights and the "Last Major Redoubt of Unfettered National Sovereignty"' (2012) 46 International Migration Review 551; Linda S Bosniak, 'Human Rights, State Sovereignty and the Protection of Undocumented Migrants under the International Migrant Workers' Convention', *Irregular Migration and Human Rights: Theoretical, European and International Perspectives* (Brill Nijhoff 2004).

[5] Niraj Nathwani, *Rethinking Refugee Law* (Martinus Nijhoff Publishers 2003).

In the context of other migrant groups and stateless peoples that are seeking immigration status, little protection exists for them in international law. This problem could be overcome by the creation of new treaties to cover other migrant groups and stateless peoples—although, there is likely little political will to develop and/or agree to be bound by such treaties because there are often significant political movements that are resistant to new migrants and often highly controversial issues surrounding groups of stateless peoples. For these reasons, states are probably not willing to exercise their sovereignty to relinquish power in this area—or to allow international law to dictate domestic immigration law to such an extent. For this reason, I developed the arguments in Chapter 2 regarding establishing clear guidelines for when state sovereignty should be overridden in favour of certain human rights—and, of course, claiming that the human right to legal personhood is one of the most important rights to establish as a right that takes precedence over state sovereignty claims. Without such guidelines—and without the possibility for the right to legal personhood to take precedence over state sovereignty claims—we have a system that looks very much like the current system in which the right to legal personhood is virtually meaningless for many migrant groups and stateless peoples. These denials of the right to legal personhood for these groups will occur because of the general lack of political will to develop legally binding treaties to protect such groups—and because of the existing international law systems that assume that states can exercise their sovereignty to deny legal personhood, largely at their discretion, to non-citizens, including migrant groups and stateless peoples.

## 3. Barriers to Legal Personhood

The core barriers to legal personhood for these groups arise due to either lack of recognition by the state (stateless peoples and undocumented immigrants, in particular) or specific limitations on their legal personhood via their allocated immigration status (some documented immigrants with specific constraints attached to their permission to remain in the jurisdiction). Applying the definition of legal personhood established in Chapter 1, these are denials of legal personhood because they either limit or deny an individual's legal standing—their ability to be a holder of rights—or they limit or deny an individual's legal agency—their ability to exercise their legal standing via, for instance, the creation or extinguishing of legal relationships. An example of these limitations or denials in practice includes a visa to remain in a jurisdiction, but not to work there (as mentioned above)—this type of visa would amount to a limitation on the individual's legal personhood via a limitation on their legal agency to engage in employment and any contracts related to employment. Another example is a state's complete lack of recognition of certain groups of people—with no meaningful avenue for that group to acquire documentation recognising their legal personhood in their present jurisdiction. This lack of recognition results, perhaps quite obviously, in that group being denied legal personhood. Both stateless peoples and undocumented migrants are at risk of experiencing this lack of recognition. In the following sections, I will reiterate a brief definition of each group and provide an initial analysis of some barriers to legal personhood that the group is facing. These analyses are not meant to provide an exhaustive examination of all barriers to legal personhood that these groups are experiencing—instead, my intention is to simply start a conversation about the barriers to legal personhood that these groups are facing, begin to explore them as human rights violations, and begin to examine what obligations the state may have in removing such barriers and better protecting the right to legal personhood for these groups.

## 3.1 Undocumented Migrants

I am using the term 'undocumented migrants' to refer to peoples who have entered a jurisdiction in which they are neither citizens nor have any formal documentation issued by the state that gives them permission to remain in the jurisdiction. An individual can be undocumented for a variety of reasons; for example, they may have been forcibly and/or urgently displaced from their home jurisdiction and either there is no avenue in the new jurisdiction for them to gain documentation for formal permission to remain in that state or they are not aware of such an avenue, or they have sought documentation from such an avenue but the processes is dysfunctional, time consuming, or for some other reason not able to provide the individual with the necessary documentation to grant formal permission to remain in the jurisdiction. Stateless people are also sometimes undocumented migrants—they would acquire this status when they cross a national border with the intention to remain in a new jurisdiction; however, there remains no jurisdiction—including the new one—that is willing to recognise the stateless people or person, and they are unable to acquire formal documentation from the state granting them permission to remain in the jurisdiction.[6]

Undocumented migrants face significant barriers to their right to legal personhood. Without documentation from the state formally permitting them to remain in the jurisdiction and recognising their presence in the jurisdiction, they essentially have no legal personhood in that jurisdiction—they have neither legal standing nor the ability to exercise that standing via legal agency (because the exercise of legal standing is predicated on that legal standing first being recognised

[6] Caroline Sawyer and Brad K Blitz, *Statelessness in the European Union: Displaced, Undocumented, Unwanted* (CUP 2011); Douglas S Massey and Chiara Capoferro, 'Measuring Undocumented Migration' (2004) 38 International Migration Review 1075; Alejandro Portes, 'Toward a Structural Analysis of Illegal (Undocumented) Immigration' (1978) 12 International Migration Review 469.

by the state). While there are likely exceptions to this in some jurisdictions—for example, in California, United States, an undocumented migrant can generally get a driver's license which provides legal standing in some limited circumstances, such as engaging with law enforcement professionals[7]—generally, however, undocumented migrants have nearly full denial of their legal personhood with little recourse to overcoming this issue and gaining documentation from the state that would recognise their existence and provide them with either full or some form of limited legal personhood. Correcting such barriers to legal personhood for undocumented migrants would likely require a new understanding of national borders—discussed in more depth below—and a de-prioritisation of claims of state sovereignty with regard to immigration law in this area. It would require that states have an explicit obligation to provide some form of recognition and documentation to all persons within their borders.

## 3.2 Documented Migrants

I am using the term 'documented migrants' to refer to people who have come into a new jurisdiction with the intention to remain and have been provided with formal documentation from the state that recognises their presence in the state and grants them some form of permission to remain in the state. Such migrants generally have significantly fewer barriers to legal personhood than undocumented migrants. They generally have their legal standing recognised via the documentation from the state granting them permission to remain in the jurisdiction. They may, however, have their ability to exercise their legal standing via their legal agency limited by restrictions indicated in their documentation from the state giving them permission to remain in the state. For example, as mentioned above, they may have documentation giving them permission to remain in the jurisdiction but not to work in the jurisdiction. This limitation on employment amounts to a limitation on their legal personhood because they are not free to exercise their legal agency to contract for employment in the jurisdiction. This limitation can have a significant impact on their power and privilege within our socio-legal structures because they are either forced to live without a source of income for themselves or they are forced to engage in work that is also 'undocumented'—meaning that it is work that occurs without the formal knowledge or recognition of the state and therefore

[7] Catalina Amuedo-Dorantes, Esther Arenas-Arroyo, and Almudena Sevilla, 'Labor Market Impacts of States Issuing of Driver's Licenses to Undocumented Immigrants' (2020) 63 Labour Economics 101805; Kevin R Johnson, 'Driver's Licenses and Undocumented Immigrants: The Future of Civil Rights Law Symposium: Pursuing Equal Justice in the West' (2004) 5 Nevada Law Journal 213; Laura E Enriquez, Daisy Vazquez Vera, and S Karthick Ramakrishnan, 'Driver's Licenses for All? Racialized Illegality and the Implementation of Progressive Immigration Policy in California' (2019) 41 Law & Policy 34.

does not engender any employment protection that the state provides workers, such as minimum wage protection, regulation of conditions of employment, and reporting avenues when abuse of workers takes place. This limitation on the legal agency is a barrier to the legal personhood of documented migrants and, I argue, should—at a minimum—be interrogated to determine whether it is a limitation on legal agency that we would like to permit in some circumstances for certain public policy reasons or whether it is an impermissible form of denying legal personhood. To break down this barrier to legal personhood for documented migrants, it would require that states are obligated to ensure that all migrants within their jurisdiction are granted permission to exercise their legal agency—either in full or specifically within the context of employment.

## 3.3 Refugees and Asylum Seekers

I am using the term 'refugees and asylum seekers' in line with the manner in which it is used in international legal instruments such as the 1951 Refugee Convention. A refugee is 'someone who is unable or unwilling to return to their country of origin owing to a well-founded fear of being persecuted for reasons of race, religion, nationality, membership of a particular social group, or political opinion'.[8] An asylum seeker is a person who has left a particular jurisdiction that is unsafe and is seeking protection in another jurisdiction. They are termed 'seekers' because their claim has not been finally decided on by the jurisdiction in which they have submitted it. If their claim is successful, they will generally become a 'refugee', and if it is not, they will likely not be recognised as a 'refugee'. Refugees are also, generally, documented migrants; however, I have chosen to identify them as a separate category here because they have unique issues related to their rights to legal personhood. Asylum seekers may be documented migrants if the jurisdiction that they are in has a process for providing them with documentation recognising their legal status in that jurisdiction while their claim for asylum is being assessed. If there is no process for receiving documentation while waiting for a claim of asylum to be assessed, then an asylum seeker may be an undocumented migrant.

Refugees and asylum seekers have unique barriers to their legal personhood because they are usually in particular hardship due to having fled an unsafe environment in another jurisdiction. They may be residing in refugee camps, which may or may not have efficient and robust processes for providing documentation to those residing there. They may also be living in fear of state processes because of past trauma in other jurisdictions related to state-sanctioned violence or state-sponsored violence or other unsafe conditions facilitated by the state. Since the

[8] Convention Relating to the Status of Refugees (adopted 28 July 1951, entered into force 22 April 1954) 189 UNTS 137 (Refugee Convention).

state is the primary source for granting or denying legal personhood, this potentially tense relationship with the state may prove to be a significant barrier for refugees and asylum seekers. In addition, those that are either documented or undocumented migrants—as discussed above—may also face the barriers to legal personhood that those groups face and that are identified above.

Refugees and asylum seekers are also in a unique position because there is a long-standing international treaty that prescribes how states should treat them. The 1951 Refugee Convention provides specific directions for states in how to deal with refugees and asylum seekers. While it does not specifically acknowledge the right of refugees and asylum seekers to have their right to legal personhood protected, it does acknowledge specific rights that must be protected, and many of those rights are part and parcel of the right to legal personhood; for example, the right to work, the right to join associations, and the right to standing before courts. Although these rights are universal, and—in theory—all persons have such rights, it is powerful that they are specifically outlined in an international treaty for refugees and asylum seekers. The convention has given advocates and individuals fuel for arguing for the protecting of such rights and for the construction of processes for enabling refugees and asylum seekers to enforce such rights. These systems are far from perfect—and refugees and asylum seekers continue to experience denials and limitations on many rights, including the right to legal personhood—however, it is beneficial to have the international structure to guide advocacy in the area. It is worth considering whether similar treaties may be useful in protecting and enforcing the right to legal personhood for other groups and whether additional detail to the right to legal personhood for refugees and asylum seekers is needed in further international instruments.

## 3.4 Stateless People

I am using the term 'stateless people', in line with its common use in international instruments, to refer to people who are not recognised by a jurisdiction that has standing as a state in international law—such people are not recognised as citizens or residents.[9] There are approximately 12 million stateless people globally.[10] Often, there are political issues—sometimes related to national borders—that have created barriers or resistance to the recognition of the particular people. At times, stateless people are also migrants. However, often, they are not migrants—they have not crossed national borders with an intention to stay and/or reside—but are simply not recognised by the jurisdiction in which they reside, which is often their

[9] Goris, Harrington, and Köhn (n 2).

[10] UNHCR, 'UNHCR Global Trends 2014: World at War' (2015) <https://www.refworld.org/docid/558292924.html> accessed 17 July 2023.

home jurisdiction or where they were born. Examples of stateless people include Palestinians that have been denied citizenship by certain jurisdictions,[11] Bidoon people in Bahrain who were denied citizenship after criticising the government,[12] and many others.[13] There are international instruments that refer to stateless peoples and attempt to regulate how states treat stateless peoples; for example, the 1954 Convention Relating to the Status of Stateless Peoples. However, there is little reference to their right to legal personhood.

As mentioned above, stateless people experience some of the most profound denials of legal personhood because they often have no legal recognition whatsoever—meaning that they often have neither legal standing nor legal agency. Their situation is likely similar to that of undocumented migrants—although, as discussed above, stateless people are often not migrants themselves. The similarity lies in both undocumented migrants and stateless people not being legally recognised by any jurisdiction—at least not any jurisdiction that is recognised as a state in international law or by the international community. They often do not have documentation that would grant them legal standing, and legal standing is required for the legally valid exercise of legal agency.

Also similar to undocumented migrants, the key solutions for breaking down barriers to legal personhood for stateless people require either new understandings of national borders or de-prioritisation of state sovereignty claims. Such measures are required because the recognition of legal personhood for stateless people likely requires forcing a state to recognise such people or requires a new source of legal personhood beyond the confines of domestic states. In order to force a sovereign state to recognise stateless people, their claims of state sovereignty would likely have to be overcome—or they would have to willingly engage in such recognition on the basis of political pressure or some other form of motivation or political will. In order to establish a source of legal personhood beyond domestic states, a new understanding of national borders would have to be established and either

[11] Abbas Shiblak, 'Passport for What Price? Statelessness among Palestinian Refugees', in *Palestinian Refugees* (Routledge 2010); Danielle C Jefferis, 'Institutionalizing Statelessness: The Revocation of Residency Rights of Palestinians in East Jerusalem' (2012) 24 International Journal of Refugee Law 202; Barzoo Eliassi, *Narratives of Statelessness and Political Otherness: Kurdish and Palestinian Experiences* (Palgrave Macmillan 2021); Shourideh C Molavi, *Stateless Citizenship* (Brill 2013); Elena Fiddian-Qasmiyeh, 'On the Threshold of Statelessness: Palestinian Narratives of Loss and Erasure' (2016) 39 Ethnic and Racial Studies 301.

[12] Faisal Mukhyat Abu Sulaib, 'Stateless "Bidoon" in Kuwait: A Crisis of Political Alienation' (2021) 57 Middle Eastern Studies 134; Ahmad Benswait, 'Language and Statelessness: The Impact of Political Discourses on the Bidoon Community in Kuwait' in Tendayi Bloom and Lindsey N Kingston (eds), *Statelessness, Governance, and the Problem of Citizenship* (Manchester UP 2021).

[13] Paul Robert Magocsi, 'Mapping Stateless Peoples: The East Slavs of the Carpathians' (1997) 39 Canadian Slavonic Papers 301; Brad K Blitz and Miguel Otero-Iglesias, 'Stateless by Any Other Name: Refused Asylum-Seekers in the United Kingdom' (2011) 37 Journal of Ethnic and Migration Studies 657; Kristy A Belton, 'Rooted Displacement: The Paradox of Belonging among Stateless People', *Theorising Noncitizenship* (Routledge 2017); Jay Milbrandt, 'Stateless' (2011) 20 Cardozo Journal of International and Comparative Law 75; Bill Berkeley, 'Stateless People, Violent States' (2009) 26 World Policy Journal 3.

a regional or international legal body would have to act as such a source. This is not beyond the realm of possibility, although there does not currently seem to be such a source. Examples of places that could act as sources of legal personhood are regional bodies, such as the European Union, or international bodies, such as the United Nations. However, such power would give these bodies significantly different roles than they have at the moment and require power distributed between the domestic jurisdiction and the region or international body in a manner that resembled a federal system, where the regional or international government had the ability to grant or deny legal personhood, likely in the form of granting or denying citizenship or some other form of association with the regional or international government (which the domestic government would then be required to recognise and respect). This solution would only serve to break down barriers to legal personhood for stateless people—or migrant groups—if the regional or international bodies were upholding the right to legal personhood for all individuals and did not seek to limit legal standing or legal agency on the basis of national origin or migration status. What I am suggesting here is that stateless people make up a quite large group of people—and their human right to legal personhood is denied or significantly limited on a widespread basis. We therefore have an obligation to—at a minimum—explore how to rectify this and how to break down any barriers to legal personhood that this group is facing. This obligation presents an opportunity to re-examine how we understand national borders and state sovereignty and whether it serves us well as a society that seeks to uphold universal human rights—with the right to legal personhood perhaps being the most important of those rights.

## 4. Evolving Responsibilities of State to Non-citizen

The proposed solutions to the barriers to legal personhood identified above are predicated on the state willingly engaging in such reform and developing practices to better protect the right to legal personhood of these groups or require external pressure from the United Nations or other states, which would require that a state's claims of sovereignty and their right to non-intervention from external powers (as discussed in detail in Chapter 2) are, at a minimum, not permitted to supersede the obligation to protect the right to legal personhood for these groups—and, indeed, for all groups. This de-prioritisation of state sovereignty claims requires that the individual is prioritised over the state—at least to some extent. It also requires that this prioritisation occurs both in relation to the right to legal personhood and in relation to citizens and non-citizens.

As established in Chapters 1 and 2, human rights law was originally primarily intended to regulate the relationship between a sovereign state and its citizens. This was initially, at least in part, to avoid the manner in which the ruling Nazi party in Germany treated its citizens before and during World War II, including segregation based on discriminatory grounds such as disability, race, and religion; state-sponsored torture and killing; among other atrocities. It was also created with a focus on regulating the state—as the primary actor—because it was created as part of the international law framework, which—as described in Chapter 1—was developed as a means of regulation of sovereign states both to mitigate the instance of war and conflict and to legitimise certain state action related to colonialism and imperialism.[14] While international law was a well-established venue for human rights and provided a ripe forum for the development of new treaties focused on regulating the matter in which the state treats its citizens, it was largely not constructed with the individual in mind as the primary legal actor. This focus on the state as the primary legal actor in international law—and therefore also in human rights law because human rights law is a form of international law—has created a system in which the state, its borders, and its sovereignty are of primary importance. The importance of those borders in determining the nature of the sovereign state and its jurisdictional coverage has meant that the impact of borders is felt strongly in human rights law—and also felt strongly by individuals that are meant to hold rights under human rights law. For example, citizenship is generally dictated by some form of presence or connection to a state within its national borders—such as birth within the borders, or ancestral connections to the jurisdiction that generally must include some territorial connection within the borders such as birth or extended residence or presence. It is generally clear that a state then has human rights obligations towards individuals that are its citizens and have the prescribed connection to its national borders. However, the nature of international law—and the focus on the sovereign state and its borders—have resulted in more ambiguity in regard to the human rights responsibilities of states to non-citizens.

As a starting point for examining the evolving responsibilities of the state to the non-citizen, it is critical to remind ourselves of the evolving position of the individual within international law. This is important because the status of the individual in international law may impact the manner in which the state's relationship to the non-citizen is also evolving. For example, as the individual becomes a more prominent holder of rights and responsibilities at the international level, the importance of the national borders and state sovereignty diminishes because the state may no longer be the primary actor in international law. Understanding the individual's role in international law is also important for deconstructing the barriers to the right to legal personhood for migrant groups and stateless peoples, in particular, who are non-citizens because these evolving responsibilities of the individual are core to how human rights law is changing—and could potentially be further changed to better address the needs of individuals beyond the restrictions of national borders and claims of state sovereignty.

[14] Frans Viljoen, 'International Human Rights Law: A Short History' (2012) 12 Journal of Humanitarian Medicine 4.

As discussed in Chapter 1, the individual is taking a new central position in the application of international law—more than ever before, rights and responsibilities derived from international legal instruments are being ascribed to individuals as opposed to states. For example, individual rights and duties are increasingly being created and/or enforced in international law in extradition treaties, double taxation agreements, transport treaties, intellectual property treaties, investment protection treaties, treaties on the legal status of foreigners, the Vienna Convention on Consular relations, and ad hoc criminal tribunals and the International Criminal Court.[15] In particular, for improved realisation of the right to legal personhood of migrant groups and stateless peoples, it is pertinent to examine whether the evolving responsibilities of the state to the individual are also extending to the non-citizen.

As international human rights law has developed, there have been increasing details provided regarding the responsibilities of the state to the non-citizen. For example, the 1951 Refugee Convention established that a refugee is someone who

> owing to well-founded fear of being persecuted for reasons of race, religion, nationality, membership of a particular social group or political opinion, is outside the country of [their] nationality and is unable or, owing to such fear, is unwilling to avail [themself] of the protection of that country; or who, not having a nationality and being outside the country of [their] former habitual residence, is unable or, owing to such fear, is unwilling to return to it.[16]

It also outlines the legal protection, rights, and assistance that a refugee is entitled to receive from a state.[17] This treaty was the culmination of a set of international guidelines and documents created starting after World War I when there were high levels of refugees fleeing due to the impact of war. World War II impacted the refugee crisis and spurred the development of the convention, a legally binding international legal instrument.[18] In addition, the 1990 International Convention on the Protection of the Rights of All Migrant Workers and Members of Their Families establishes how states parties must treat migrant workers, including non-citizens.[19] It does maintain a distinction between documented and undocumented workers—in an apparent nod to state sovereignty to determine domestic immigration law—but it simultaneously acknowledges the universality of human rights law and the entitlement of all people to the enjoyment of their fundamental human rights. While conventions such as these have re-enforced the universality of human rights, and have—to some extent—undermined the notion that states only have

15 Anne Peters, *Beyond Human Rights* (CUP 2016).
16 Refugee Convention.
17 ibid.
18 Nathwani (n 5).
19 Juhani Lönnroth, 'The International Convention on the Rights of All Migrant Workers and Members of Their Families in the Context of International Migration Policies: An Analysis of Ten Years of Negotiation' (1991) 25 International Migration Review 710.

a responsibility to protect the human rights of their own citizens or documented immigrants, there remain widespread denials and limitations of the right to legal personhood for migrant groups and stateless peoples around the world—such as the barriers identified above.

Overall, the new prominence of the individual in international law, including increased ascription of rights and responsibilities separate from the state, and the growing understanding of the state's responsibilities to the non-citizen provide fertile ground for the re-examination of the position of the non-citizen in human rights law. I argue that this re-examination should focus on the full protection of the human rights of non-citizens, which again requires breaking down our current understanding of national borders and the importance placed on them. Therefore, in this book, my arguments for—to some extent—de-commissioning national borders is both to de-prioritise state sovereignty and to facilitate the realisation of certain human rights, such as the right to legal personhood, as a matter of urgency and for it to take precedence over claims of state sovereignty—and also to break down our current understanding of national borders to ensure that citizenship or immigration status does not dictate our level of human rights protection—that instead, we are all entitled to realisation and protection of our human rights on an equal basis, regardless of citizenship or immigration status. These fundamental changes to our understandings of national borders are essential for the realisation of the right to legal personhood, in particular, because—as I have, hopefully, demonstrated in this chapter—national borders are a significant barrier to the right to legal personhood for migrant groups and stateless people. As they are currently understood and prioritised, they give states an avenue to use state sovereignty claims to deny or restrict the right to legal personhood of migrant groups and stateless peoples and they create a murky understanding of what the state's obligations are to non-citizens and whose rights—including the right to legal personhood—they are obligated to realise and protect. At the moment, state's widespread and rampant denial and limitation of legal personhood to migrant groups and stateless peoples indicates that states generally interpret their obligations under international law to be relatively weak with regard to the realisation and protection of the right to legal personhood for these groups.

## 5. Conclusion

My aim in setting out these barriers to legal personhood that migrant groups and stateless peoples are experiencing is to demonstrate how widespread such denials and limitation on legal personhood are for these groups—and also to highlight that these denials and limitations on their legal personhood have been largely ignored, both by human rights activist and scholar community and by state parties and UN monitoring bodies. This is not to say that there are no activists and scholars, in particular, who are providing robust analysis and resistance to many immigration policies by domestic governments around the world—as well as advocating for the recognition of stateless peoples in various contexts.[20] However, very few—if any—are making these arguments using the right to legal personhood. I am not suggesting that the current arguments around immigration reform and the recognition of stateless peoples should be abandoned—I am, however, suggesting that arguments regarding the right to legal personhood could provide a novel tool for exploring state obligations for ensuring equality and realising the human rights of individuals in these groups. I am also suggesting that—if we take the human rights framework seriously, as a society—we have an obligation to look closer at the right to legal personhood, especially in cases such as that of migrant groups and stateless people who are experiencing widespread denials or limitations on the right.

Similarly, I am not suggesting that there is an overnight solution to these limitations or denials on the right to legal personhood for these groups. Instead, I am suggesting that—again, if we take the human rights framework seriously—we have an obligation to, at a minimum, engage in a discussion of these denials or limitations on the right to legal personhood for these groups and begin to explore if there are situations in which we are happy to permit states to exercise their sovereignty and to engage in such denials and limitations. As I have hinted at—or perhaps argued quite strongly for—above and in Chapter 2, my view is that in undertaking a human rights analysis of such denials and limitations, we cannot ignore that if we allow states to exercise their sovereignty and deny or limit legal personhood for migrant groups and stateless peoples in the manner in which we are currently doing, we are not doing justice to the human rights framework or to these individuals. The situation, as it is currently, prioritises state sovereignty and a history of imperialism and colonialism that established national borders and the foundations of international law. I am arguing that we need to re-examine such priorities and apply more pressure on states to realise and protect the right to legal personhood for all groups, but particularly for groups such as migrants and stateless peoples who are experiencing widespread denials and limitations on the basis of antiquated imperialist and colonial understandings of the state and its relationship to the individual.

[20] Kingston (n 3); Owen (n 3).

# 6
# Legal Personhood, Racial Minorities, and Indigenous Peoples

## 1. Introduction

Limitations or denials of legal personhood are being experienced by racial minorities and indigenous peoples in the previous groups of persons discussed—described in Chapters 3–5, including migrant groups, stateless peoples, and disabled people—as well as in the groups that are discussed in the following chapters—including women and gender minorities. However, racial minorities and indigenous peoples are also experiencing limitations or denials of legal personhood that are unique to them. The limitations or denials of legal personhood that they are experiencing both as racial minorities and/or indigenous peoples and as members of one or more of the other groups amount to intersectional forms of marginalisation (as discussed in Chapters 1 and 3), and they likely experience those limitations and denials in a manner that is unique to that intersectional experience. For example, black women who are stateless likely experience a unique form of denial or limitation on legal personhood, which is likely quite distinct from limitations or denials of legal personhood experienced by black men who are stateless or white women who are stateless. In this chapter, I am describing how racial minorities and indigenous peoples experience legal personhood, including limitations and denials on legal personhood. I am also exploring those limitations and denials in the context of intersectional identities, such as black women who are stateless. However, the limitations and denials to legal personhood that I identify in this chapter are not an exhaustive identification or exploration of such limitations or denials of either of the discrete groups—racial minorities and indigenous peoples—or of the possible combinations of forms of intersectional marginalisation that is occurring in the form of such limitations or denials on legal personhood. I am also exploring solutions to these limitations and denials; these solutions are also not an exhaustive list of solutions—they are, instead, simply the beginning of an exploration of what solutions could look like and an invitation for others to continue to explore the barriers to legal personhood for these groups and possible solutions for breaking down these barriers.

I have chosen to include both racial minorities and indigenous people in this chapter because there are some parallels in the limitations and denials of legal personhood that they are experiencing. In addition, many indigenous peoples are also racial minorities, which makes it particularly relevant to analyse their legal

*The Right to Legal Personhood of Marginalised Groups*. Anna Arstein-Kerslake, Oxford University Press.
 DOI: 10.1093/9780191926549.003.0006

personhood in tandem. It gives me the opportunity to explore the commonalities and differences of each group, as well as the unique intersectional experiences that may be occurring for indigenous peoples that are also racial minorities.

I am using the term 'racial minority' to refer to any group of people that are experiencing marginalisation and/or a lack of power and privilege on the basis of their race. Such groups are often 'black', 'brown', and/or 'coloured'—I am using the term 'racial minority' as a general term in order to accurately indicate that my analysis is focused not on a particular racial group but instead on how race impacts legal personhood, and the follow-on impacts for power and privilege. Much more research is needed on legal personhood limitations and denials for specific racial groups.

I am using the term 'indigenous peoples' here for a similar reason—I am focusing my analysis on the impact of indigeneity on legal personhood. Again, there is a need for more research on how legal personhood is being limited and denied to particular indigenous groups. This chapter only provides an introductory analysis to the impact of race and indigeneity on legal personhood. It explores how the right to such legal personhood could be better protected; however, a much more detailed analysis is needed to identify concrete solutions for particular groups in specific jurisdictions.

In order to undertake this analysis of the right to legal personhood for racial minorities and indigenous peoples, I am using a critical race theory lens. Using this critical social theory lens provides an in-depth examination of limitations and denials of legal personhood that goes beyond the realities of what is currently happening and explores the underlying socio-legal and historical structures that may have led to such limitations and denials of legal personhood for these groups.[1] I have chosen to use a critical race theory lens because I believe that an analysis without this lens would be sorely lacking—it may be able to identify current limitations or denials, but it would likely not provide a sufficient exploration of the origin or sources of those limitations or denials, which is essential for developing meaningful and sustainable solutions that address the roots of the various problems and barriers to legal personhood for these groups.

I am also choosing to use a critical race theory lens because it aligns with the social model of disability, which arises from critical disability theory.[2] The social model underlies the Convention on the Rights of Persons with Disabilities (CRPD), including Article 12 of the CRPD, which provides the most detail to the right to legal personhood of any international human rights instrument—as

[1] Richard Delgado and Jean Stefancic, *Critical Race Theory: An Introduction* (3rd edn, New York UP 2017).

[2] Dan Goodley, 'Dis/Entangling Critical Disability Studies' (2013) 28 Disability & Society 631; Melinda C Hall, 'Critical Disability Theory' <https://plato.stanford.edu/ENTRIES/disability-critical/> accessed 6 September 2023; Helen Meekosha and Russell Shuttleworth, 'What's So "Critical" about Critical Disability Studies?' (2009) 15 Australian Journal of Human Rights 47.

described in Chapters 1 and 4. Utilising critical race theory to analyse the right to legal personhood creates a platform for the analysis that is symbiotic with Article 12, which demands both a breaking down of socio-legal barriers to legal personhood (Article 12(1 and 2)) and an analysis of how the state can provide access to support for the exercise of legal personhood (Article 12(3)) in a manner that meaningfully breaks down the socio-legal and historical barriers that have been erected over centuries of discrimination and marginalisation of racial minorities and indigenous peoples.

## 2. Colonisation and Imperialism as an Infringement on Legal Personhood

Colonialism and imperialism have profoundly shaped legal personhood for most racial minorities and indigenous peoples. In addition, using a critical race theory lens demands an initial analysis of the institutional and systemic structures contributing to marginalisation—and colonialism and imperialism are often at the root of marginalisation and factors limiting power and privilege for racial minorities and indigenous people.

Racial minorities and indigenous peoples have experienced colonialism and imperialism differently—and it has impacted on their legal personhood differently. However, both groups have experienced slavery either directly or indirectly as a result of colonisation and imperialism. For example, a direct result of colonisation and imperialism was the displacement of millions of African and Indian persons as slaves and indentured servants as a source of cheap labour for colonisers and imperial forces around the world. Similarly, indigenous peoples were enslaved by colonisers in jurisdictions around the world.[3] In addition, an indirect result of colonisation and imperialism—caused by the resulting unequal distribution of wealth to certain jurisdictions around the world and the resulting economic disparities and lack of opportunities in certain areas of the world—is the millions of migrant workers that are subjected to very poor migration conditions amounting to either slavery or indentured servitude.[4] Some of these individuals are even specifically exploited by organised criminal enterprises that capitalise on the economic disparities created by the global socio-economic situation, which was heavily impacted

[3] Robin Blackburn, *The Overthrow of Colonial Slavery, 1776–1848* (Verso 1988); James Walvin, *A Short History of Slavery* (Penguin 2007); Craig Perry and others (eds), 'The Cambridge World History of Slavery', *The Cambridge World History of Slavery: Volume 2: AD 500–AD 1420*, vol 2 (CUP 2021).

[4] PC Emmer (ed), *Colonialism and Migration: Indentured Labour before and after Slavery* (Martinus Nijhoff Publishers 1986); Lucy Mayblin and Joe Turner, *Migration Studies and Colonialism* (John Wiley & Sons 2020); Ernst Van Den Boogaart and PC Emmer, 'Colonialism and Migration: An Overview' in PC Emmer (ed), *Colonialism and Migration: Indentured Labour before and after Slavery* (Martinus Nijhoff Publishers 1986).

by the existence of colonialism and imperialism.[5] These slaves and indentured servants—and others in similar situations—are often racial minorities and/or indigenous peoples, and they often have their legal personhood either fully denied via a denial of their legal standing or significantly limited via denials or restrictions on their legal agency. Individuals in these circumstance are often also undocumented migrants or documented migrants with significant limitations on their legal agency via either formal restrictions on their immigration status in the jurisdiction or informal restrictions on their legal agency by human traffickers or others controlling either their physical environment or their access to legal documentation or other means necessary for the exercise of their legal agency. These individuals are often experiencing unique forms of legal personhood denial based on their intersecting identities as racial minorities and indigenous peoples, and/or migration status.

For racial minorities, generally, such slavery, indentured servitude, or other form of forced labour may be one of the most profound forms of denials or restrictions on their legal personhood caused by colonialism and imperialism. However, there are also insidious forms of denial or limitation on legal personhood that racial minorities experience that are likely due to the long history of discrimination, prejudice, and institutional violence that has been spurred by colonialism and imperialism and has resulted in profound social inequalities for racial minorities, which can lead to limitations or denials of legal personhood; for example, both racial minorities and indigenous peoples experience disproportionately high rates of incarceration, which carries with it inherent limitations on legal personhood.[6] For example, limitations on legal agency to contract—both formally due to private parties not wishing to contract with individuals who are incarcerated or have been convicted of a crime and informally due to physical limitations related to being held in an incarceration facility and significantly restricted from interacting with socio-legal structures outside of the incarceration facility. Many other forms of legal personhood limitations or denials likely exist for racial minorities and/or indigenous peoples that are a result of colonialism and imperialism or the social inequalities that have resulted.

For indigenous peoples there were also unique experiences of colonialism and imperialism that specifically limited their legal personhood. For example, when

[5] Andreas Schloenhardt, 'Organized Crime and the Business of Migrant Trafficking' (1999) 32 Crime, Law and Social Change 203; Raimo Väyrynen, 'Illegal Immigration, Human Trafficking and Organized Crime' in George J Borjas and Jeff Crisp (eds), *Poverty, International Migration and Asylum* (Palgrave Macmillan 2005).

[6] Glenn C Loury, *Race, Incarceration, and American Values* (MIT Press 2008); Marc Mauer, 'Addressing Racial Disparities in Incarceration' (2011) 91 The Prison Journal 87S; Reuben Jonathan Miller, 'Race, Hyper-incarceration, and US Poverty Policy in Historic Perspective' (2013) 7 Sociology Compass 573; Robert Nichols, 'The Colonialism of Incarceration', *Legal Violence and the Limits of the Law* (Routledge 2017); Devah Pager, *Marked: Race, Crime, and Finding Work in an Era of Mass Incarceration* (University of Chicago Press 2008); Julian V Roberts and Anthony N Doob, 'Race, Ethnicity, and Criminal Justice in Canada' (1997) 21 Crime and Justice 469.

colonial forces invaded and settled a particular jurisdiction, then often completely ignored, or actively pushed aside, existing socio-legal structures of indigenous populations, which likely had their own mechanisms for recognising legal personhood—or some version of recognition of individuals as entities with rights and responsibilities to the community and to socio-legal structures. Furthermore, colonial forces often either specifically created limited forms of legal personhood that applied to indigenous people or carried out practices that served to limit the legal personhood of indigenous peoples.[7]

In addition, ongoing prejudice and discrimination, as well as unequal socio-economic situations created by colonialism and impacting some indigenous peoples, have resulted in many modern practices that continue to limit or deny the legal personhood of indigenous peoples today. For example, in Australia, indigenous peoples are much more likely to be found 'unfit to plead' to criminal charges and are denied legal standing to enter a plea or even engage in a trial.[8] This limitation on legal standing results in indigenous people being held indefinitely in incarceration facilities in some states in Australia or can result in them being held substantially longer than they would have been held if they were permitted to engage in the trial process. The result is disproportionate limitations on both the legal standing of indigenous peoples and their ability to exercise their legal agency in the trial process and when they are incarcerated. There are likely many other examples of such modern denials or limitations on the legal personhood of indigenous peoples—much more research is needed, and it is important to continue to identify when such limitations or denials are either a direct or indirect result of colonialism and imperialism.

The identification of connections with colonialism or imperialism is important in order to appropriately take responsibility for historical wrongs, as well as in order to fully understand why such limitations or denials of legal personhood

[7] Val Napoleon, 'Gitxsan Legal Personhood: Gendered' in Austin Sarat, George Pavlich, and Richard Mailey (eds), *Interrupting the Legal Person*, vol 87A (Emerald Publishing 2022); Michael J Heckenberger, *The Ecology of Power: Culture, Place and Personhood in the Southern Amazon, AD 1000–2000* (Routledge 2004); Martuwarra RiverOfLife and others, 'Yoongoorrookoo' (2021) 30 Griffith Law Review 505; Richard Jenkins and Mark Nuttall (eds), 'States and Categories: Indigenous Models of Personhood in Northwest Greenland', *Questions of Competence: Culture, Classification and Intellectual Disability* (CUP 1998); Nicolas Peterson, 'On the Persistence of Sharing: Personhood, Asymmetrical Reciprocity, and Demand Sharing in the Indigenous Australian Domestic Moral Economy' (2013) 24 The Australian Journal of Anthropology 166.

[8] Anna Arstein-Kerslake and others, 'Human Rights and Unfitness to Plead: The Demands of the Convention on the Rights of Persons with Disabilities' (2017) 17 Human Rights Law Review 399; Bernadette McSherry and others, 'Unfitness to Plead and Indefinite Detention of Persons with Cognitive Disabilities' (Report, Melbourne Social Equity Institute 2017) <https://apo.org.au/node/312445> accessed 6 May 2022; Anna Arstein-Kerslake and others, 'Implementing a Participatory Human Rights-Based Research Methodology: The Unfitness to Plead Project' (2019) 11 Journal of Human Rights Practice 589; Piers Gooding and others, 'Unfitness to Stand Trial: The Indefinite Detention of Persons with Cognitive Disabilities in Australia and the United Nations Convention on the Rights of Persons with Disabilities' (Social Science Research Network 2016) SSRN Scholarly Paper 3288278 <https://papers.ssrn.com/abstract=3288278> accessed 6 May 2022.

are occurring and develop solutions that serve to better realise the human right to legal personhood of indigenous peoples and accurately take into consideration how such limitations or denials came to be and how they can be corrected. For example, in the case of the disproportionate findings of 'unfit to plead' for indigenous peoples in Australia, an understanding of colonial history allows us to see that the criminal justice system, as a whole, is one that was imposed by white settlers on the indigenous community (Aboriginal and Torres Straight Islanders) and is ill suited to meet their needs. Such a recognition can then lead to solutions that either allow for alternative justice systems that are led by indigenous communities themselves or reform of the existing criminal justice system to better incorporate the needs and cultural context of indigenous communities; for example, more support within the justice system that is tailored for indigenous communities, more justice professionals that are from indigenous communities, better understanding of communication methods of indigenous communities (even when those are non-verbal or unorthodox for the white settler community), and any other measure that takes into account the profound impact that colonialism has had on indigenous communities and the need to account for that in white settler systems that have been imposed on indigenous communities, such as Western criminal justice systems. This is just one, relatively discrete, example of how legal personhood can be limited or denied for indigenous peoples as a result of the socio-legal systems that have arisen out of colonial and imperial forces; much more research is needed to explore how we can better realise the right to legal personhood for indigenous peoples and how an understanding of colonial and imperial experiences and forces have shaped those denials and limitations of legal personhood and how we can create solutions that take these experiences and forces into consideration, as mentioned above.

## 3. Eugenics and Historical Denials of Personhood

As I have discussed elsewhere in the context of disability, the eugenics movement had a profound impact on our socio-legal understandings of legal personhood and moral personhood. I will not discuss its impact on moral personhood here, simply due to lack of space and wanting to stay focused on issues directly related to legal personhood; however, I wanted to note that the impact of the eugenics movement on personhood goes beyond simply legal personhood. The eugenics movement was a professed 'scientific' movement that largely started in England and spread to Continental Europe, the United States, and around the world.[9] It was developed largely by white, able-bodied, cisgender males. Its core precepts are that there exists a human ideal, and we should utilise medicine, science, and other means to

[9] Stephen Garton, 'Eugenics in Australia and New Zealand: Laboratories of Racial Science' in Alison Bashford and Philippa Levine (eds), *The Oxford Handbook of the History of Eugenics* (OUP 2010).

tailor the population to this human ideal. The human ideal upheld by the movement is one of a white, European, able-bodied, cisgender person.

In the context of disability, I have previously discussed its impact on legal personhood in the form of forced sterilisation, forced medical experimentation, institutionalisation, and the insidious notion that was allowed to creep into the public consciousness that disabled people are less valuable than others and the knock-on effect that may have occurred in legal structures in terms of limitations and/or denials of their legal personhood.[10] Unfortunately, in some places, the eugenics movement impacted the legal personhood of racial minorities and indigenous peoples in much the same way that it impacted disabled people. Racial minorities and indigenous peoples were subjected to forced sterilisation in places like the United States, Canada, Sweden, and Australia.[11] Forced sterilisation is a limitation on legal personhood because it is a denial of legal agency to consent to medical treatment. There is also evidence that racial minorities and indigenous peoples were subjected to forced medical experimentation under the premise that their lives were less valuable—in line with eugenic ideology.[12] Forced medical experimentation is a limitation on legal personhood for the same reason that forced sterilisation is—it is a limitation on legal agency to consent to medical treatment. Racial minorities and indigenous peoples—both children and adults—were also institutionalised across the United States, Australia, Europe, and elsewhere.[13] Institutionalisation is a limitation on legal personhood because it is the forced placement of an individual in a congregated setting where they do not have the option to leave. This

[10] Tom Shakespeare, 'Choices and Rights: Eugenics, Genetics and Disability Equality' (1998) 13 Disability & Society 665; Anna Arstein-Kerslake, *Restoring Voice to People with Cognitive Disabilities* (CUP 2017); Anna Arstein-Kerslake, *Legal Capacity & Gender: Realising the Human Right to Legal Personhood and Agency of Women, Disabled Women, and Gender Minorities* (Springer 2021); Anna Arstein-Kerslake, 'Understanding Sex: The Right to Legal Capacity to Consent to Sex' (2015) 30 Disability & Society 1459.

[11] Paul A Lombardo, *Three Generations, No Imbeciles: Eugenics, the Supreme Court, and Buck v. Bell* (JHU Press 2022); Garton (n 9); Nina Lemieux, 'Australian Eugenics from 1900 To 1961' (Honor's thesis, University of Texas at Austin 2017) <https://repositories.lib.utexas.edu/handle/2152/63658> accessed 6 September 2023; Michael L Wehmeyer, 'Eugenics and Sterilization in the Heartland' (2003) 41 Mental Retardation 57; Leonardo Pegoraro, 'Second-Rate Victims: The Forced Sterilization of Indigenous Peoples in the USA and Canada' (2015) 5 Settler Colonial Studies 161; Stephanie Hyatt, 'A Shared History of Shame: Sweden's Four-Decade Policy of Forced Sterilization and the Eugenics Movement in the United States' (1997) 8 Indiana International & Comparative Law Review 475.

[12] Edwin Black, *War against the Weak: Eugenics and America's Campaign to Create a Master Race, Expanded Edition* (Dialog Press 2012); Greg Blyton, 'Australia: Tainted Blood—Scientific Racism, Eugenics and Sanctimonious Treatments of Aboriginal Australians: 1869–2008' in Bruce E Johansen and Adebowale Akande (eds), *Get Your Knee Off Our Necks: From Slavery to Black Lives Matter* (Springer 2022); Mary Cawte, 'Craniometry and Eugenics in Australia: R.J.A. Berry and the Quest for Social Efficiency' (1986) 22 Historical Studies 35; Paul A Lombardo and Gregory M Dorr, 'Eugenics, Medical Education, and the Public Health Service: Another Perspective on the Tuskegee Syphilis Experiment' (2006) 80 Bulletin of the History of Medicine 291.

[13] Delan Devakumar and Rochelle Burgess, 'Legacies of Eugenics' (2023) 401 The Lancet 725; Greta Jones, 'Eugenics in Ireland: The Belfast Eugenics Society, 1911–15' (1992) 28 Irish Historical Studies 81; Allison C Carey, 'Beyond the Medical Model: A Reconsideration of "Feeblemindedness", Citizenship, and Eugenic Restrictions' (2003) 18 Disability & Society 411; Garton (n 9).

is a limitation on their legal agency to choose where to live; in addition, in many institutional settings, the residents' legal standing is denied and is held by the institution or the administrative staff of the institution.[14] Such a situation amounts to a full denial of legal personhood because both their legal standing and their legal agency are denied.

Many of these limitations and denials occurred outside the context of Nazi Germany; however, the eugenics movement also heavily influenced Nazi Germany and the concentration camps that were part of the holocaust and carried out campaigns of forced sterilisation, forced medical experimentation, forced detention, and other atrocities and forms of limitations and denials of legal agency and standing. Disabled people, racial minorities (such as the Roma people), and indigenous groups were among those subjected to such violations.[15] In addition, it is likely that the paradigms that the eugenics movement fostered and upheld insidiously infiltrated the public consciousness and continue to impact our understandings of personhood today.

My purpose in highlighting the impact of the eugenics movement on racial minorities and indigenous peoples here is to demonstrate the deep historical prejudice that exists against the full realisation of the right to legal personhood for racial minorities and indigenous groups. This is in line with critical race theory and is similar to my purpose for highlighting the impact of colonialism and imperialism. Again, more research is needed—here I am hoping to open up the conversation around what the historical context is for the high level of limitations and denials on the legal personhood of racial minorities and indigenous peoples, to identify the modern barriers that exist, and to explore solutions that take into account this historical context and seek to break down the resulting modern barriers.

## 4. Barriers to Legal Personhood

Modern barriers to legal personhood for racial minorities and indigenous peoples are often directly caused by or heavily influenced by historical and systemic issues such as colonialism, imperialism, and eugenics, as described above. It is important to identify these sources of barriers to legal personhood—and to specifically identify the modern barriers, their practical implications, and potential solutions. This identification is essential for doing more than just recognising past wrongs that

[14] Series Lucy, *Deprivation of Liberty in the Shadows of the Institution* (Policy Press 2022); Lucy Series, 'The Mental Capacity Act 2005 and the Institutional Domination of People with Learning Disabilities' (University of Exeter 2013) <https://ore.exeter.ac.uk/repository/handle/10871/9941> accessed 3 May 2019.

[15] Stefan Kuhl, *The Nazi Connection: Eugenics, American Racism, and German National Socialism* (OUP 2002); Lawrence A Zeidman, 'Neuroscience in Nazi Europe Part I: Eugenics, Human Experimentation, and Mass Murder' (2011) 38 Canadian Journal of Neurological Sciences 696.

racial minorities and indigenous groups face—it allows for a more practical analysis of the current situation and how it can be improved (of course, while taking into considering the historical and systemic issues).

Although this list is not exhaustive, key barriers to legal personhood that racial minorities and indigenous peoples are facing include: disproportionate incarceration leading to limitations on legal standing and legal agency; migration status leading to limitations on legal standing and legal agency; educational disadvantage leading to restricted opportunity and potentially limitations on legal agency; discrimination and prejudice leading to disproportionate denials of legal standing and legal agency; among others. Disproportionate incarceration of racial minorities and indigenous peoples is discussed above and can lead to the disproportionate denial or limitation of legal standing and legal agency. One example, in addition to the examples provided above, is voting rights—in many jurisdictions, individuals who are either convicted of a crime or incarcerated are either denied their legal agency to vote or have it severely limited.[16] Many racial minorities and indigenous people are also migrants and face similar barriers to legal personhood as those described in Chapter 5. Of course, as intersectional marginalisation is often a unique experience—they also likely experience compounding disadvantage in relation to power and privilege related to barriers to legal personhood that are faced by racial minorities and indigenous peoples, as described in this chapter. Education disadvantage is also widely experienced by racial minorities and indigenous peoples around the world; this likely impacts denials or limitations on legal personhood because it leaves individuals with fewer tools to interact with and challenge the socio-legal structures that have the power to grant, deny, or limit legal personhood.[17] Finally, discrimination and prejudice, more broadly, are likely still impacting the disproportionate denial and limitation of legal personhood to racial minorities and indigenous groups—across various areas of the law, where the power to grant, deny, or limit legal personhood is held by socio-legal structures that are not led by racial minorities or indigenous peoples, they will likely not be acting squarely within the interests of these groups, as critical race theory

[16] John Dittmer, *Local People: The Struggle for Civil Rights in Mississippi* (University of Illinois Press 1994); Frank R Parker, *Black Votes Count: Political Empowerment in Mississippi After 1965* (University of North Carolina Press 1990); Kathleen M Olivares and Velmer S Burton, 'The Collateral Consequences of a Felony Conviction: A National Study of State Legal Codes 10 Years Later' (1996) 60 Federal Probation 10.

[17] Lilly Brown, 'Indigenous Young People, Disadvantage and the Violence of Settler Colonial Education Policy and Curriculum' (2019) 55 Journal of Sociology 54; Kevin Gillan, Suzanne Mellor, and Jacynta Krakouer, 'The Case for Urgency: Advocating for Indigenous Voice in Education' [2017] Australian Education Review <https://research.acer.edu.au/aer/16> accessed 11 January 2024; Gawaian Bodkin-Andrews and Bronwyn Carlson, 'The Legacy of Racism and Indigenous Australian Identity within Education' (2016) 19 Race Ethnicity and Education 784; Vincent J Roscigno, 'Race and the Reproduction of Educational Disadvantage' (1998) 76 Social Forces 1033; George Farkas, 'Racial Disparities and Discrimination in Education: What Do We Know, How Do We Know It, and What Do We Need to Know?' (2003) 105 Teachers College Record 1119.

has taught us. This will be discussed a bit more below and is generally important to keep in mind whenever assessing a potential denial or limitation on legal personhood that is appearing to impact any marginalised group disproportionately, but especially racial minorities and indigenous peoples because of the profound history of discrimination, prejudice, and state violence that they have experienced.

## 5. Legal Personhood and Legal Sovereignty for Indigenous Peoples: Impact of Power and Privilege

Indigenous groups likely experience unique issue with legal personhood related to it being granted or denied by the settler state—I touched on these issues above, but I think that it is important to also highlight the tensions related to legal sovereignty of indigenous peoples and state sovereignty claims from settler states that may be resistant to recognising full legal personhood for indigenous peoples. There is both the tension of the larger indigenous group being recognised as a sovereign jurisdiction and the tension of individual indigenous peoples being recognised by the settler state as legal persons. It varies across the world which indigenous groups are recognised as sovereign jurisdictions—many are still struggling for such recognition.[18] Groups that do have their sovereignty recognised, such as tribal governments in the United States, have the ability to grant, deny, or limit the legal personhood of the individuals within their jurisdiction—although, in most cases, even the federal government also maintains some powers to do so.[19] Groups that do not have their sovereignty recognised, such as the Aboriginal and Torres Strait Islanders peoples of Australia, do not have the same formal legal power to grant, deny, or limit individual's legal personhood—instead that power primarily lies with the settler state. Although there is not space here to fully explore these issues, it is important to recognise the lack of autonomy that many indigenous groups are facing, and the knock-on effect that has on the legal personhood of indigenous individuals.

[18] Catherine J Iorns, 'Indigenous Peoples and Self Determination: Challenging State Sovereignty' (1992) 24 Case Western Reserve Journal of International Law 199; Aileen Moreton-Robinson, *Sovereign Subjects: Indigenous Sovereignty Matters* (Routledge 2020); Federico Lenzerini, 'Sovereignty Revisited: International Law and Parallel Sovereignty of Indigenous Peoples' (2006) 42 Texas International Law Journal 155; Siegfried Wiessner, 'Indigenous Sovereignty: A Reassessment in Light of the UN Declaration on the Rights of Indigenous People' (2008) 41 Vanderbilt Journal of Transnational Law 1141.

[19] Steven Paul McSloy, 'Back to the Future: Native American Sovereignty in the 21st Century' (1992) 20 New York University Review of Law & Social Change 217; Robert A Fairbanks, 'Native American Sovereignty and Treaty Rights: Are They Historical Illusions?' (1995) 20 American Indian Law Review 141; KC Abraham and Bernadette Mbuy-Beya, *Spirituality of the Third World: A Cry for Life: Papers and Reflections from the Third General Assembly of the Ecumenical Association of Third World Theologians, January, 1992, Nairobi, Kenya* (Wipf and Stock Publishers 2005).

For indigenous people where the particular indigenous group does not enjoy sovereignty and the power to grant, deny, or limit legal personhood is lying almost completely with the settler state, they are likely significantly disadvantaged. In line with understandings of power and privilege coming from critical social theory and critical race theory, where a significant source of power—such as legal personhood recognition—is held by one group, that group often shapes the granting of that power in a manner that is most advantageous for their members, and those most similar to them, and others are often disadvantaged because the manner of granting power is ill-suited to their needs or is withheld from them based on the group holding power placing their needs for power above that of other groups.

For legal personhood, where the power to grant, deny, or limit an individual's personhood lies with the settler state—and where the settler state has very few structures within it that are controlled by indigenous leaders—indigenous people are likely highly disadvantaged because individuals within the settler state and structures within the settler state are often ill-suited to the needs and cultural understandings of indigenous peoples both in relation to when and how legal standing is needed and when and how it is exercised via legal agency. The unfitness to plead law situation in Australia, described above, is one example.[20] Another example is the disproportionate denial of parental rights to indigenous people around the world, including in North American and Australia. The denial of parental rights is a limitation of legal agency—and therefore a limitation on legal personhood—and indigenous groups are experiencing disproportionate limitations of legal agency in this way via the disproportionate removal of indigenous children from families, as well as high levels of state involvement in indigenous family life, while this disproportionate limitation on legal agency seems to be occurring in both jurisdictions where indigenous peoples do not enjoy group sovereignty and jurisdictions where they do enjoy some level of sovereignty.[21]

Indigenous groups seem to be at risk of disadvantage in relation to legal personhood in both jurisdictions where they enjoy group sovereignty (eg United States) and jurisdictions where they do not (eg Australia). This may be due to deeply rooted socio-economic disadvantage caused by prejudice, discrimination, and state violence experienced by indigenous peoples that continues to impact them in profound ways. However, I would argue that where an indigenous group enjoys

[20] Arstein-Kerslake and others, 'Human Rights and Unfitness to Plead: The Demands of the Convention on the Rights of Persons with Disabilities' (n 8); McSherry and others (n 8); Gooding and others (n 8).

[21] Vinita B Andrapalliyal, 'History Repeats Itself: Parallels between Current-Day Threats to Immigrant Parental Rights and Native American Parental Rights in the Twentieth Century' (2013) 8 University of Massachusetts Law Review 562; Christopher Wildeman, Frank R Edwards, and Sara Wakefield, 'The Cumulative Prevalence of Termination of Parental Rights for US Children, 2000–2016' (2020) 25 Child Maltreatment 32; Chris Cunneen and Terry Libesman, 'Postcolonial Trauma: The Contemporary Removal of Indigenous Children and Young People from Their Families in Australia' (2000) 35 Australian Journal of Social Issues 99.

sovereignty and their own governing bodies have at least some control with regard to the granting, denying, and limitation of legal personhood of their own people, there is a greater chance that legal personhood will be granted, denied, and limited in a manner that is more culturally appropriate and better meets the needs of indigenous individuals.

## 6. Conclusion

While significantly more research is needed into the legal personhood denials and limitations that racial minorities and indigenous peoples are facing, hopefully, this chapter has opened a door to conversations and discussions in this area. As discussed throughout this book, I am arguing that the human right to legal personhood of all people—including these groups—should supersede any claims to state sovereignty. This argument has a particular significance for indigenous peoples, as discussed above. It likely does not require the same reimagining of national borders that is required for migrants and stateless peoples, as discussed in Chapter 5. However, it will require a new prioritisation of the right to legal personhood for racial minorities and indigenous peoples within domestic governments. This new prioritisation will require both an examination of current barriers to legal personhood and a deep exploration of the historical and systemic sources of those barriers—in line with critical race theory. Solutions must include the practicalities of modern times as well as an understanding and compensation for the foundations of denials and limitations on legal personhood.

# 7
# Legal Personhood and Gender
## Women and Gender Minorities

### 1. Introduction

As with the previous groups discussed, women and gender minorities are experiencing marginalisation due to legal personhood limitations and denials both as distinct social groups and intersectionally when they are also members of the social groups discussed in this book (racial minorities, indigenous peoples, migrants, stateless peoples, and disabled people), as well as other groups. This chapter focuses on those limitations and denials and the resulting marginalisation.[1]

To provide context, it introduces the historical discrimination that women have experienced regarding their decision-making skills and that gender minorities have experienced as a result of assumptions related to their mental health. It discusses the myth of female hysteria and irrationality that has permeated our culture in the past and continues to be seen in law, policy, and practice.[2] It also discusses the historical fallacy that gender minorities—especially those that do not conform to gender binaries—are experiencing mental health disability.[3] In other words, it explores the pathologisation of gender. It argues that these historical prejudices may have led to modern discrimination, including the denigration of female and non-binary cognition and the resulting limitations or denials on legal personhood. Using the definition of legal personhood established in Chapter 1, it also outlines specific barriers to legal personhood that women and gender minorities are experiencing.

[1] For an in-depth discussion of legal personhood (or legal capacity) and gender, see Anna Arstein-Kerslake, *Legal Capacity & Gender: Realising the Human Right to Legal Personhood and Agency of Women, Disabled Women, and Gender Minorities* (Springer 2021). Portions of this chapter are based on research carried out for that book, and some text from that work has been included here; the arguments related to legal personhood and gender are further developed here.

[2] Maya Manian, 'The Irrational Woman: Informed Consent and Abortion Decision-Making' (2009) 16 Duke Journal of Gender Law & Policy 223; Cecily Devereux, 'Hysteria, Feminism, and Gender Revisited: The Case of the Second Wave' (2014) 40 English Studies in Canada 19, 20.

[3] Pieter Cannoot, '"#WontBeErased": The Effects of (De)Pathologisation and (De)Medicalisation on the Legal Capacity of Trans* Persons' (2019) 66 International Journal of Law and Psychiatry 101478; Pieter Cannoot, 'The Pathologisation of Trans* Persons in the ECtHR's Case Law on Legal Gender Recognition' (2019) 37 Netherlands Quarterly of Human Rights 14; David O Cauldwell, 'Psychopathia Transexualis' in Susan Stryker and Stephen Whittle (eds), *The Transgender Studies Reader* (Routledge 2006).

*The Right to Legal Personhood of Marginalised Groups.* Anna Arstein-Kerslake, Oxford University Press.
 DOI: 10.1093/9780191926549.003.0007

## 2. Hysteria and the Denigration of Female Cognition

In many instances, legal personhood is denied on the basis of irrationality—in other words, the actual or perceived inability to make legal decisions. This is particularly true for disabled people, women, and gender minorities. As discussed in Chapter 4, disabled people are often presumed to lack sufficient cognitive skills to make legal decisions, and their legal personhood is therefore removed from them and granted to a representative in order for them to make legal decisions on the disabled person's behalf. These type of legal personhood denials occur through guardianship and other similar legal mechanisms, including in discrete areas of the law, such as unfitness to plead legislation in criminal law, and others. Similar limitations and denials of legal personhood occur for women and gender minorities based on assumptions (which are often inaccurate) related to their rationality and cognition. For women, the historical evolution of 'hysteria' as an inherent female trait may have been a strong driver which created modern assumptions regarding the irrationality of women and may have resulted in various limitations and denials of legal personhood, including guardianship as well as more informal denials in interpersonal relationships where others (often men) are informally given the legal decision-making power over women.

There is a long history of women being perceived as having inferior cognitive skills to that of men.[4] At many points in history, women have been viewed as prone to 'hysteria' or other mental health issues that would lead to decision-making impairments.[5] 'Hysteria' was presented as evidence of the instability of the female mind and the purported limitations of women that were perceived to be due to their reproductive organs.[6] It can be debated whether this perception of women as irrational led to restrictions on legal personhood—or whether restrictions on legal personhood led to an inability to demonstrate decision-making skills on an equal basis with men, which led to perceptions of irrationality. It may be that one contributed to the other in a vicious cycle of deeply imbedded prejudice and accompanying rights denial.

The term 'hysteria' has multiple meanings. One is its use in common parlance to delineate overemotional people—predominately women or people displaying what is perceived as 'female behaviour'.[7] Another is the disease of hysteria, described by French physician and psychologist Pierre Brique in 1859.[8] Sometimes,

[4] Arstein-Kerslake, *Legal Capacity & Gender* (n 1); Mark S Micale, *Approaching Hysteria: Disease and Its Interpretations* (Princeton UP 1995).

[5] HE Lerner, 'The Hysterical Personality: A "Woman's Disease"' (1974) 15 Comprehensive Psychiatry 157; Mark S Micale, *Approaching Hysteria: Disease and Its Interpretations* (Princeton UP 2019); Devereux (n 2) 19, 20; Sander L Gilman, *Hysteria beyond Freud* (University of California Press 1993).

[6] Devereux (n 2) 20.

[7] Paul Chodoff, 'The Diagnosis of Hysteria: An Overview' (1974) 131 American Journal of Psychiatry 1073, 1074.

[8] ibid.

hysteria was perceived to be caused by the functioning and distress of female reproductive organs and sometimes simply attributed to being female.[9] One commonality in the use of the term 'hysteria' is that it refers to dysfunction of the mind of primarily women or those demonstrating what are considered to be female characteristics.

The father of psychoanalysis, Sigmund Freud, is often credited with the modern ascription of hysteria to woman.[10] He coined the term 'anxiety hysteria'.[11] Much of his work pathologised the experiences and expressions of women and largely discarded them as 'hysterical' or irrational.[12] He is credited with the creation of the concept of 'hysterical conversion', which emphasised the repression of unpleasant and traumatic experiences that are 'converted' into physical symptoms.[13] He argued that hysteria was caused by repressed traumatic memories that were likely sexual in nature. One of the most famous cases that Freud wrote about was that of 'Anna O'. She displayed 'hysterical' symptoms, and after discussing the traumatic events that led to her hysterical symptoms, the symptoms disappeared—this was the beginning of 'the talking cure' and was a part of the creation of Freud's psychoanalysis that remains heavily influential on modern psychology.[14]

Freud, however, was by no means the first to attribute hysteria or irrationality to women. From almost the earliest written records, there has been an association between femininity and hysteria.[15] For example, the word 'hysteria' is derived from the Greek word for uterus, 'hystera', and has been associated with female psychological dysfunction ever since.[16] The Greek use of the word was derived from the Sanskrit word for stomach or belly. There is evidence that Egyptian medicine from around 1900 BC documented what was perceived as abnormal behaviour in adult women, and they interpreted it as abnormalities caused by the movement of the uterus, in an autonomous manner, upward, which put pressure on the diaphragm. Treatment for such 'hysteria' included placement of scented substances on the vulva to lead the uterus back down and the smelling and consumption of foul-tasting and rotting substances to move the uterus away from the diaphragm.[17]

9 Micale (n 5).
10 Micale (n 4) 3; Gilman (n 5).
11 Paul Chodoff and Henry Lyons, 'Hysteria, the Hysterical Personality and "Hysterical" Conversion' (1958) 114 American Journal of Psychiatry 734, 734.
12 Dianne Hunter, 'Hysteria, Psychoanalysis, and Feminism: The Case of Anna O.' (1983) 9 Feminist Studies 465; Beret E Strong, 'Foucault, Freud, and French Feminism: Theorizing Hysteria as Theorizing the Feminine' (1989) 35 Literature and Psychology 10.
13 Carol S North, 'The Classification of Hysteria and Related Disorders: Historical and Phenomenological Considerations' (2015) 5 Behavioral Sciences 496, 499; Chodoff (n 7) 1073; Sigmund Freud and Joseph Breuer, *Studies in Hysteria* (Penguin Classics 2004).
14 Micale (n 4) 27.
15 Paul Chodoff, 'Hysteria and Women' (1982) 139 American Journal of Psychiatry 545, 545.
16 ibid; Phebe Cramer, 'What Has Happened to Hysteria?' (2019) 207 The Journal of Nervous and Mental Disease 705, 705; Micale (n 4) 19.
17 Micale (n 4) 19.

These Egyptian views on hysteria formed the foundations for the classical Greek medical and philosophical theories of hysteria.[18] In referring to the 'nature' of women, Plato wrote:

> The womb is an animal which longs to generate children. When it remains barren too long after puberty it is distressed and sorely disturbed and straying about in the body and cutting off the passages of the breath, it impedes respiration and brings the sufferer into the extremist anguish, and provokes all manner of diseases besides. [The disturbance continues until the womb is appeased by passion and love.] Such is the nature of women and all that is female.[19]

Here, women were viewed as burdened with their reproductive organs, which were perceived to control their lives—both physically and mentally. They were perceived as incapable of rational thought on par with men—in part, because their biology would not allow it.[20] Therapy for such perceived illness was often immediate marriage.[21]

Ancient Romans also wrote about hysteria. They moved on from the Greek notion of a wandering uterus; however, it remained an illness tied exclusively to the female reproductive tract. Cases were identified primarily in unmarried women, in particular—virgins, those never married, and widows—and the treatment prescribed was often marital fornication. The Egyptian, Greek, and Roman conceptions of hysteria provided the basis for the concept of hysteria in Western civilisation. Until the early twentieth century, the notion of gynaecological determinism of hysteria remained, which was the idea that hysteria was caused by the female reproductive organs.[22]

From the 5th to the 13th centuries, with the increasing strength of Christian civilisation in Europe, there was a shift towards viewing hysteria as a manifestation of evil and a consequence of original sin. The female hysteric was seen either as a victim of bewitchment to be pitied or a soulmate of the devil to be feared. In the late medieval and Renaissance periods, there was a shift from treating hysteria in hospitals to subjecting women deemed as hysterics to the courtroom. Women were tortured and executed on the basis of being a witch or hysteric. In response to this, in the following period—during the scientific revolution—hysteria was returned to the field of medicine and became re-pathologised and was, once again, treated as a medical disorder and mental illness. In the mid-1800s, medical scholars began to treat hysteria as a behavioural disorder, as opposed to a physical illness. Traits that were ascribed to hysteria during this time included eccentricity, impulsiveness,

18 ibid.
19 Plato and Benjamin Jowett, *Timaeus* (Project Gutenberg 360AD); Chodoff (n 15) 546.
20 Chodoff (n 15) 546; Cramer (n 16) 705.
21 Micale (n 4) 19.
22 ibid 20.

emotionality, coquettishness, deceitfulness, and hypersexuality. It was not until the late 1800s that hysteria began to be discussed as a psychological phenomenon.[23]

Just prior to Freud's work on hysteria, which took place in the 1880s and 1890s, Briquet was one of the first to discuss 'hysteria' as a disease. He identified it as a disease of women that has an onset before the age of 35. It is characterised by multiple physical complaints and hospitalisation.[24] He defined hysteria as 'neurosis of the brain in which the observed phenomena consist chiefly of a perturbation of vital activities, which serve as the manifestation of affective feeling and passions'.[25] Briquet based much of his work on a study he conducted with 430 cases of 'hysteria' over a ten-year period at the Hôpital de la Charité in Paris. In this study he identified several predisposing factors for hysteria: sex, age, heredity, physical constitution and 'moral disposition', social class, mode of education, influence of emotions and 'moral affections', occupation, sexual continence, and general health.[26] He identified that women are at least 20 times more at risk of becoming hysterics than men.[27] He noted,

Amongst women, there exists a more lively sensitiveness than amongst men. Feelings are more easily aroused, are experienced more intensely, and have more repercussions in the whole economy than amongst men. Everything is an occasion for feeling, and all feelings exercise their influences on the splanchnic viscera.[28]

Briquet found that there were certain phenomena that provided alleviation of hysteria:

The return of regular menses, an improvement in social position, the development of an intercurrent disease (eg, tuberculosis), 'violent moral emotions', and the imagination and the will had a favorable effect on the course of hysteria, whereas marriage and pregnancy had an unfavorable effect. In general, those influences that calmed the nervous system improved hysteria, and those that excited the nervous system aggravated the illness.[29]

In his work, there is a clear connection between assumptions about women, rationality, and illness.

Prominent psychiatrist and scholar Paul Chodoff engaged in significant scholarly work exploring the history, meaning, and application of hysteria.[30] In the early 1980s, he queried whether hysteria was inherently female or whether it was, in fact, predominantly seen in women due to social and cultural forces such as male

[23] ibid 21–26.
[24] Chodoff (n 7) 1074.
[25] Pierre Briquet, *Traite de l'Hysterie* (JB Bailliere et Fils 1859) 3; Francois M Mai and Harold Merskey, 'Briquet's Treatise on Hysteria: A Synopsis and Commentary' (1980) 37 Archives of General Psychiatry 1401, 1401.
[26] Mai and Merskey (n 25) 1401–1402.
[27] Briquet (n 25) 36.
[28] ibid 47; Mai and Merskey (n 25) 1401.
[29] Briquet (n 25) 498–514; Mai and Merskey (n 25) 1403.
[30] Chodoff (n 7); Chodoff (n 15); Chodoff and Lyons (n 11).

domination.[31] His work, at the time, appeared to be quite progressive for the psychiatric profession—he concluded that hysteria is not a natural attribute of women. Instead, he found that hysteria is developed in women under the stress of male dominance. He does not appear to engage with the question of whether 'hysteria' exists at all or whether it is merely a creation of the male-dominated medical and psychiatric professions. He does not question whether it is simply a gendered label to further stigmatise and oppress the already marginalised female population.

Feminists at the time had already begun to query the foundations of 'hysteria' and its use as a tool of oppression.[32] Interestingly, in the 1970s and 1980s, in the midst of the Second Wave of feminism, feminist scholars began to reclaim hysteria. The involuntary, physical symptoms of hysteria that had been ascribed as a medical condition were being re-understood as a cultural phenomenon—an embodied manifestation of paternalistic oppression. They were beginning to be understood as an individual assertion of feminism—a kind of individual rebellion against the patriarchy.[33] It is paradoxical that this coincided with the removal of the diagnosis of 'hysteria' from the Diagnostic and Statistical Manual of Mental Disorders (DSM). Both the conservative medical profession and radical feminists were asserting that hysteria is something other than a physical malady.[34]

The evolution of the concept of hysteria in the DSM is evidence of the ongoing modern prevalence of the remnants of the notion of female persons being inherently cognitively flawed. The DSM is the classification of what are believed to be 'mental disorders' using a common language and standard criteria. It is published by the American Psychiatric Association (APA) and is widely used by clinicians, researchers, psychiatric drug regulation agencies, health insurance companies, pharmaceutical companies, the legal system, and policymakers.[35] The DSM included some form of hysterical (histrionic) personality disorder until 1980.[36] The current version, *DSM-5*, does not include a specific reference to hysteria. However, it has retained 'conversion disorder', which is drawn from Freud's psychoanalytic theory and, as described above, was developed from notions of female hysteria.[37]

Hysteria is far from an antiquated, under-used concept. In 1995, scholar Mark Micale wrote of the 'new hysteria studies'—documenting a new surge in academic interest in hysteria.[38] In addition, hysteria is ever-present in popular culture,

[31] Chodoff (n 15).
[32] Devereux (n 2).
[33] ibid; Gilman (n 5) 21.
[34] Devereux (n 2) 21.
[35] American Psychiatric Association, *Diagnostic and Statistical Manual of Mental Disorders (DSM-5®)* (5th edn, American Psychiatric Publishing 2013).
[36] North (n 13) 503; Kendra Cherry, 'Understanding Hysteria in the Past and Present' (2020) *Verywell Mind* <https://www.verywellmind.com/what-is-hysteria-2795232> accessed 13 May 2020; Devereux (n 2) 19; American Psychiatric Association, *Diagnostic and Statistical Manual of Mental Disorders (DSM-3®)* (3rd edn, American Psychiatric Publishing 1987); Cramer (n 16) 705.
[37] North (n 13) 503.
[38] Micale (n 5).

including recent feature films and television series centred on the concept.[39] It continues to be part of modern vernacular, and the oppression inherent in hysteria's insistence that women are irrational and cognitively unstable continues to permeate social consciousness.

This is only a snapshot of the long and winding history of the discreditation of female cognition. On the basis of their gender, women's intellects, rationality, and decision-making skills have been questioned pervasively and continuously.[40] In law, this has manifested itself as the repeated denial of legal decision-making power through the denial of legal personhood in various different realms. This denial of decision-making power coupled with the disregard and disrepute for women's decision-making skills have had a profound effect on women's power and privilege—it has decidedly held them back.

## 3. Stigma, Medicalisation, and Invisibility of Gender Minorities

Gender minorities experience a different—but equally detrimental—form of prejudice that leads to others questioning their decision-making skills. Gender minorities—transgender people, in particular, but intersex and other gender minorities have experienced it as well—have been erroneously labelled as having mental health illnesses as a result of their gender identity and the way that they experience gender. This has happened on both a formal level with the psychiatric profession and an informal, interpersonal level with widespread misunderstanding and prejudice expressed in popular culture and in interpersonal interactions.[41]

The existence of gender minorities is not a new phenomenon. Throughout human history there is evidence of non-binary and non-traditional gender identity and expression. Many cultures did not have negative associations with non-binary gender expression. Some cultures have even revered such experiences and expressions as having important religious or spiritual value. However, European-centric cultures have relatively consistently pathologised non-binary gender experiences and expressions.[42] In these cultures, non-conforming gender identity has been considered a medical condition to be treated instead of simply an individual characteristic.[43] The late 1800s and early 1900s saw an increase in the medicalisation

[39] Devereux (n 2) 41.

[40] Devereux (n 2).

[41] Cannoot, '"#WontBeErased"' (n 3); Friedemann Pfäfflin, 'Transgenderism and Transsexuality: Medical and Psychological Viewpoints' in Jens M Scherpe (ed), *The Legal Status of Transsexual and Transgender Persons* (Intersentia 2015); Stacee Reicherzer, 'Evolving Language and Understanding in the Historical Development of the Gender Identity Disorder Diagnosis' (2008) 2 Journal of LGBT Issues in Counseling 326, 328; Dean Spade, *Normal Life: Administrative Violence, Critical Trans Politics, and the Limits of Law* (Duke UP 2015).

[42] Reicherzer (n 41) 327.

[43] Cannoot, 'The Pathologisation of Trans* Persons in the ECtHR's Case Law on Legal Gender Recognition' (n 3) 3.

of non-binary and non-traditional gender expression, which came about with the advent of forensic psychiatry and sexology in Europe—particularly in Austria and Germany. During this time, patients with non-binary or non-traditional gender identities or gender expression were often classified as having delusions. In addition, because transsexual individuals, in particular, were often having sexual relationships with people of their same biologically expressed gender, their sexual relationships were criminalised and there were many individuals that were imprisoned.[44]

In order to understand the pathologisation and medical classification of non-binary and non-traditional gender expressions and experiences, it helps to understand the history of the treatment of sexuality and gender more broadly. While gender minorities vary significantly in their sexualities and sexual expression—including heterosexual, homosexual, and bisexual individuals—the history of treatment of sexuality provides a window into the oppressive atmosphere that exists in relation to non-traditional sexual and gender identities and expressions. It was in the late 1940s and 1950s that Alfred Kinsey and Evelyn Hooker produced some of the first substantial research work on sexuality. Both were highly controversial and professionally censured by many in the academic and psychological communities of the time. This history demonstrates the lack of knowledge and the resistance to seeking knowledge regarding gender and sexual identity and expression.[45]

Just over a decade later, in 1968, the gay rights movement was well underway—demonstrated by the Stonewall Rebellion in which a demonstration for the human rights of gay, lesbian, and transgender people erupted into riots prompted by violence by police against protestors in the iconic gay bar the Stonewall Inn in New York City.[46] While this struggle for recognition and equality was gathering momentum, sexuality and gender were also being increasingly medicalised. In 1968, the DSM produced a new volume that included the diagnosis of 'sexual orientation disturbance [homosexuality]' (the DSM continued to include some form of diagnosis of homosexuality until 1987).[47] It was amidst this climate of prejudice and ignorance that the ongoing medicalisation of gender minorities was taking place.

Medicalisation of non-binary gender experiences and expressions began occurring via formal identification and classification of what was considered gender non-conformity in the early 1900s.[48] Some of the first sex reassignment

[44] Pfäfflin (n 41).
[45] Reicherzer (n 41) 327.
[46] Vern L Bullough, *Before Stonewall: Activists for Gay and Lesbian Rights in Historical Context* (Routledge 2014); Lillian Faderman, *The Gay Revolution: The Story of the Struggle* (Reprint edition, Simon & Schuster 2016); Martin F Manalansan, 'In the Shadows of Stonewall: Examining Gay Transnational Politics and the Diasporic Dilemma' (1995) 2 GLQ: A Journal of Lesbian and Gay Studies 425.
[47] Reicherzer (n 41) 327.
[48] ibid 330.

surgeries also occurred in Europe in the early 1900s. Two were performed in London, England, on two individuals that were born with male genitalia and identified as female. The decision to perform the surgery was made due to the doctor's concern that the individuals would self-mutilate otherwise.[49] Several other reassignment surgeries were performed around the same time in Berlin, Germany, at Magnus Hirshfield's Institute for Sexual Science.[50] Hirshfield has been described as a 'Jew, transvestite, and effeminate homosexual', and his institute sought to provide both scientific rigor to studies of gender and sexuality and assistance to gender minorities, and to begin to seek equality and equal rights for gender and sexual minorities.[51] It appears that sex reassignment surgeries were occurring both at the behest of individuals themselves that sought to have their physical bodies altered to better reflect their gender identities and at the behest of medical professionals who sought to correct non-conforming gender binary behaviour that they perceived to be an illness.

World War II impacted this medicalisation of non-binary gender expression and experiences. In 1933, Hirshfield's institute and his work were largely dismantled by the Nazis in Germany.[52] This was effectively the loss of the first significant hub of progressive work towards the realisation of gender minority rights. It was also the loss of one of the first significant efforts towards scientific discovery in the area of sexuality and gender. Scientific medical research continued in the area, but most of it did not include the same effort towards social justice for gender and sexual minorities. For example, Dr David Cauldwell, a sexologist who worked on gender non-conforming individuals from 1947 to 1956, began to classify gender non-conforming expression and experiences as 'psychopathia transexualis';[53] he made the following assertions:

When an individual fails to mature according to his (or her) proper biological and sexological status, such an individual is psychologically (mentally) deficient. The psychological condition is in reality the disease ... When an individual who is unfavorably affected psychologically determines to live and appear as a member of the sex to which he or she does not belong, such an individual is what may be called a psychopathic transexual. This means, simply, that one is mentally unhealthy and because of this the person desires to live as a member of the opposite sex.[54]

Cauldwell concluded that individuals who he labelled as 'psychopathic transexuals' acquired this disease as a result, largely, of unfavourable childhood

[49] ibid.

[50] Pfäfflin (n 41); Cannoot, '"#WontBeErased"' (n 3) 3; Reicherzer (n 41) 330.

[51] Magnus Hirschfeld, *Die Homosexualität des Mannes und des Weibes* (L Marcus 1914); Magnus Hirschfeld, *Berlin's Third Sex* (Rixdorf Editions 2017) <https://www.rixdorfeditions.com/hirschfeld-third-sex> accessed 5 June 2020; Ralf Dose, *Magnus Hirschfeld: The Origins of the Gay Liberation Movement* (Monthly Review Press 2014).

[52] Reicherzer (n 41) 331.

[53] ibid.

[54] Cauldwell (n 3) 41.

environments and overindulgent caregivers. He believed that a cure for psychopathic transexualis was inevitable and imminent.[55] Cauldwell's pathologisation of non-binary gender expression and experiences assumes that individuals having such experiences and generally not conforming to the gender binary are unwell and 'mentally unhealthy'. It is easy to see how such pathologisations and assumptions can lead to gender minorities being considered to be unable to make decisions for themselves or that they generally lack decision-making skills because they are mentally unwell.

There were also two widely known cases of sex reassignment surgery that brought significant medical attention to the transgender world, in particular. The first was Christine Jorgensen, a transwoman from the United States who travelled to Denmark to receive sex reassignment surgery in 1952, and Laurence Michael Dillon, a transman from the United Kingdom who underwent sex reassignment surgery in the 1940s and published a book on his experience.[56] Paradoxically, gender reassignment surgery became increasingly available for those that sought to exercise agency and choose to change their physical gender characteristic, while, at the same time, the increased medicalisation of non-binary gender experiences and expressions also served to increasingly discredit and disregard the experiences of gender minorities as delusions or struggles of the mentally ill. This likely has contributed to the devaluing of the cognition and decision-making skills of gender minorities.

Until the mid-1960s, psychotherapy to 'cure' non-conforming gender expression was the dominant form of treatment for what was considered a disease and mental illness. In 1966 endocrinologist and sexologist Harry Benjamin published his book *The Transsexual Phenomenon*, which became the foundation of the modern medical approach to non-conforming gender expression. He argued that the physical body should be changed to match the gender that the individual identifies with psychologically. However, he believed that this should be done only for those that he designated as 'true transsexuals'—and he only believed that the individual's experience could be designated as 'true' via diagnosis by a psychiatrist. This continues to be a prevalent requirement for those undergoing sex reassignment surgery and those seeking to legally change their gender. The requirement of a diagnosis for sex reassignment or legal gender recognition inherently pathologises non-conforming gender expression and experiences. It makes having a non-conforming gender identity a medical problem to be cured instead of simply an aspect of identity.[57] It also devalues the personhood and agency of the individual who has a non-conforming gender identity. The decisions of the individual

[55] ibid; Reicherzer (n 41) 331.

[56] Cannoot, '"#WontBeErased"' (n 3) 3; Pfäfflin (n 41); Michael Dillon, *Self: A Study in Ethics and Endocrinology* (Elsevier 2013).

[57] Cannoot, '"#WontBeErased"' (n 3) 3; Harry Benjamin, *The Transsexual Phenomenon* (Julian Press, Incorporated Publishers 1966).

themselves regarding sex reassignment surgery and legal gender recognition are not sufficient—they are not given full legal recognition. Instead, the decisions of a psychiatrist are used to make decisions on behalf of the individual. This devaluing of the decision-making of those who have non-conforming gender experiences or expression is particularly striking when compared with other individuals who seek cosmetic plastic surgery. Generally, there is no requirement for a psychiatrist or other doctor to provide a diagnosis before an individual can undergo significant plastic surgery that has significant health implications and may alter their appearance significantly. As long as an individual is seeking surgery that conforms with the gender binary, generally no diagnosis is needed. In this way, because gender minorities do not fit in to traditional gender expression and roles, they are pathologised and their decision-making is often discredited.

Judith Butler discusses the myth of illness in relation to gender minorities. She acknowledges that from a practical perspective there are many advantages to being diagnosed with what the medical profession calls gender identity disorder (GID). For example, the medicalisation of gender non-conforming expressions and experiences into GID can provide a means for some to access medical and technological means for transitioning. Medical diagnosis is often required for health insurance companies to cover costs of sex reassignment surgery or other medical treatment related to gender identity needs. For these reasons, and others, it can be critical that medical treatment and sex reassignment surgery not be conceived of as 'elective'. However, she cautions that a diagnosis is an instrument of pathologisation.[58] She asserts:

To be diagnosed with GID is to be found, in some way, to be ill, sick, wrong, out of order, abnormal, and to suffer a certain stigmatization as a consequence of the diagnosis being given at all.[59]

She notes that those that argue for the continued inclusion of the GID in the DSM and as a medical illness often do so because they are seeking the means to conform appropriately to external societal and legal obligations before they can exercise their autonomy in choosing to undergo treatment or surgery that will allow them to express their gender as they choose. She also notes that those that seek to stop the pathologisation of non-binary gender experiences and expressions also often do so in order to have their autonomy recognised. They seek for their gender expression to be recognised as an exercise of their autonomy and to be understood as simply an aspect of human diversity—not a sickness to be cured.[60]

Butler also notes that the two positions—one arguing for a medical diagnosis of gender dysphoria and one arguing against any diagnosis—have fundamentally different views of autonomy. Those arguing against a medical diagnosis are often

[58] Judith Butler, *Undoing Gender* (Routledge 2004) 75.
[59] ibid 76.
[60] ibid 76–77.

coming from an individualistic perspective similar to liberal political theory. They seek for non-binary gender identity and experiences to be recognised as a natural part of the human experience in order for each individual to be free to exercise autonomy and make their own choices regarding their gender identity and experiences. Those arguing for the inclusion of gender dysphoria as a medical diagnosis are acknowledging that there are material conditions for the exercise of liberty. They would like GID to remain a medical diagnosis in order for them to be able to have the medical community and insurance companies, in particular, recognise and provide resources towards the potential necessity of medical treatments in order for people to have the gender expressions and experiences of their choosing. In this way, the resources gained from insurance companies are a material condition for the expression of autonomy.[61] The medicalisation of non-binary gender expression and experiences, therefore, inhibits autonomy assuming illness instead of choice—and also fosters autonomy, when it is the means by which an individual can access the medical treatment necessary in order for them to exercise autonomy in gender expression.[62]

Butler's work provides a succinct analysis of the impact of medicalising non-binary gender expression and experiences. It both hampers freedom and facilitates it. However, it only facilitates it within a world in which the gender binary and heteronormativity dominate. In a changed world—where gender expression was not stigmatised, the gender binary was broken down, and same-sex relationships were accepted in the same manner as heterosexual relationships—there would be no need for the medicalisation of non-binary gender expression and experiences to facilitate autonomy or, in other words, to facilitate the exercise of legal personhood to choose gender expression. This would be vastly preferable because while the medicalisation of non-binary gender expression and experiences can facilitate autonomy in the way described, it even more frequently and insidiously undermines autonomy. Similar to stigmatisation from disability labelling described above,[63] pathologising and medicalising non-binary gender expression experiences can be profoundly damaging. When something is medicalised or pathologised, it is a label of wrongness—of something that needs to be corrected; of a person who is not whole. It is socially and psychologically dehumanising. As Butler puts it, '[T]he diagnosis intensifies the very suffering that requires alleviation.'[64] It sends a message to the world that the individual is not complete, and when the label is one of a mental health diagnosis—as GID is—it sends a message to the world that the individual cannot make decisions for themselves and should not be allowed to make decisions

[61] ibid 85.

[62] ibid 92.

[63] Ian Hacking, 'Making Up People' in Thomas C Heller, Morton Sosna, and David E Wellbery (eds), *Reconstructing Individualism: Autonomy, Individuality, and the Self in Western Thought* (Stanford UP 1986); Bruce J Winick, 'The Side Effects of Incompetency Labeling and the Implications for Mental Health Law' (1995) 1 Psychology, Public Policy, and Law 6.

[64] Butler (n 58) 100.

for themselves. It is easy, in such a context, for an individual to be denied legal personhood to make decisions—either minute decisions or significant decisions, such as medical or financial decisions. In this way, the myth of non-binary gender expression and experiences as an illness significantly contributes to the widespread erection of barriers to and denial of legal personhood for gender minorities.

Gender minorities have their own unique history of prejudice and legal personhood denial. Much of it centres around forced treatment for what was perceived to be mental illness, as discussed in Chapter 3, and the criminalisation of non-gender conforming behaviours.[65] In addition, as will be discussed below, law, policy, and practice that continue to prevent gender minorities from having their gender identity legally recognised create barriers to the recognition and exercise of their legal personhood in many ways, including the inability to obtain legal identification and documentation, which is often a prerequisite for the recognition of legal personhood and the exercise of legal agency.[66]

Forced treatment has been an unfortunate presence in the lives of gender minorities. In the late 1800s and early 1900s, sex reassignment surgery began to be available, and the medical profession began to pay attention to non-binary gender experiences and expressions.[67] This attention from the medical profession—including surgeons and psychiatrists—facilitated the exercise of autonomy for some transgender people because they were able to get medical assistance to achieve, physically, their gender identity.[68] However, for other transgender people and other gender minorities, it accompanied a medicalisation of non-binary gender experiences and expressions that led both to informal pressures to undergo medical treatment and to formal legal requirements of medical treatment and surgery.[69] For example, intersex infants and children began to be surgically altered to adhere to the dominant gender binary expectations.[70] In addition, some jurisdictions began to require surgery, medical treatment (such as hormone treatment), and psychiatric treatment before an individual could legally change their gender.[71] Many of these requirements remain today.[72]

[65] Corinne Lennox and Matthew Waites (eds), *Human Rights, Sexual Orientation and Gender Identity in the Commonwealth: Struggles for Decriminalisation and Change* (University of London Institute of Commonwealth Studies 2013); 'Map of Countries That Criminalise LGBT People | Human Dignity Trust' <https://www.humandignitytrust.org./lgbt-the-law/map-of-criminalisation/?type_filter=crim_gender_exp> accessed 10 August 2020.

[66] Cannoot, '"#WontBeErased"' (n 3).

[67] ibid.

[68] Pfäfflin (n 41).

[69] Butler (n 58) 75–77.

[70] Suresh, 'Pendulous Penises and Couture Clitorises: What Medical Men Do to Intersex Infants' in Arvind Narrain and Vinay Chandran (eds), *Nothing to Fix: Medicalisation of Sexual Orientation and Gender Identity* (Sage 2015).

[71] Dean Spade, 'Documenting Gender' (2009) 8 Dukeminier Awards—Best Sexual Orientation and Gender Identity Law Review 137.

[72] Chinyere Ezie, 'Deconstructing the Body: Transgender and Intersex Identities and Sex Discrimination—the Need for Strict Scrutiny' (2011) 20 Columbia Journal of Gender and Law 141.

Some surgery and treatment that gender minorities have been forced to undergo due to informal pressures or formal legal requirements has the potential for significant downsides—including sterilisation, permanence, health risks, and others.[73] For example, a transgender person may not want to engage in certain surgeries or medical treatment because it poses a risk to fertility or for other reasons; however, that individual may identify as a gender other than their birth gender and may have a need to legally change their gender. In some jurisdictions, it may not be possible to legally change their gender without undergoing certain surgeries or medical treatment.[74] This is due, in part, to this history of the medicalisation of gender minorities and their non-binary gender experiences and expressions. In addition, the surgical alteration of intersex children that was also precipitated by the medicalisation of non-binary gender experiences or expressions has had profoundly negative impacts—because it denies the child the ability and the autonomy to discover for themselves their gender identity, but also because the medical treatments themselves have similar negative effects as those described above—health risks, permanence, and sterilisation.[75]

This history of forced treatment of gender minorities is a history of legal personhood denial. Gender minorities, such as transgender people, experienced overt denial of their legal personhood to consent to medical treatment when they have been subjected to forced mental health treatment and other forced medical treatment on the basis that their non-binary gender experiences and expressions are a form of mental illness. This could fall under the prohibition of legal personhood denial on the basis of disability under Article 12 of the Convention on the Rights of Persons with Disabilities (CRPD).

They have also been subjected to more insidious forms of forced treatment via laws that require medical and surgical treatment as a prerequisite for legal gender recognition. This is a form of legal personhood denial because it places gender minorities in a position that requires them to undergo medical treatment in order to have their legal personhood recognised. Gender recognition is a form of legal personhood recognition when it is required before an individual will be recognised as a legal person. For example, in order to be recognised as a legal person,

[73] R Rossi Neto and others, 'Gender Reassignment Surgery—a 13 Year Review of Surgical Outcomes' (2012) 38 International Brazilian Journal of Urology 97; Shane D Morrison and others, 'Long-Term Outcomes of Rectosigmoid Neocolporrhaphy in Male-to-Female Gender Reassignment Surgery' (2015) 136 Plastic and Reconstructive Surgery 386; Lily C Wang and Dix P Poppas, 'Surgical Outcomes and Complications of Reconstructive Surgery in the Female Congenital Adrenal Hyperplasia Patient: What Every Endocrinologist Should Know' (2017) 165 The Journal of Steroid Biochemistry and Molecular Biology 137.

[74] Jason Allen, 'A Quest for Acceptance: The Real ID Act and the Need for Comprehensive Gender Recognition Legislation in the United States' (2007) 14 Michigan Journal of Gender & Law 169; Ezie (n 72).

[75] Katrina Alicia Karkazis, *Fixing Sex: Intersex, Medical Authority, and Lived Experience* (Duke UP 2008); Suresh (n 70).

identity documents are often required. Many jurisdictions required the gender binary identification of gender on identity documents.[76] If gender minorities are prevented from having their accurate gender (the gender that they identify with) on their identity documents, then they often cannot get appropriate documents and are then prevented from having the documentation that is often required for others to recognise them as legal persons. If medical treatment, including surgery, is required in order for an individual to be able to access appropriate documentation that accurately reflects their gender and allows them to be recognised as a legal person, then they are being forced into medical treatment in order to be recognised as a legal person. In this way, their legal personhood to consent to medical treatment is effectively denied because the alternative is the inability to have their legal personhood recognised (which is an element of legal personhood).

The denial of legal personhood to consent to medical treatment—including irreversible surgery—of intersex children raises some more complex questions. The first is whether children have the same right to legal personhood as adults. There is not space here to thoroughly address this question. However, if children do enjoy the same right to legal personhood as adults, then this is an impermissible denial of the right to legal personhood on the basis of gender identity and group membership as a gender minority. I am inclined to argue that children are entitled to protection of the right to legal personhood; however, there is language in the Convention on the Rights of the Children (CRC) that could be used to argue otherwise—for example, the consistent use of the 'best interest' standard throughout the CRC, which indicates that it is not the will and preference of the child that must be protected (as is required by Article 12 of the CRPD for the protection of the right to legal personhood). The profound impact of forced medical treatment in this area, however, leads me to seek arguments for the protection of the right to legal personhood of children to consent to such medical treatment.

Gender minorities have been impacted by multiple forms of criminalisation. The criminalisation of same-sex sexual activity is perhaps the most widespread form of criminalisation that affects gender minorities. There is a striking correlation between colonisation and the criminalisation of same-sex sexual activity. It was criminalised across the British Empire in the 19th century, and decriminalisation did not begin until 1967 in England and Wales.[77] Many countries in the British Commonwealth, the former British Empire, and elsewhere continue to criminalise same-sex sexual activity—at the time of writing, there remain 72 countries that criminalise private, consensual, same-sex sexual activity, and in 11 of those jurisdictions the death penalty is a potential sentence for these crimes.[78] Gender

[76] Shelby Hanssen, 'Beyond Male or Female: Using Nonbinary Gender Identity to Confront Outdated Notions of Sex and Gender in the Law Notes' (2017) 96 Oregon Law Review 283, 302.

[77] Lennox and Waites (n 65) 1.

[78] 'Map of Countries That Criminalise LGBT People | Human Dignity Trust' (n 65).

minorities are also impacted by laws that criminalise the gender identity and expression of transgender people. This criminalisation occurs via laws that criminalise 'cross-dressing', 'impersonation', and 'disguises'.[79] For example, in Brunei, Syariah Penal Code Order 2013, Section 198 criminalises anyone who 'dresses and poses' as the opposite sex in a public place. In Lebanon, Article 521 of Penal Code 1943 makes it an offense for a man to 'disguise himself as a woman'. In Indonesia, Article 281 of Penal Code 1999 criminalises any person who 'offends against decency', and in Sri Lanka, Section 399 of Penal Code 1883 criminalises cheating 'by pretending to be some other person'—both of which can be used to criminalise non-binary gender experiences or expression.[80]

Laws that criminalise non-binary gender experiences or expressions are also often rooted in colonial history.[81] For example, in the 1800s in Iran, gender was much more fluid, and there was not a strict binary between female and male. In addition, same-sex sexual relationships were common—in fact, homoeroticism was a large part of Persian literature. With increased contact with the West—and with Britain, in particular—Iranian culture began to disavow same-sex practices and to solidify the gender binary categories of female and male. This was reflected in laws, such as the criminalisation of sodomy.[82] In addition, in countries that were under colonial rule, such as Pakistan and India, explicit laws were created to criminalise non-binary gender experiences and expressions. Prior to these laws, non-binary gender experiences and expressions were often celebrated and sometimes even deified.[83]

The criminalisation of same-sex sexual activity has had significant implications for sexual minorities; it has also made the position of many gender minorities very difficult. Not all gender minorities engage in same-sex sexual relationships—although some do. Many gender minorities also engage in sexual relationships that they may not consider same-sex, due to the gender that they identify with; however, the law may consider them same-sex and may have criminalised them in some circumstances. This could occur because in a particular jurisdiction there were no appropriate legal mechanisms for altering one's gender ascribed at birth. It could also occur because a particular individual did not engage existing gender recognition laws due to the oppressive nature of some laws. Nonetheless, the history of criminalisation of same-sex sexual relations has had an impact on the freedom of gender minorities to exercise sexual agency.

[79] ibid.

[80] ibid.

[81] Michael Kirby, 'The Sodomy Offence: England's Least Lovely Criminal Law Export?', *Human Rights, Sexual Orientation and Gender Identity in The Commonwealth* (University of London Press 2013); Lennox and Waites (n 65); Mahso Gichki, 'Deconstructing Transgender Identities in Pakistan, India, and Iran in Colonial and Post-Colonial Context' (2020) 63 Development 31, 33.

[82] Gichki (n 81) 34.

[83] ibid 33–35.

This criminalisation of same-sex sexual activity and non-binary gender experiences and expressions is a denial of the right to legal personhood to consent to sexual activity and to exercise agency in asserting one's gender identity. The right to legal personhood to consent to sex requires that all people have an equal right to consent to sex—therefore, the right to consent to sex cannot be denied on the basis of an individual's group membership.[84] In this way, the right to legal personhood to consent to sex requires that gender and sexual minorities have the same right to legal personhood to consent to sex as others. Similarly, it requires that gender minorities have the same right to experience and express their gender identity as others. In this way, the historical (and ongoing) criminalisation of same-sex sexual activity and non-binary gender experiences and expression is a denial of the right to legal personhood on an equal basis.

## 4. Barriers to Legal Personhood

### 4.1 Women

The perceived irrationality of women, described above, has presented significant barriers to their enjoyment of the right to legal personhood. This is similar to disabled people—a perception of irrationality and a lack of decision-making skills is often cited as the reasons for denying disabled people the recognition of full legal personhood. However, as described in Chapter 1, the interpretation of the right to legal personhood, as described by the CRPD Committee, specifically distinguishes the concepts of mental capacity and legal capacity and asserts that legal personhood must not be denied on the basis of mental capacity. Instead, it demands that all people—regardless of cognitive ability or decision-making skills—be recognised as having full legal personhood and that the state provide access to support for the exercise of legal personhood, where needed and desired. The argument has been largely discredited that women lack sufficient rationality or cognitive skills to have their legal personhood recognised on the same level as men. However, even if that argument was thought to be valid, according to the interpretation of the right to legal personhood from the CRPD Committee, it would not be a legitimate argument for the denial of the right to legal personhood for women (or for any other group).

Nonetheless, the historic disregard for women's cognition and rationality has likely contributed to the denial of legal personhood—including legal personhood and agency—to women. This section explores these legal personhood denials that

[84] Anna Arstein-Kerslake, 'Understanding Sex: The Right to Legal Capacity to Consent to Sex' (2015) 30 Disability & Society 1459.

are uniquely experienced by women. It embraces the CRPD Committee definition of the right to legal personhood and the interpretation that the right to legal personhood includes the right to legal personhood and legal agency, as described in Chapter 1.[85] It uses this definition to examine the history of gendered denials of legal personhood and explore where existing systems continue to deny legal personhood in unique ways to women.

Historically, gender has been a predicate to full legal personhood and agency.[86] Until relatively recently in history, women were often considered to be the property of their fathers or husbands.[87] They often did not enjoy separate legal personhood from these men; instead, the law viewed women as objects, and these men held the power to make legal decisions on their behalf.[88] This was a denial of women's legal personhood because their personhood was generally not independently recognised and their legal agency was largely divested to their father or husband.

For example, the practice of coverture dictated that a woman's legal rights and obligations were subsumed by her husband upon marriage—husband and wife became one legal person. The wife was no longer a separate legal person. She had no legal rights or obligations separate from those of her husband. She could not own property, inherit, enter into contracts, or keep a wage.[89] The first major reform of coverture in England came in 1870 with the Married Women's Property Act. The act came about after significant lobbying and activism by feminist groups.[90] It allowed women to keep their own wages and to inherit a certain amount of wealth.[91] Shortly thereafter, the Married Women's Property Act of 1882 further secured the right of married women to own, buy, and sell property. It also established married women as separate legal entities from their husbands—it granted legal personhood

[85] Anna Arstein-Kerslake and Eilionóir Flynn, 'The General Comment on Article 12 of the Convention on the Rights of Persons with Disabilities: A Roadmap for Equality before the Law' (2016) 20 The International Journal of Human Rights 471; Committee on the Rights of Persons with Disabilities, 'General Comment No 1 Article 12: Equal Recognition Before the Law' (19 May 2014) UN Doc CRPD/C/GC/1.

[86] Saru M Matambanadzo, 'Embodying Vulnerability: A Feminist Theory of the Person' (Fall 2012) 20 Duke Journal of Gender Law & Policy 45-83 (Fall 2012) Available at: https://scholarship.law.duke.edu/djglp/vol20/iss1/2.

[87] Jane F Gardner, *Women in Roman Law & Society* (Croom Helm 1986); Ellen E Kittell, 'Guardianship over Women in Medieval Flanders: A Reappraisal' (1998) 31 Journal of Social History 897; Matambanadzo (n 86); Claudia Zaher, 'When a Woman's Marital Status Determined Her Legal Status: A Research Guide on the Common Law Doctrine of Coverture' (2002) 94 Law Library Journal 459.

[88] Matambanadzo (n 86).

[89] Amy Louise Erickson, 'Coverture and Capitalism' (2005) History Workshop Journal 1; Lee Holcombe, *Wives & Property: Reform of the Married Women's Property Law in Nineteenth-Century England*; Matambanadzo (n 86); Zaher (n 87).

[90] Carole Shammas, 'Re-assessing the Married Women's Property Acts' (1994) 6 Journal of Women's History 9; Mary Lyndon Shanley, *Feminism, Marriage, and the Law in Victorian England* (Princeton UP 1993).

[91] Mary Beth Combs, '"A Measure of Legal Independence": The 1870 Married Women's Property Act and the Portfolio Allocations of British Wives' (2005) 65 The Journal of Economic History 1028.

to wives.[92] It is notable that coverture was not significantly reformed in England until the late 19th century—meaning that women in England have only been guaranteed legal personhood separate from their husbands for less than 150 years.[93]

The coverture laws of England heavily influenced common law countries. Similarly, the Married Women's Property Act in England coincided with a cascade of reforms to coverture laws across common law jurisdictions.[94] However, in the United States, the last significant laws related to coverture were not reformed until the 1950s and 1960s.[95] In California, for example, the 1954 case of *Follansbee v Benzenberg* was the landmark decision which secured separate legal personhood for women from their husbands. It states, 'The legal status of a wife has changed. Her legal personality is no longer merged in that of her husband. Generally, a husband and wife have, in the marriage relation, equal rights which should receive equal protection of the law.'[96] As such, women in some parts of the United States have only enjoyed a formal recognition of their legal personhood independent of their husbands for less than 75 years.[97]

Laws such as these were often propagated by the notion that women are objects incapable of reason or self-governance. Women were viewed to need a male counterpart to provide the cognitive capabilities necessary for the exercise of legal personhood.[98] While many such laws have been abolished or significantly stripped back, the notion that women are less able to make legal decisions appears to continue to permeate modern legal personhood law. Laws securing the right to exercise legal personhood in the context of reproductive choice for women are continually challenged and remain non-existent or ineffectual in many jurisdictions.[99] The ability to exercise legal personhood to consent to sex is frequently

[92] Shanley (n 90); Married Women's Property Act 1882 ch 75.

[93] Shanley (n 90).

[94] Shammas (n 90).

[95] Norma Basch, 'The Emerging Legal History of Women in the United States: Property, Divorce, and the Constitution' (1986) 12 Signs 97; Eleanor Flexner and Ellen Frances Fitzpatrick, *Century of Struggle: The Woman's Rights Movement in the United States* (Harvard UP 1996); Matambanadzo (n 86).

[96] *Follansbee v Benzenberg*, 265 P 2d 183 (California District Court of Appeal 1954); W Robert Wilson, 'Rights of Married Women: Liabilities and Dealings with Third Persons Symposium on the Law of Domestic Relations in Oklahoma—Student Comments' (1961) 14 Oklahoma Law Review 317.

[97] Ursula Vogel, 'Under Permanent Guardianship: Women's Condition under Modern Civil Law' in Anna G Jonasdottir and Kathleen B Jones (eds), *The Political Interests of Gender: Developing Theory and Research with a Feminist Face* (Sage 1990).

[98] Libby Assassi, 'Property and Gender: Irrational Women and Rational Men' in Libby Assassi, *The Gendering of Global Finance* (Palgrave Macmillan 2009); Maggie Cheu, 'Now and Then: How Coverture Ideology Informs the Rhetoric of Abortion' (2012) 22 Texas Journal of Women and the Law 113; Jennifer Ward, *Women in Medieval Europe: 1200–1500* (Routledge 2014).

[99] Cheu (n 98); Máiréad Enright and others, 'Abortion Law Reform in Ireland: A Model for Change' (2015) 5(1) Feminists@Law <https://journals.kent.ac.uk/index.php/feministsatlaw/article/view/173> accessed 11 January 2024; Rosalind P Petchesky, *Abortion and Woman's Choice: The State, Sexuality, and Reproductive Freedom* (rev edn, Northeastern UP 1990); Lisa Smyth, 'Feminism and Abortion Politics: Choice, Rights, and Reproductive Freedom' (2002) 25 Women's Studies International Forum 335.

framed as a passive permission that the female may grant to a male who is viewed as the decision-maker and holder of power.[100] There is also evidence that women are denied legal personhood under guardianship regimes at higher rates than men and that they have unique needs under guardianship, which are often unexamined and unmet.[101] In these ways and others, women continue to have their legal personhood restricted in ways that men do not experience.

### 4.1.1 Denying reproductive and sexual choice of women

Reproductive and sexual choice are a poignant example of laws and policies that deny legal agency to women and gender minorities on a differential basis from men. There is a long history of denial of reproductive and sexual choice on the basis of gender. Coverture laws, described above, and other laws that prevented married women from making legal decisions without their husbands were likely applied to issues of reproductive and sexual choice.[102] Even legal personhood to consent to sexual acts has been removed from married women for centuries through laws that permit rape within the confines of marriage.[103]

In addition, rape law itself has a long history of prioritising male autonomy at the expense of female autonomy.[104] For example, the concept of consent is often conceived as a female passively submitting to a male decision-maker, as opposed to an active process of negotiation and agreement between two equal parties.[105] Rape law has also erroneously ascribed autonomy to women in order to create consistency with male choices, for example, when women's clothes and past choices are permitted to be used as evidence that she consented to a man's choices regarding sexual acts.[106] This is not a granting of autonomy, but instead a masking of the women's true choices with the effect of further entrenching the notion that a man's

[100] Michelle J Anderson, 'Sex Education and Rape Symposium: Rhetoric & Relevance: An Investigation into the Present and Future of Feminist Legal Theory' (2010) 17 Michigan Journal of Gender & Law 83; Arstein-Kerslake, 'Understanding Sex' (n 84); Anna Arstein-Kerslake and Eilionóir Flynn, 'Legislating Consent: Creating an Empowering Definition of Consent to Sex That Is Inclusive of People with Cognitive Disabilities' (2016) 25 Social & Legal Studies 225.

[101] Sonia R Grover, 'Menstrual and Contraceptive Management in Women with an Intellectual Disability' (2002) 176 Medical Journal of Australia 108; Joseph A Rosenberg, 'Poverty, Guardianship, and the Vulnerable Elderly: Human Narrative and Statistical Patterns in a Snapshot of Adult Guardianship Cases in New York City' (2009) 16 Georgetown Journal on Poverty Law & Policy 315; Victoria Office of the Public Advocate, 'Annual Report 2016–2017' (2017).

[102] Cheu (n 98); Petchesky (n 99).

[103] Jill Elaine Hasday, 'Contest and Consent: A Legal History of Marital Rape' (2000) 88 California Law Review 1373; Diana EH Russell, *Rape in Marriage* (rev edn, Indiana UP 1990).

[104] Anderson (n 100); Stephen J Schulhofer, 'Taking Sexual Autonomy Seriously: Rape Law and Beyond' (1992) 11 Law and Philosophy 35.

[105] Anderson (n 100).

[106] Michelle J Anderson, 'From Chastity Requirement to Sexuality License: Sexual Consent and a New Rape Shield Law' (2002) 70 George Washington Law Review 51; Theresa L Lennon, Sharron J Lennon, and Kim KP Johnson, 'Is Clothing Probative of Attitude or Intent—Implications for Rape and Sexual Harassment Cases' (1992) 11 Law and Inequality: A Journal of Theory and Practice 391; Alinor C Sterling, 'Undressing the Victim: The Intersection of Evidentiary and Semiotic Meanings of Women's Clothing in Rape Trials' (1995) 7 Yale Journal of Law and Feminism 87.

autonomy—his legal personhood—take precedence over a women's in the realm of sexual choice.

Sexual choice is also frequently denied to disabled women, particularly those with cognitive disability, including mental health disability, intellectual disability, dementia, and others.[107] In some jurisdictions, there are laws that criminalise all sexual activity with intellectually disabled women.[108] Disabled women are often prevented from exercising legal personhood to consent to sex through policies or informal arrangements that discourage sexual relationships. For example, there is significant evidence that disabled women and girls often have limited access to sex education, which would facilitate the meaningful and informed exercise of legal personhood to consent to sex.[109] In addition, there is evidence that some residential service providers for disabled people discourage romantic and sexual relationships and may even act to prevent sexual relationships.[110]

This denial of the freedom to exercise legal personhood to consent to sex for disabled women often leaves disabled women without the tools necessary to exercise legal personhood to consent to sex because when they are restricted from doing so, they do not have the opportunity to develop the skills necessary for exercising choice related to sexual activity.[111] (Decision-making is well documented as largely a learned skill in all people which requires education, training, and repeated experience in order to develop and grow.[112] This is true for all decision-making, including sexual decision-making.[113]) For example, when faced with a situation of sexual abuse, an individual may not be able to identify or distinguish it as abuse if they were not previously exposed to sexual choices in an appropriate

[107] Arstein-Kerslake, 'Understanding Sex' (n 84); Barbara Faye Waxman, 'Up against Eugenics: Disabled Women's Challenge to Receive Reproductive Health Services' (1994) 12 Sexuality and Disability 155.

[108] Arstein-Kerslake and Flynn, 'Legislating Consent' (n 100); Brendan D Kelly, 'Dignity, Human Rights and the Limits of Mental Health Legislation' (2014) 31 Irish Journal of Psychological Medicine 75.

[109] E Dukes and BE McGuire, 'Enhancing Capacity to Make Sexuality-Related Decisions in People with an Intellectual Disability' (2009) 53 Journal of Intellectual Disability Research 727; Gillian Eastgate and others, 'Women with Intellectual Disabilities: A Study of Sexuality, Sexual Abuse and Protection Skills' (2011) 40 Australian Family Physician 226; Shaniff Esmail and others, 'Attitudes and Perceptions towards Disability and Sexuality' (2010) 32 Disability and Rehabilitation 1148; Michelle McCarthy and David Thompson, 'A Prevalence Study of Sexual Abuse of Adults with Intellectual Disabilities Referred for Sex Education' (1997) 10 Journal of Applied Research in Intellectual Disabilities 105; Mitchell S Tepper, 'Sexuality and Disability: The Missing Discourse of Pleasure' (2000) 18 Sexuality and Disability 283.

[110] Monica Cuskelly and Rachel Bryde, 'Attitudes towards the Sexuality of Adults with an Intellectual Disability: Parents, Support Staff, and a Community Sample' (2004) 29 Journal of Intellectual & Developmental Disability 255; Esmail and others (n 109); Kelly (n 107).

[111] Dukes and McGuire (n 109).

[112] James P Byrnes, *The Nature and Development of Decision-Making: A Self-Regulation Model* (Psychology Press 2013).

[113] Dukes and McGuire (n 109); Anne McCreary Juhasz, 'A Chain of Sexual Decision-Making' (1975) 24 The Family Coordinator 43.

sexual relationship. This is a significant risk, and there is a growing body of evidence to indicate that many disabled women experience this.[114]

Reproductive choice is also denied to women through the criminalisation of abortion. Biologically, men are not able to get pregnant and are therefore not subjected to laws that do not permit reproductive choice in the form of abortion. However, due to the historical and ongoing socio-political power that men hold, if men were able to get pregnant, they may not be subjected to the denial of their autonomy—the denial of their legal personhood—to make decisions regarding reproductive choice, such as abortion.[115] This is evidenced by the long history of laws, described above, that remove autonomy from women disproportionately to that of men. This includes abortion laws which continue to restrict women's exercise of their legal personhood to make reproductive choices: for example, laws that restrict abortion to only certain circumstances, such as when the health of the mother is at risk or where there is evidence of incest or a sexual assault; policies that exclude abortion from health-care insurance cover—making it prohibitively expensive and consequentially removing it as a possible choice for many women; and a lack of measures to ensure that clinics where abortions are performed are safe and accessible environments for women.[116] There is not space in this chapter to provide a full debate on where the right to legal personhood to reproductive choice should begin and end in the context of abortion. However, the lack of widespread availability of abortion and the ongoing overbroad restrictions on abortion in law and policy amount, at a minimum, to denial of the right to legal agency to exercise reproductive choice for women.

Legal agency to exercise reproductive choice is also denied to women in the form of forced sterilisation. This occurs particularly in the context of disabled women and girls. There are laws in some jurisdictions that allow for the forced sterilisation of disabled women and girls.[117] In addition, some disabled women

[114] Eastgate and others (n 109); McCarthy and Thompson (n 109).

[115] Sherryl Kleinman, Martha Copp, and Kent Sandstrom, 'Making Sexism Visible: Birdcages, Martians, and Pregnant Men' (2006) 34 Teaching Sociology 126; Anuradha Kumar, Leila Hessini, and Ellen MH Mitchell, 'Conceptualising Abortion Stigma' (2009) 11 Culture, Health & Sexuality 625; Carmel Shalev, 'Rights to Sexual and Reproductive Health: The ICPD and the Convention on the Elimination of All Forms of Discrimination against Women' (2000) 4 Health and Human Rights 38; Gloria Steinem, 'If Men Could Menstruate' (2019) 6 Women's Reproductive Health 151 (originally published in 1978 in *Ms* magazine).

[116] Louise Finer and Johanna B Fine, 'Abortion Law around the World: Progress and Pushback' (2013) 103 American Journal of Public Health 585; Phillip B Levine, Amy B Trainor, and David J Zimmerman, 'The Effect of Medicaid Abortion Funding Restrictions on Abortions, Pregnancies and Births' (1996) 15 Journal of Health Economics 555; Iqbal H Shah, Elisabeth Åhman, and Nuriye Ortayli, 'Access to Safe Abortion: Progress and Challenges since the 1994 International Conference on Population and Development (ICPD)' (2014) 90 Contraception S39; Reva B Siegel, 'Dignity and the Politics of Protection: Abortion Restrictions under Casey/Carhart Feature' (2007) 117 Yale Law Journal 1694; Christina Zampas and Jaime M Gher, 'Abortion as a Human Right—International and Regional Standards' (2008) 8 Human Rights Law Review 249.

[117] Roberta Cepko, 'Involuntary Sterilization of Mentally Disabled Women' (1993) 8 Berkeley Women's Law Journal 122; Priti Patel, 'Forced Sterilization of Women as Discrimination' (2017) 38 Public Health Reviews 15; Hoangmai H Pham and Barron H Lerner, 'In the Patient's Best Interest?

are only offered methods of contraception that may jeopardise their reproductive health.[118] There is also evidence that sterilisations are performed at the request of family members or others, without attention paid to the will or preference of the woman or girl.[119] Both contexts of forced sterilisation result in a denial of the individual's legal agency to choose sterilisation, as well as in her legal agency to make reproductive choices for the remainder of her life.

### 4.1.2 Women under guardianship with limited decision-making control over their own lives

Guardianship, and other forms of interdiction and conservatorship, are one of the most complete forms of legal personhood denial. It occurs when the law provides a mechanism for the removal of legal personhood in relation to one or more decisions. The most all-encompassing form is plenary guardianship, where an individual's legal personhood can be completely removed and ascribed to another individual or group of people—for example, a family member, a group home or institution, or a court. There are also more limited forms which include either limited guardianship or laws, such as the *Mental Capacity Act* in England and Wales, which allow for the removal of legal personhood in regard to either a specific decision or a specified area of life.[120]

There is evidence that women experience guardianship uniquely.[121] There is also evidence that women may be disproportionately placed under guardianship—potentially, due to the lasting impacts of historical notions of women as less rational and in more need of protection than men.[122] For example, until recently, it was widely accepted that women with intellectual disability living in institutional settings would either almost automatically be given medication to end the menstrual cycle or undergo surgery for sterilisation or some form of management of the menstrual cycle. This was often done in the 'best interests' of the individual—the individual or entity that maintained guardianship or was ascribed her legal personhood in another form made the decision based on what they believed to be in the woman's best interest.[123] While, in many places, this policy has changed in

Revisiting Sexual Autonomy and Sterilization of the Developmentally Disabled' (2001) 175 Western Journal of Medicine 280.

[118] Waxman (n 107).

[119] Stephen A Rosenbaum and Julia Epstein, 'Revisiting Ashley X: An Essay on Disabled Bodily Integrity, Sexuality, Dignity, and Family Caregiving' (2019) 35 Touro Law Review 101.

[120] Anna Arstein-Kerslake, *Restoring Voice to People with Cognitive Disabilities* (CUP 2017); Eilionóir Flynn and Anna Arstein-Kerslake, 'Legislating Personhood: Realising the Right to Support in Exercising Legal Capacity' (2014) 10 International Journal of Law in Context 81; Lucy Series, 'The Mental Capacity Act 2005 and the Institutional Domination of People with Learning Disabilities' (PhD thesis, University of Exeter 2013).

[121] Grover (n 101); Rosenberg (n 101); Victoria Office of the Public Advocate (n 101).

[122] Raia Prokhovnik, *Rational Woman: A Feminist Critique of Dichotomy* (Routledge 2012); Rosenberg (n 101); Carol Tavris, 'The Mismeasure of Woman' (1993) 3 Feminism & Psychology 149; Victoria Office of the Public Advocate (n 101).

[123] Grover (n 101).

institutional settings,[124] young women under guardianship and other substituted decision-making regimes that do not respect the rights, will, and preference of the individual are still faced with menstrual and sterilisation decisions that are made on their behalf, in their 'best interests'.[125]

The loss of legal personhood under guardianship or other forms of substituted decision-making is often accompanied by loss of financial control—the substituted decision-maker can be given control over financial decisions for the individual. There is significant evidence that financial abuse under guardianship is common and often accompanied by few safeguards or avenues for recourse for the individual experiencing abuse.[126] There is also evidence that women experience such financial abuse at higher rates than men.[127]

### 4.1.3 Forced psychiatric treatment of women

Forced psychiatric treatment of women has a long history tied to the concept of women as 'hysterical' and suffering from madness. While psychiatry has been deeply criticised by some of the leading scholars of our time (Erving Goffman, Michel Foucault, and others), most scholars overlooked the role that gender played in psychiatry until second-wave feminists identified it in the 1970s.[128] For example, Phyllis Chesler's book *Women and Madness* and Elaine Showalter's book *The Female Malady* identified these gendered practices within psychiatry and, indeed, the gendered nature of the concept of 'madness' itself.[129] While psychiatry has evolved significantly, women continue to experience both internalised

[124] Eleanor Atkinson and others, 'Consensus Statement: Menstrual and Contraceptive Management in Women with an Intellectual Disability' (2003) 43 Australian and New Zealand Journal of Obstetrics and Gynaecology 109.

[125] ibid; Grover (n 101); Lan-Ping Lin and others, 'Caregiver Attitudes to Gynaecological Health of Women with Intellectual Disability' (2011) 36 Journal of Intellectual & Developmental Disability 149; M Wingfield, DL Healy, and A Nicholson, 'Gynaecological Care for Women with Intellectual Disability' (1994) 160 The Medical Journal of Australia 536; M Wingfield and others, 'Endometrial Ablation: An Option for the Management of Menstrual Problems in the Intellectually Disabled' (1994) 160 The Medical Journal of Australia 533.

[126] John B Bond and others, 'The Financial Abuse of Mentally Incompetent Older Adults: A Canadian Study' (2000) 11 Journal of Elder Abuse & Neglect 23; Johnny Coker and Bobby Little, 'Investing in the Future: Protecting the Elderly from Financial Abuse' [1997] FBI Law Enforcement Bulletin 1; Carolyn L Dessin, 'Financial Abuse of the Elderly: Is the Solution a Problem' (2002) 34 McGeorge Law Review 267; Kathleen H Wilber and Sandra L Reynolds, 'Introducing a Framework for Defining Financial Abuse of the Elderly' (1996) 8 Journal of Elder Abuse & Neglect; London 61.

[127] Bond and others (n 126).

[128] Michel Foucault and Richard Howard, *Madness and Civilization: A History of Insanity in the Age of Reason* (Routledge 2001); Erving Goffman, *Asylums: Essays on the Social Situation of Mental Patients and Other Inmates* (Routledge 2017); Susan J Hubert, *Questions of Power: The Politics of Women's Madness Narratives* (University of Delaware Press 2002); Peter R Sedgwick, *Psycho Politics: Laing, Foucault, Goffman, Szasz, and the Future of Mass Psychiatry* (1st Harper & Row ed., Harper & Row 1982).

[129] Phyllis Chesler, *Women and Madness* (Allen Lane 1974); Hubert (n 128); Elaine Showalter, *The Female Malady: Women, Madness and English Culture 1830–1980* (Virago 1987).

oppression from these early emanations of psychiatry and systemic and socially imposed oppression.[130]

Rates of psychiatric disorder are virtually the same for men and women; however, there are significant differences in how women are diagnosed and treated.[131] Women remain the majority of psychiatric patients.[132] Women are more likely to be treated with psychotropic drugs and are more likely to be diagnosed with depression and anxiety.[133] Stereotypically female traits are also more likely to be regarded as indications of mental health issues, for example, expression of emotions, deference to others, lack of assertiveness, and others.[134] In this way, women who are performing in accordance with gender stereotypes are at risk of being diagnosed as mentally unwell. However, women who are performing outside their gender role may also be at risk of being diagnosed as mentally unwell because they are straying from societal expectations for females.[135] As women are more likely to be involved in the psychiatric treatment systems, it follows that they are at risk for being denied legal personhood within these systems and forcibly treated or detained. A recent study has noted how little research exists in this area and how much more research needs to be done to accurately understand the needs of women in psychiatric care.[136]

The vulnerability that is produced from these gendered perspectives and practices in psychiatry is pervasive. Within the psychiatric system, there is evidence that women are vulnerable to sexual and physical abuse due to systems that are ill-suited to their needs.[137] More generally, the ongoing notion that women are overemotional and prone to irrationality—including extremes of panic and anxiety—undermines women as decision-makers and leaders. It may contribute to the ever-persistent pay gap between men and woman as well as the lack of women in political leadership roles which remains in most countries. Employment,

[130] Hubert (n 128).

[131] Ronald C Kessler and others, 'Lifetime and 12-Month Prevalence of DSM-III-R Psychiatric Disorders in the United States: Results from the National Comorbidity Survey' (1994) 51 Archives of General Psychiatry 8.

[132] Katherine Hodges, 'The Invisible Crisis: Women and Psychiatric Oppression' (2003) 33 Off Our Backs 12.

[133] Mark Linzer and others, 'Gender, Quality of Life, and Mental Disorders in Primary Care: Results from the PRIME-MD 1000 Study' (1996) 101 The American Journal of Medicine 526; M Piccinelli and F Gomez Homen, 'Gender Differences in the Epidemiology of Affective Disorders and Schizophrenia' (World Health Organization 1997); Linda Simoni-Wastila, 'The Use of Abusable Prescription Drugs: The Role of Gender' (2000) 9 Journal of Women's Health & Gender-Based Medicine 289.

[134] Denise Russell, 'Psychiatric Diagnosis and the Oppression of Women' (1987) 5 Women & Therapy 83.

[135] Denise Russell, 'Psychiatric Diagnosis and the Oppression of Women' (1985) 31 International Journal of Social Psychiatry 298.

[136] Michaela Archer, Yasmine Lau, and Faisil Sethi, 'Women in Acute Psychiatric Units, Their Characteristics and Needs: A Review' (2016) 40 BJPsych Bulletin 266.

[137] ibid; Mental Health Complaints Commissioner, 'The Right to Be Safe: Ensuring Sexual Safety in Acute Mental Health Inpatient Units' (Victorian Government 2018) <https://www.mhwc.vic.gov.au/right-be-safe-sexual-safety-project-report> accessed 30 November 2023.

financial resources, and political leadership are all areas of significant social capital that women are currently missing out on. While it is not only the psychiatric systems that may be creating and contributing to this problem, the gendered aspects of the psychiatric system—including the ever-present reality that the labelling of a psychiatric diagnosis could result in the removal of legal personhood and an experience of forced detention or treatment—are likely contributing to these negative social phenomena that women are experiencing.

## 4.2 Gender Minorities

### 4.2.1 Gender recognition, marriage, and reproductive choice

Gender minorities are also experiencing ongoing modern denials of the right to legal personhood. They are facing the history of assumptions that they are mentally ill (as discussed in Chapter 3), which sometimes has resulted in forced medical treatment (as discussed above in Section 4.1.3). They also face historical legal personhood denials in the form of criminalisation of non-binary gender experiences and expressions as well as same-sex sexual activity. Some of these denials of legal personhood continue today. They are accompanied by other modern forms of legal personhood denial that affect gender minorities. In this section, I have chosen to focus on legal personhood denials related to gender recognition, marriage, and consent. There are likely other ways in which gender minorities face legal personhood denials; however, these three areas highlight the challenges that gender minorities face—and legal personhood denials in relation to gender recognition, in particular, go to the heart of much of the legal personhood denials that gender minorities are subjected to.

### 4.2.2 Gender recognition

Gender binary requirements for legal documents necessitate identification as either female or male.[138] Some gender minorities are non-binary; they do not identify as female or male.[139] In addition, some gender minorities do identify as female or male; however, their gender identification does not align with their legal gender as listed on their birth certificate and other documents. In many jurisdictions, there are significant barriers and restrictions to a formal change of gender on such documents.[140] While the intention of gender binary requirements may not explicitly be to remove legal personhood of gender minorities, it can often have this effect.

[138] George Dvorsky and James Hughes, 'Postgenderism: Beyond the Gender Binary' (2008) 20 Institute for Ethics and Emerging Technologies 44–57; Franklin H Romeo, 'Beyond a Medical Model: Advocating for a New Conception of Gender Identity in the Law Note' (2004) 36 Columbia Human Rights Law Review 713.

[139] Jessica A Clarke, 'They, Them, and Theirs' (2019) 132 Harvard Law Review 894.

[140] Allen (n 74); Spade (n 71); Spade (n 41).

When there is a requirement of an identification of gender, and a person from a gender minority either is not given the appropriate gender choice, is not legally allowed to make a particular gender choice, or fears the repercussions of identifying as a particular gender, they may be prevented from exercising their legal personhood to make a legal decision regarding their gender. This, in and of itself, is a denial of legal personhood. In addition, because they do not have a formal method for the appropriate recognition of their gender, they may be prevented from obtaining legal documentation such as a driver's license or passport, which is required for the exercise of legal personhood in many other circumstances. For example: signing a rental agreement; becoming an employee; entering into most contractual relationships; getting married; voting; and others. Without the required legal documentation and identification, all of these exercises of legal personhood become virtually impossible—creating impediments to the individual's participation in society and their enjoyment of equality.[141]

Currently, the law in many jurisdictions is inflexible and does not accommodate gender minorities due to a long history of prejudice and stigma, as discussed above and in Chapter 3.[142] Some of this prejudice and stigma is related to the erroneous notion that gender minorities are inherently experiencing mental health disorders that result in gender confusion as well as a decreased ability to reason or make independent decisions regarding their gender identity, as discussed in Chapter 3. This rejection of the decision-making of gender minorities is similar to the historical assumption, also discussed in Chapter 3, of women's lack of rational decision-making skills—both have resulted in law and policy that do not respect the legal decision-making of individuals in these groups.

It may also be considered a denial of legal personhood when there are laws that require surgery, medical treatment, psychological services, or other prohibitive measures before an individual is legally permitted to change their gender on legal documentation or be legally recognised as a particular gender in another way, such as by a court.[143] This may be considered a denial of legal personhood because it presents significant barriers to gender recognition—which is often required for the exercise of legal personhood, as described above—and it only applies to gender minorities. Therefore, such requirements for formal gender changes on legal documents is a barrier to legal personhood that only gender minorities experience. It may be considered a denial of legal personhood on the basis of group membership as a gender minority.

141 Romeo (n 138).

142 Allen (n 74); Spade (n 71); Spade (n 41); Susan Stryker and Stephen Whittle, *The Transgender Studies Reader* (Routledge 2006).

143 Allen (n 74); Spade (n 71); Ezie (n 72) 162–168; Spade (n 41); Anna James (aj) Neuman Wippler, 'Identity Crisis: The Limitations of Expanding Government Recognition of Gender Identity and the Possibility of Genderless Identity Documents' (2016) 39 Harvard Journal of Law & Gender 491.

Non-binarity in gender requirements on its own may not be sufficient to allow for the full realisation of the right to legal personhood for gender minorities.[144] There may be a need for a form of gender designation that, instead, actively challenges the gender binary status quo.[145] This could take many different forms; however, the most important quality of any type of gender designations is the freedom for everyone, including gender minorities, to maintain self-determination in their identifications.[146] Importantly, breaking down gender binary requirements will likely never occur if gender recognition laws maintain medical and biological definitions of gender or if they simply place all those that do not fit in to gender binary requirements in a category designated as a blank space. This can perpetuate existing stigma and discrimination and further marginalise gender minorities.[147] While it may allow for some limited additional exercises of legal personhood for gender minorities, on the whole, it will likely result in more barriers to legal personhood due to the ongoing discrimination that it may engender.

### 4.2.3 Marriage

Gender minorities are denied the right to legal personhood to choose to enter into or maintain a marriage contract via gender recognition laws and laws that prohibit same-sex marriage. There are several jurisdictions in which gender recognition laws exist that allow an individual to formally change their gender—however, one of the prerequisites to the formal change of gender is that the individual divorce their partner.[148] These laws appear to be primarily based on a desire to outlaw same-sex marriages that would result from one partner legally changing their gender to that of the other partner. These laws have the effect of denying individuals the legal personhood to choose to maintain their marriages and their marriage contract.

In addition, restrictions on same-sex marriages can deny gender minorities the right to legal personhood to choose to enter into a marriage contract. Some gender minorities are in same-sex relationships; if there are legal restrictions on same-sex

[144] Cannoot, 'The Pathologisation of Trans* Persons in the ECtHR's Case Law on Legal Gender Recognition' (n 3).

[145] Neuman Wippler (n 144).

[146] Christopher Hutton, 'Legal Sex, Self-Classification and Gender Self-Determination' (2017) 11 Law and Humanities 64.

[147] Cannoot, 'The Pathologisation of Trans* Persons in the ECtHR's Case Law on Legal Gender Recognition' (n 3); Sonia K Katyal, 'The Numerus Clausus of Sex Article Award Winners: The Dukeminier Prize Awarded To' (2018) 17 Dukeminier Awards: Best Sexual Orientation and Gender Identity Law Review 195; Neuman Wippler (n 144); Jens T Theilen, 'Beyond the Gender Binary: Rethinking the Right to Legal Gender Recognition' (2018) 3 European Human Rights Law Review 249.

[148] Allen (n 74); Andrew N Sharpe, 'Endless Sex: The Gender Recognition Act 2004 and the Persistence of a Legal Category' (2007) 15 Feminist Legal Studies 57; United Nations Free and Equal, 'Transgender' <https://www.unfe.org/wp-content/uploads/2017/05/UNFE-Transgender.pdf> accessed 11 January 2024; Cannoot, 'The Pathologisation of Trans* Persons in the ECtHR's Case Law on Legal Gender Recognition' (n 3).

marriage, then they are denied the right to legal personhood to choose to engage in a marriage contract with their same-sex partner. In addition, in jurisdictions that allow legal gender changes, but have restrictions on same-sex marriages, an individual may be able to legally change their gender to the gender that they identify with, but they may then be restricted from entering into a marriage contract with a partner that is of the same sex as the individual has changed their gender to. This may also amount to a restriction on the right to legal personhood of the individual to choose to engage in a marriage.

### 4.2.4 Reproductive choice

Gender minorities experience lack of reproductive choice when law or policy requires sterilisation before granting gender recognition. In many jurisdictions, there remain no formal options for an individual to change their sex on legal documentation.[149] In some jurisdictions where there is a formal legal entitlement to apply for a change in gender status on legal documentation, there is also a requirement that the individual undergo sterilisation.[150] This denies the individual the opportunity to exercise their legal personhood to make reproductive choices. They are faced with a choice between living an uncertain and often unsafe life with an incorrect gender on legal documents or having their gender accurately reflected on legal documents but losing the ability to exercise legal personhood to make reproductive choices.

## 5. Interpersonal Restrictions on Legal Personhood and Role of Law

As described above, legal personhood denials that disproportionately affect women—or are specifically designed to impact women—are enshrined in many areas of the law. However, women's lives, in particular, are held—to a large extent—in private.[151] This is due to the patriarchal system actively hiding away the lives of women via a process of systemically objectifying women as objects of the home to serve the needs of men and the family. It is also due to women being excluded from political decision-making and law creation, leading to a legal system that often does not address the needs of women or specifically discriminates against them.[152] For these reasons, many of the rights violations that women experience are also in the private realm—in the home or in interpersonal relationships.

[149] Allen (n 74); Spade (n 71); Spade (n 41).

[150] Peter Dunne, 'Transgender Sterilisation Requirements in Europe' (2017) 25 Medical Law Review 554; Spade (n 41).

[151] Jean Bethke Elshtain, *Public Man, Private Woman: Women in Social and Political Thought* (2nd edn, Princeton UP 1993).

[152] ibid; Ngaire Naffine, 'Women and the Cast of Legal Persons' in Jackie Jones and others, *Gender, Sexualities and Law* (Routledge 2011).

Barriers to the recognition or expression of legal personhood for women often occur in this private, interpersonal sphere. For example, oppressive relationships that keep the woman in the home and do not allow her to participate equally in society, even though she may legally be allowed to do so. There are also less severe examples—husbands who are culturally or individually inclined to be the household decision-maker and do not seek input from the women of the house or do not allow them to make most decisions—especially those with legal implications. Even more insidious examples may occur in professional roles, where the opinion and decision-making of women is overlooked in favour of that of men. Situations such as these may prevent or inhibit women from making decisions and exercising their legal personhood.

Issues such as these, in the private, interpersonal sphere, may, in fact, present the most pervasive form of barriers to the recognition and exercise of legal personhood for women. However, in such situations, the application of international law—and the right to legal personhood in Article 12 of the CRPD and Article 15 of the Convention on the Elimination of Discrimination Against Women (CEDAW)—can be difficult. First, the right to legal personhood only applies to an individual's legal personhood or legal agency. This means that it only applies to decision-making that has legal implications. Those decisions that do not have the potential to create, extinguish, or alter a legal relationship are likely not exercises of legal agency, and they may not be protected under the right to equal recognition before the law. Many of the decisions in the private, interpersonal realm—where many women spend a significant portion of their time—may not be considered exercises of legal agency. For example, if an oppressive partner is emotionally manipulative and controls what a woman wears, who she sees, and where she goes, but does so with subtle, non-violent threats and other forms of intimidation that do not rise to the level of criminal violations and do not implicate the law, then it may not be that the partner is preventing her from exercising legal agency.

To solve this uncertainty, the definition of legal agency outlined in Chapter 1 can be applied to discover whether an action or decision can be considered legal agency and whether it is, therefore, protected by the right to legal personhood. The definition of legal agency in Chapter 1 is as follows:

> an action or inaction that the individual intended and which
>
> 1. has legal consequences, or
> 2. creates, modifies, or extinguishes a legal relationship.[153]

[153] Anna Arstein-Kerslake and Eilionóir Flynn, 'The Right to Legal Agency: Domination, Disability and the Protections of Article 12 of the Convention on the Rights of Persons with Disabilities' (2017) 13 International Journal of Law in Context 22.

Using this definition, it can be argued that legal agency is being exercised pervasively throughout all people's lives. Following liberal political theory and social contract theory, every individual agrees to inhabit society and social spaces in a way that follows democratically agreed upon laws. In this way, potentially all the actions that individuals take and decisions that they make are some form of exercise of legal agency because everything individuals do exists inside this social contract in which they have agreed (implicitly, usually) to live—and all actions within this social contract have the potential to have legal consequences and to affect the individual's legal relationship with individuals and entities in their social environment. This is reflected in modern laws in several different ways. Deciding what to wear in the morning, for example, may generally be considered a non-legal decision or non-legal action. However, in many places, it may be dictated by the law—in many places women are not permitted to wear a head covering or burka[154]; conversely, in many other places women are required by law to wear a head covering.[155] Therefore, the decision to do so, or not to do so, has legal implications; it is a choice between either following the law or not following the law—and a woman may be held legally responsible depending on which choice she makes. A more indirect example may be where an individual chooses to go. A decision to leave the house may not, on its face, appear to be an exercise of legal agency; however, where a person is physically present can have legal implications in a multitude of ways. If they are on private property, they may be trespassing and may be held liable for trespassing. If they are on public property, trespassing law may not be implicated, but there are a variety of other ways that the law could be implicated. For example, if there are traffic laws, even as a pedestrian, the individual's presence in the public space has legal implications in accordance with whether they are or are not following traffic laws. If legal agency is viewed in this way, then there is the potential that virtually every action that an individual takes or decision that they make has legal consequences and therefore is an exercise of legal agency. In this way, the right to legal personhood may apply to virtually every decision and action because virtually every decision and action has the potential to have legal implications and is therefore an exercise of legal agency.

This is important, in particular, for women. As discussed above, women live much of their lives in the private, interpersonal sphere. In order for decisions and actions to be protected by the right to legal personhood in that sphere, it must be

[154] Pascal Bruckner, 'UNVEILED: A Case for France's Burqa Ban' (2010) 173 World Affairs 61; Pascale Fournier, 'Headscarf and Burqa Controversies at the Crossroad of Politics, Society and Law' (2013) 19 Social Identities 689; Jennifer Fredette, 'Becoming a Threat: The Burqa and the Contestation Over Public Morality Law in France' (2015) 40 Law & Social Inquiry 585.

[155] Hauwa Mahdi, 'The Hijab in Nigeria, the Woman's Body and the Feminist Private/Public Discourse' (2009) (Institute for the Study of Islamic Thought in Africa (ISITA) Working Paper No 09–003; Ziba Mir-Hosseini, 'The Politics and Hermeneutics of Hijab in Iran: From Confinement to Choice' (2007) 4(1) Muslim World Journal of Human Rights [i]; Z Shirafkan Fadihe, 'Compulsory Hijab in Iran: A Site of "Authenticity", Intervention and Resistance' (Master's thesis, Utrecht University 2018).

established that those decisions and actions are exercises of legal agency and therefore fall within the right to legal personhood and are protected by the right to legal personhood. If the expansive view of legal agency is taken, as described above and in accordance with the definition outlined above, a significant portion, if not all, of the decisions and actions taken by women in the private or interpersonal sphere may also be protected by the right to legal personhood. For example, the decision to wear a head scarf or burka.

If it is accepted that even private, interpersonal actions and decisions are often exercises of legal agency and are therefore protected by the right to legal personhood, the next question is how such actions and decisions can be protected, from a practical perspective. There is a risk of both over-regulation and under-protection. It is likely that it would not be desirable for the state or actors of the state to enter uninhibited into the private, interpersonal lives of women in order to protect their right to legal personhood, including legal agency and legal personhood. However, it may be necessary for some level of intrusion to occur in order for the right to be protected in the private, interpersonal sphere. More research is needed to discover the best way for the state to protect the right to legal personhood of women in the interpersonal sphere, and it is likely that solutions will need to be developed that are culturally specific because the role of women in interpersonal realms varies so significantly across jurisdictions.

## 6. Conclusion

Women and gender minorities have been denied the right to legal personhood pervasively across history. This has, in many instances, been legitimised by a belief that women lack the necessary cognitive skills or decision-making skills and gender minorities are experiencing mental illness and therefore cannot be granted recognition of their legal personhood, including legal standing and legal agency. This can be seen in coverture laws that dictated that a woman's legal personhood be held by her husband, as well as in forced treatment of gender minorities, and many other examples discussed above. The right to legal personhood, as articulated by the CRPD Committee, disallows the denial of legal personhood on the basis of group membership, such as gender, as discussed in Chapter 1. It also disallows the denial of legal personhood on the basis of an actual or perceived deficit in mental capacity, as also discussed in Chapter 1. Therefore, denials of legal personhood on the basis of gender amount to a denial of the right to legal personhood—as do denials of legal personhood on the basis that women and gender minorities lack sufficient mental capacity, such as decision-making skills or rationality.

# 8

# Identifying Implications and Creating Solutions

## Breaking Down the Barriers to Legal Personhood

### 1. Introduction

In this book, I have applied the right to equal recognition before the law to various different marginalised groups. In order to do this, I first outlined the history of the right to equal recognition before the law throughout the international human rights system. I also provided an interpretation and a definition of the right—drawing on key human rights bodies, such as the UN Committee on the Rights of Persons with Disabilities. I establish that the right to equal recognition before the law is enshrined throughout international human rights law (eg Universal Declaration of Human Rights (Article 6), International Covenant on Civil and Political Rights (Article 16), Convention on the Elimination of Discrimination Against Women (Article 15), and the Convention on the Rights of Persons with Disabilities (Article 12)). I also establish that the right includes the right to legal capacity, which I have termed 'legal personhood' in this book in order to ensure clarity across multiple fields and to avoid confusion with the concept of 'mental capacity'—a wholly different concept that pertains to an individual's decision-making and cognitive skills. Legal capacity and legal personhood, on the other hand, refer not to an individual's decision-making skills or cognitive abilities but instead to an individual's right to legal standing and legal agency—their entitlement to be a holder of rights and to exercise those rights.

I have been involved in the development of this interpretation and definition via both engagement with the committee and with my own scholarship. As explained in the early chapters of this book, the critical importance of the right to equal recognition before the law as a foundational right, without which most other rights are largely ineffectual, makes the precise interpretation and definition of the right both an essential component of its application and a key to developing the right as a social justice tool with teeth. For this reason, it is critical that the right to legal personhood is clearly understood as distinct from the concept of mental capacity and that the right to legal personhood is firmly accepted to include both standing and agency. It is this understanding of the right that I have used and applied throughout this book.

*The Right to Legal Personhood of Marginalised Groups.* Anna Arstein-Kerslake, Oxford University Press.
 DOI: 10.1093/9780191926549.003.0008

To further explore how those figurative teeth can be sharpened to facilitate the development of the right to equal recognition before the law as a potentially transformative tool of equality and equity, I went on to explain the role of state sovereignty and to argue that the right to equal recognition before the law should take precedence over state sovereignty—or that there should, at least, be a clear understanding of when it does take precedence over state sovereignty. This argument is critical because, as explained in the early chapters, there are many areas where state sovereignty currently takes precedence over the right to equal recognition before the law, which results in the impossibility of the realisation of the right for many groups, for example, migrant groups who are at the mercy of state sovereignty claims regarding immigration law and are often denied legal personhood as a result.

I also explored the evolving role of the individual in international law—looking at the move from human rights law's inception, when it was merely conceived as a tool to control state action, to the current increasing use of international law as a regulatory structure that directly attaches to individuals, for example, the growth of international criminal law and treaties regarding cross-national taxation of individuals. I explored this new role of the individual in the context of human rights law—a type of international law—in order to identify the potential for the right to equal recognition before the law to be established as a right that attaches directly to the individual and, as such, supersedes claims of state sovereignty.

Once I had established the interpretation and definition of the right to legal personhood and outlined my arguments regarding the right attaching to the individual and taking precedence over state sovereignty claims, I used the remainder of the book to apply the right to various marginalised groups. I did this in order to highlight the vast number of areas in which marginalised groups are experiencing denials or limitations of the right to legal personhood and to begin to explore the further marginalisation that those denials and limitations are causing. This is the first piece of scholarly work to explore the right to legal personhood in this way and across this range of social groups. My aim was to begin to demonstrate the potential power of the right—if the right to legal personhood is realised for these marginalised groups, it has the potential to achieve significant social justice goals for each group.

## 2. Implications for Human Rights Law and Global Legal Order

The implications of the realisation of the right to equal recognition before the law—and the right to legal personhood—are quite extensive. As discussed throughout this book, it would require a new understanding of state sovereignty—one which prioritises the right to legal personhood. This would have implications for national borders and for our global legal order more broadly. It has implications for our global legal order because it removes power from domestic states and places it more centrally in international law. In other words, it would require states to be bound by the right to equal recognition before the law in international human rights law and require them to reform their laws accordingly to ensure that all people enjoy legal personhood on an equal basis. From the perspective of social justice, this change would likely be highly beneficial in achieving greater equality for marginalised groups for the reasons outlined in the chapters of this book. However, it does raise the question of whether we are ready for more power to be placed in the hands of international law and for the scales to tip towards the centre in the hierarchy of the global legal order. It is worth remembering the Euro-centric and colonial origins of international law and human rights law. There is also the problem of enforcement at the international level—it remains very difficult. Even so, a shift in rhetoric that prioritises the right to legal personhood over claims of state sovereignty has the potential to be a very powerful message and to lead to real change at the domestic level.

## 3. Conclusion

Creating solutions for the vast number of legal personhood denials and restrictions that marginalised groups face is a difficult and daunting task. However, I believe that it is the key—or *a* key—to the achievement of social justice goals. I have discussed some of the barriers to legal personhood for the various groups addressed in this book in order to begin to show the impact of the right to legal personhood and also to identify some of the areas where, if change occurs, the realisation of the right to legal personhood could significantly lift the marginalisation that some of these groups are experiencing. I am not suggesting that the right to legal personhood is an easy fix for social justice challenges—nor that the right could be realised overnight, or even over a decade. Instead, my aim here was to turn our attention to a long-overlooked right—and a long overlooked potential advocacy tool. If we—and domestic governments—start taking the right to legal personhood seriously, it has the potential to shift power and privilege towards groups that have been marginalised for centuries. For example, if we acknowledge and rectify law, policy, and practice that denies legal personhood based on gender, it will place greater power in the hands of women and gender minorities. Similarly, if we stop allowing domestic governments to deny legal personhood based on individuals' ties to national borders, it will allow migrants to have legal standing and agency on an equal basis with others, returning power to them, and giving them more equal footing in many areas of law and society. Ultimately, what I hope I have done with this book is present the right to legal personhood as a new lens for analysing social inequality and a new tool for reaching social justice goals.

# Index

*For the benefit of digital users, indexed terms that span two pages (e.g., 52–53) may, on occasion, appear on only one of those pages.*